Robust Speech Recognition and Understanding

Robust Speech Recognition and Understanding

Editor

Danel Jaso

scitus
academics

Robust Speech Recognition and Understanding
Edited by **Danel Jaso**

ISBN: 978-1-68117-466-2
Library of Congress Control Number: 2016942828

SCITUS Academics LLC,
www.scitusacademics.com
Box No. 4766, 616 Corporate Way,
Suite 2, Valley Cottage,
NY 10989

Printed in United States of America on Acid Free Paper

Preface

Speech recognition systems have in the recent past become much more powerful in terms of both voice variability and acoustic variability. Automatic speech recognition (ASR) systems are increasingly being used in everyday life. Many of the common environments in which systems are used are loud, e.g. users who call up a voice search system from a fast-paced cafeteria or a street. This could lead to poor speech recordings and the overall performance of speech recognition systems. In addition to the independence of speakers, many current systems can also automatically compensate for moderate acoustic degradation caused by unknown noise and unknown linear filtering. Since speech recognition and spoken language technologies are now being transferred to real applications, the demand for greater robustness in recognition technology is becoming more evident. In the last ten years, considerable progress has been made in the powerful adaptation of speech recognition systems to new speakers, with strategies that modify or may distort the phonetic representations of the systems to reflect the acoustic characteristics of the speakers themselves. Speech recognition systems are also recently powerful, in particular with regard to slowly varying acoustic degradation sources. As the use of ASR systems increases, the knowledge of state-of-the-art techniques to deal with these problems becomes important for system and application engineers and researchers working with ASR technologies or possibly with them.

Compiling many different aspects of current research into automatic speech recognition and understanding of language, this book provides a comprehensive survey of the state of the art in techniques used to improve the robustness of speech recognition systems against these degrading external influences.

Table of Contents

1

CHAPTER

Multi-Candidate Missing Data Imputation for Robust Speech Recognition

Yujun Wang and Hugo Van hamme

Department of ESAT, Katholieke Universiteit Leuven, Kasteelpark Arenberg 10, B-3001 Leuven, Belgium

ABSTRACT

The application of Missing Data Techniques (MDT) to increase the noise robustness of HMM/GMM-based large vocabulary speech recognizers is hampered by a large computational burden. The likelihood evaluations imply solving many constrained least squares (CLSQ) optimization problems. As an alternative, researchers have proposed frontend MDT or have made oversimplifying independence assumptions for the backend acoustic model. In this article, we propose a fast Multi-Candidate (MC) approach that solves the per-Gaussian CLSQ problems approximately by selecting the best from a small set of candidate solutions, which are generated as the MDT solutions on a reduced set of cluster Gaussians. Experiments show that the MC MDT runs equally fast as the uncompensated recognizer while achieving the accuracy of the full backend optimization approach. The experiments also show that exploiting the more accurate acoustic model of the backend does pay off in terms of accuracy when compared to frontend MDT.

Keywords: speech recognition constrained optimization missing data noise robustness

1. INTRODUCTION

One of the major concerns in deploying Automatic Speech Recognition (ASR) applications is the lack of robustness of the technology when compared to human listeners. A key aspect is the sensitivity to background noise. This effect is caused by the differences between the conditions in which the statistical models for speech are trained and those in which they are applied in real-life situations. Many approaches which reduce the mismatch to improve the noise robustness of speech recognition have been proposed earlier. They modify either the frontend signal preprocessing or the backend acoustic model of the recognizer. A popular frontend method is the Advanced Front-End [1] which applies multiple stages of Wiener filtering to remove the background noise from the corrupted observations. Other techniques working in the frontend are, e.g., spectral subtraction [2], Stereo Piecewise Linear Compensation for Environment [3] and the Vector Taylor series compensation algorithm [4]. Some examples of backend approaches are Parallel Model Combination (PMC) [5] and model adaption algorithms, such as Maximum Likelihood Linear Regression (MLLR) [6] and Maximum A Posterior probability (MAP) based adaptation [7].

In the late 1990s, Missing Data Techniques (MDT) were introduced in speech recognition as a perceptually motivated approach to improve the noise robustness of a speech recognizer. Research in Auditory Scene Analysis (ASA) [8] proposed models for the capability of human listeners to deal with concurrent signals. The human auditory system is able to extract sufficient information from the speech source of interest in order to recognize what is said, even if parts of the target signal are masked by other signals. It exploits the redundancy in the speech signal and can thus handle missing data. The motivation of MDT is to explore these capabilities of human listeners and exploit them in ASR to reduce the performance gap between humans and computers. It relies on the model that a given spectral band at a given time is dominated by either speech or noise. In the frontend preprocessing, the time-frequency regions of a speech signal are labeled as reliable or as unreliable. This labeling information is encoded into a so-called *missing data mask*. In the backend decoding, features in the unreliable regions are either ignored or predicted to alleviate the mismatch. This compensation strategy relies only on the speech model and unlike PMC for instance, it does not require a model of the noise, though some assumptions about the noise are required instead while generating the missing data mask [9, 10]. In recent years, the MDT was extended to techniques such as the glimpsing model [11] and speech fragment decoding [12]. Other related work includes the propagation of uncertainty [13] where the authors transform the uncertainty encoded in the binary mask from the spectral domain to the cepstral domain, and handle the transformed uncertainty with the cepstral backend acoustic models. The authors of [14] introduce a two-pass MDT system, where the lattice generated by the MDT recognizer in the first pass is rescored. In the second pass, a state-based hypothesis test then generates the so-called "integrated mask", yielding better recognition results.

The two major problems in MDT are first estimating the mask and then exploiting these masks during recognition. Identifying the 'missing' part during recognition is an essential step in MDT as proposed by Cooke et al. [15] and Lippmann and Carlson [16]. A missing data detector makes a binary decision about which spectro-temporal components are unreliable due to noise distortions and which remain reliable, i.e., are dominated by speech. Approaches of missing data mask estimation, such as Bayesian classification [17], harmonic mask estimation [10], local SNR-based mask estimation [18, 19], and VQ mask estimation [9] mainly exploit characteristics of the speech signal. The authors of [20] estimate the missing data masks based on computational ASA. More approaches can be found in a survey on missing data mask estimation by Cerisara et al. [21]. The concept of binary reliability masks can be extended to *soft masks*[22] when uncertainty about the reliability information is taken into account. The mask then assumes continuous values instead of binary values. Soft masks are not considered in this article, as we have found them to provide little benefit in [23].

Several paradigms have been designed to apply MDT once the masks are computed. MDT was first formulated for a spectral acoustic model [15], which is referred to as *spectral MDT* in this article. The spectral energy within each unreliable component can be either reconstructed based on the acoustic model and the reliable information, or marginalized out of the probability density functions (PDF) of the HMM states. The former scheme is defined as *imputation* and the latter is defined as *marginalization*. In order to improve the performance of MDT, Raj et al. [24], Van hamme [25], Cerisara [26], Häkkinen and Haverinen [27], and Faubel et al. [28] applied MDT using cepstral acoustic models, which are referred to as *cepstral MDT* in this article. The experimental results of cepstral MDT demonstrate its advantage over the spectral model. The authors of [24] used MDT imputation to enhance the speech features in the front-end, while in Maximum Likelihood (ML) Gaussian-based imputation [25] and in conditional mean imputation [28], the authors consider MDT imputation associated with Gaussians in the backend.

The above work addresses the robustness of the MDT system rather than its efficiency. MDT systems involve much more intensive computation in the backend, as explained in Section 3. This was already noticed in [15], where the problem was addressed by compromising on the acoustic model (diagonal Gaussians for log-spectral features). An alternative solution is to formulate MDT as a front-end technique [24]. In this article, we propose a Multi-Candidate (MC) MDT which not only produces competitive recognition accuracy, but also possesses the same efficiency as a conventional large vocabulary recognizer under noisy conditions. We advocate the backend approach, since it exploits the most accurate speech model that is available in the recognizer to compensate for the missing data. Each HMM state represents an accurate hypothesis about what the missing speech could be, integrating all knowledge that is available in the decoder: acoustics, lexical information, and language model. Hence, we expect more accurate missing data imputation than with frontend MDT approaches, where such sophistication is not available. In our setting, we go beyond the state level and compute a clean speech vector per Gaussian. In addition to the entire set of Gaussians embedded in the HMM, a fairly small set of Gaussians are trained to function as cluster Gaussians (CG). They provide feasible candidates (i.e., they satisfy the constraints for the imputed data, as described in Section 2.1) of imputations for the entire set of Gaussians. As such, instead of solving the full optimization problem for each Gaussian in the acoustic model, candidate solutions are selected from the CG and the most likely one is retained. Therefore, implementation of MC MDT requires only a modest modification of conventional HMM-based recognizers. The MC MDT forms the main contribution of this article. It is an algorithm that aims at *computational gains for large vocabulary speech recognizers without sacrificing accuracy or robustness*. It provides a solution for applying MDT to an existing backend model trained for the speech feature vector of one's choice. Furthermore, we show experimentally that we gain more immunity to noise than if MDT is applied as a frontend feature-enhancement technique [24] and compare several methods for solving the imputation problem.

Figure 1 shows the architecture of the MC MDT system. This article is focused on the three blocks in the middle, i.e., the imputation of the (cluster of) CG and MC imputation for the backend Gaussians (BGs). The rest of this article is arranged as follows: in Section 2, we introduce the conventional state-based imputation and marginalization [15] as well as the spectral reconstruction [24]. In Section 3, we discuss MDT imputation under the framework of ML decoding and why it becomes difficult when using a model trained with decorrelated features such as cepstral features or features generated by, e.g., linear discriminant analysis (LDA) [29]. Section 4 describes the approach of MC MDT imputation using CG to speed up the Gaussian-based imputation. Section 5 explains how to further speed up the imputation of the CG by selecting a subset of the CG dynamically. Section 6 describes several experimental results. Finally, in Section 7 we present our conclusions and propose future work.

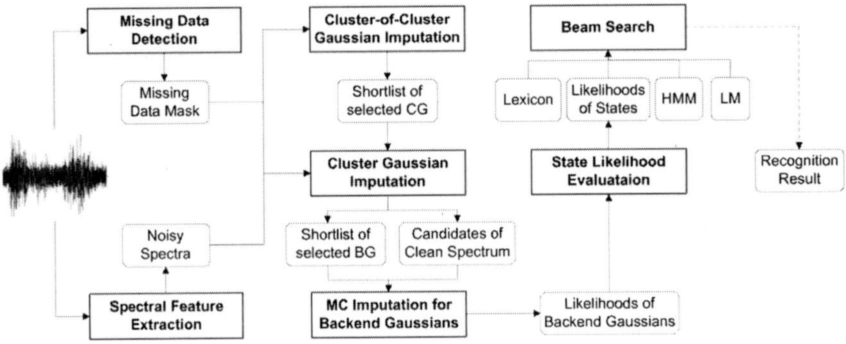

Figure 1. The block diagram of the MC MDT system.

The noisy spectrum is extracted and the missing data mask is estimated from the speech waveform. Two layers of CG, namely the CG and the CCG are trained before decoding. For each frame, the imputation is performed firstly on the CCGs using the mask and the noisy observation. Their likelihoods are calculated on the corresponding imputed spectrum. A shortlist of selected CGs is derived from these likelihoods. The imputed clean spectrum of each selected CG is then calculated based again on the noisy observation and the mask. The likelihoods of the CGs are calculated on their imputed spectra and used to determine which BGs are worth calculating. Each selected BG is evaluated on multiple related imputed spectra proposed by the CGs and the largest likelihood is retained as the final BG likelihood. The beam search can then proceed as in a conventional HMM system, integrating acoustical evidence, lexical information and a language model to generate the recognition result.

2. SPECTRAL AND CEPSTRAL MDT SYSTEMS

In this section, we review some of the concepts of MDT that lead to approaches that are most related to the proposed system.

2.1. Bounds

Environmental noises are assumed to be additive in the spectral domain. Hence, at frame t, the log-spectra of the underlying complete clean speech $\mathbf{x}_t$ can be assumed to be approximately bounded above by the observed noisy feature vector $\mathbf{y}_t$, namely:

$$\mathbf{x}_t \leq \mathbf{y}_t \tag{1}$$

where the inequality sign for vectors applies component-wise. Both $\mathbf{x}_t$ and $\mathbf{y}_t$ can be partitioned into their reliable and unreliable sub-vectors according to the mask:

$$\mathbf{x}_t = \begin{bmatrix} \mathbf{x}_{t,r} \\ \mathbf{x}_{t,u} \end{bmatrix} \text{ and } \mathbf{y}_t = \begin{bmatrix} \mathbf{y}_{t,r} \\ \mathbf{y}_{t,u} \end{bmatrix}$$

For the reliable spectro-temporal regions, the observed noisy features are deemed to be pure speech:

$$\mathbf{x}_{t,r} = \mathbf{y}_{t,r},$$

whereas for the unreliable regions, the observed features act merely as upper bounds for the clean speech:

$$\mathbf{x}_{t,u} \leq \mathbf{y}_{t,u}$$

2.2. State-based imputation and marginalization

The authors of [15] formulated several MDT approaches which use the acoustic models trained in the same domain in which the masks are expressed and in which the constraints of Equation (1) hold. In their experiments, the acoustic feature vectors are obtained via a 64-channel auditory filter bank with center frequencies spaced linearly on an ERB scale from 50 Hz to 8 kHz. The HMM-based speech recognizer is adapted to accommodate MDT by modifying the state likelihood evaluation as outlined below. Each HMM state is expressed as a mixture of multivariate Gaussians with a diagonal covariance matrix. The MDT here is carried out frame-by-frame and is assumed independent across frames. The authors proposed both state-based imputation and marginalization. Besides the upper bound $\mathbf{y}_{t,u}$, a lower bound can also be applied to control the arbitrariness of compensation for the unreliable components. This idea can be applied to all methods described in this article. However, for consistency, we will omit lower bounds from this article.

In state-based marginalization, each state output PDF is a function of the reliable components only, while the unreliable components are marginalized out, i.e., each unreliable component is integrated over the range of values it can assume. The PDF of a state *s* is given by:

$$p(\mathbf{y}_{t,r}|s) = P(k|s) \sum_{k \in G(s)} p(\mathbf{y}_{t,r}|k,s) \int_{-\infty}^{\mathbf{y}_{t,u}} p(\mathbf{x}_{t,u}|k,s) d\mathbf{x}_{t,u}$$

where $G(s)$ represents the set of Gaussians belonging to the Gaussian Mixture Model (GMM) of state *s*. The integral of Gaussian *k* can be calculated using the component-wise error function because its covariance matrix is assumed to be diagonal.

In state-based imputation, the clean speech is imputed for every state *s*, followed by calculating the likelihoods using the imputed values, which will be utilized to expand hypotheses in the search space during decoding. Two ways of imputing the clean speech per state are given: linear combination or winner-takes-all.

In linear combination, the Minimum Mean Squar Error (MMSE) estimate of the imputation from state *s* is

$$\hat{\mathbf{x}}_{t,u,s} = \sum_{k \in G(s)} P(k|\mathbf{y}_{t,r}, s) \boldsymbol{\mu}_{u,k}$$

where $\boldsymbol{\mu}_{u,k}$ is the unreliable sub-vector of mean of Gaussian *k* and

$$P(k|\mathbf{y}_{t,r}, s) = \frac{P(k|s) p(\mathbf{y}_{t,r}|k) \int_{-\infty}^{\mathbf{y}_{t,u}} p(\mathbf{x}_{t,u}|k) d\mathbf{x}_{t,u}}{\sum_{j \in G(s)} P(j|s) p(\mathbf{y}_{t,r}|j) \int_{-\infty}^{\mathbf{y}_{t,u}} p(\mathbf{x}_{t,u}|j) d\mathbf{x}_{t,u}}$$

In winner-takes-all, after the clean speech is imputed for each Gaussian belonging to state *s*, the mixture's likelihood is evaluated for all imputed values and the most likely imputation is selected as the imputation of the state. In other words, the imputation of state *s* is approximated by the clean speech vector imputed from its k^$\hat{k}$ th member Gaussian:

$$\hat{\mathbf{x}}_{t,u,s} \cong \hat{\mathbf{x}}_{t,u,\hat{k}}$$

Where $\hat{k} = \arg\max_{k \in G(s)} p(\hat{\mathbf{x}}_{t,u,k}|s)$ $\hat{\mathbf{x}}_{t,u,k}$ is the maximum likelihood imputation of the unreliable subsector $\mathbf{x}_{t,u,k}$ for Gaussian *k* included in G(*s*):

$$\hat{\mathbf{x}}_{t,u,k} = \arg\max_{\mathbf{x}_{t,u,k} \leq \mathbf{y}_{t,u}} p(\mathbf{x}_{t,u,k}|k) \quad k \in G(s)$$

This problem has a closed form solution:

$$\hat{x}_{t,u,k} = \begin{cases} \mu_{u,k} & \text{if } \mu_{u,k} \le y_{t,u} \\ y_{t,u} & \text{if } \mu_{u,k} > y_{t,u} \end{cases} \quad k \in G(s) \tag{2}$$

where it should be understood that we have written the solution vectorially for convenience, but the top or bottom case in (2) may apply to different vector components. The imputation using a spectral acoustic model containing Gaussians with a diagonal covariance matrix has an analytical solution because the components of the log-spectral features are considered to be independent. However, the spectral features do have correlation among their components and the spectral GMM used above is not very effective to model this. The performance of HMM speech recognizers using GMMs with diagonal covariance is significantly better when using decorrelated features, e.g., MEL Frequency Cepstral Coefficients (MFCC). Therefore, a cepstral MDT model with diagonal covariance-Gaussians is introduced in the following section.

2.3. Spectral reconstruction

In [24], the authors reconstruct the spectral features using either a correlation-based method or a cluster-based method. The reconstructed spectra are then transformed into cepstra for processing by the speech recognizer.

The correlation-based approach solves the imputation of unreliable components at each frame by exploiting the correlations among the components in the spectro-temporal representation. The correlation is modeled by a Gaussian wide-sense stationary (WSS) process whose parameters are learned from training data. The core of the algorithm is a bounded MAP estimate:

$$\hat{x}_{t,u} = \underset{x_{t,u} \le y_{t,u}}{\arg\max}\, p(x_{t,u} | y_{t,n}) \tag{3}$$

where $\mathbf{y}_{t,n}$ is the neighborhood vector containing all the related reliable components which are spectrally and temporally sufficiently close to $\mathbf{x}_{t,u}$ as defined by the WSS model. The likelihood $p(\mathbf{x}_{t,u} | \mathbf{y}_{t,n})$ is modeled with a full covariance Gaussian conditioned on the observed $\mathbf{y}_{t,n}$. The authors establish an iterative approach to solve (3).

In the cluster-based approach, the distribution of the observation is modeled by a spectral GMM with M mixture components with full covariance. Each of these mixture components is called *CG*, trained by the

Expectation-Maximization (EM) algorithm. The unreliable components of the reconstructed spectra are obtained from a linear combination of the values imputed for the CG:

$$\hat{\mathbf{x}}_{t,u} = \sum_{m=1}^{M} P(m \,|\mathbf{x}_{t,u,m} \leq \mathbf{y}_{t,u}, \mathbf{y}_{t,r})\hat{\mathbf{x}}_{t,u,m} \tag{4}$$

where

$$\hat{\mathbf{x}}_{t,u,m} = \underset{\mathbf{x}_{t,u,m} \leq \mathbf{y}_{t,u}}{\arg\max}\, p(\mathbf{x}_{t,u,m} | \mathbf{y}_{t,r}, m) \tag{5}$$

is the imputation resulting from the m th CG, a bounded optimization problem which can be solved by the MAP algorithm as in the correlation-based approach. $P(m|\mathbf{x}_{t,u,m} \leq \mathbf{y}_{t,u}, \mathbf{y}_{t,r})$ is the posterior probability of the CG given the reliable data and the feasible region for the unreliable data.

$$P(m \,|\mathbf{x}_{t,u,m} \leq \mathbf{y}_{t,u}, \mathbf{y}_{t,r}) = \frac{P(m) \int_{-\infty}^{\mathbf{y}_{t,u}} P(\mathbf{x}_{t,u,m}, \mathbf{y}_{t,r} \,|m)\, d\mathbf{x}_{t,u,m}}{\sum_{j=1}^{M} P(j) \int_{-\infty}^{\mathbf{y}_{t,u}} p(\mathbf{x}_{t,u,j}, \mathbf{y}_{t,r} \,|j)\, d\mathbf{x}_{t,u,j}} \tag{6}$$

To make computation of this posterior probability tractable, the spectral CGs are assumed to be diagonal in this circumstance.

In both the correlation-based and the cluster-based method, the reconstruction is separated from the decoding and there is only one single imputation per frame, while in the spectral state-based imputation of Section 2.2, each state or Gaussian has its own imputation, which is theoretically more suitable for an ML-based recognizer. The likelihood of each state is calculated at its imputed value and used in the backend of the recognizer which incorporates the lexical and grammatical knowledge to drive the path pruning in the beam.

It should be noted that the authors of [15] show that state-based marginalization outperforms state-based imputation. Therefore, it would be natural to formulate marginalization for cepstral or other decorrelated models as well. However, this leads to definite integration of full covariance Gaussians. Even if approximations described in [28] would be applied to marginalization, the computational complexity is not acceptable for a practical speech recognizer. Hence, we only focus on imputation with decorrelated models.

3. MISSING DATA IMPUTATION FOR MAXIMUM LIKELIHOOD DECODING

State-of-the-art automatic speech recognizers take a Bayesian approach, i.e., the decoding process is to find a sequence of words $\hat{\mathbf{W}}$whose posterior probability is maximal given a T-frame sequence of observations $\mathbf{y}_{1...T}$:

$$\hat{W} = \arg\max_{W} P(W|y_{1...T}) \approx \arg\max_{W} p(y_{1...T}|s_{1...T})P(W)$$

where the language model $P(\mathbf{W})$ is the probability of a hypothesized word sequence $\mathbf{W}$. In practice, the most likely state sequence $s_{1...T}$that realizes $\mathbf{W}$ is found. In MDT, the maximization should be additionally taken over the unreliable features to be imputed, i.e., $\mathbf{x}_{1...T,\,u}$, to find out the optimal imputation x^1...T,u$\hat{\mathbf{x}}_{1...T,u}$ bounded by the noisy observation $\mathbf{y}_{1...T,\,u}$.

$$(\hat{W}, \hat{x}_{1...T,u}) = \arg\max_{W, x_{1...T,u} \leq y_{1...T,u}} p(x_{1...T,u}, y_{1...T,r}|s_{1...T})P(W).$$

For a given state sequence $s_{1...T}$with $\mathbf{W}$ embedded, the complete speech is given by the following expression, where we have assumed state-conditional independence of $\mathbf{x}_{1...T,\,u}$:

$$\hat{x}_{s_{1...T},u} = \arg\max_{x_{1...T,u} \leq y_{1...T,u}} p(x_{1...T,u}, y_{1...T,r}|s_{1...T}) = a \prod_{t=1}^{T} \arg\max_{x_{t,u} \leq y_{t,u}} p(x_{t,u}, y_{t,r}|s_t) \quad (7)$$

where a is the product of the transition probabilities between the states on the hypothesized path. The maximization in Equation (7) can be accomplished frame-by-frame, i.e., the optimal clean speech at time t is obtained by the maximization of the output PDF of state s over the complete speech $\mathbf{x}_t$bounded by the observation $\mathbf{y}_t$:

$$\hat{x}_{t,u,s} = \arg\max_{x_{t,u,s} \leq y_{t,u}} p(x_{t,u,s}, y_{t,r}|s) = \arg\max_{x_{t,u,s} \leq y_{t,u}} \sum_{k \in G(s)} P(k|s)p(x_{t,u,s}, y_{t,r}|k) \quad (8)$$

Equation (8) formulates an ML state-based missing data imputation. The constrained optimization in (8) is not computationally tractable. If each member Gaussian in a state output PDF is assumed to impute its own clean speech using MLE:

$$\hat{x}_{t,u,k} = \underset{x_{t,u,k} \leq y_{t,u}}{\arg\max}\, p(x_{t,u,k}, y_{t,r} | k) \tag{9}$$

MDT imputation becomes ML Gaussian-based imputation, which is an approximation of the state-based imputation but is computationally more tractable. It will be shown in Section 6.4.4 that (8) and (9) yield comparable recognition accuracy.

If the model used for imputation is trained with cepstral features or other decorrelated features, such as LDA [29] or HLDA [30] features, Gaussian k can be formulated in the log-spectral domain after the corresponding linear transformation $\mathbf{C}$ of full row-rank is applied:

$$\begin{aligned} p(x_{t,k}|k) &= \frac{1}{\sqrt{(2\pi)^{D_m}|\Sigma_k|}} \exp\left(-\frac{1}{2}(Cx_{t,k} - \mu_k)'\Sigma_k^{-1}(Cx_{t,k} - \mu_k)\right) \\ &= \frac{1}{\sqrt{(2\pi)^{D_m}|\Sigma_k|}} \exp\left(-\frac{1}{2}(x_{t,k} - C^+\mu_k)'C'\Sigma_k^{-1}C(x_{t,k} - C^+\mu_k)\right) \end{aligned}$$

where $\mathbf{C}^+$ represents the pseudo inverse of $\mathbf{C}$, $\boldsymbol{\mu}_k$, $\boldsymbol{\Sigma}_k$ are the mean and diagonal covariance of the transformed features and D_m denotes the dimension of the decorrelated feature vectors. Instead of maximizing probabilities, we can equivalently minimize the cost function:

$$Q_k = (x_{t,k} - C^+\mu_k)'C'\Sigma_k^{-1}C(x_{t,k} - C^+\mu_k) \tag{10}$$

with the precision matrix

$$\mathbf{H}_k = \mathbf{C}'\boldsymbol{\Sigma}_k^{-1}\mathbf{C}$$

the maximization of (9) over $\mathbf{x}_{t,k}$ becomes:

$$\hat{x}_{t,u,k} = \underset{x_{t,u,k} \leq y_{t,u}}{\arg\min} \left(\begin{bmatrix} x_{t,u,k} \\ y_{t,r} \end{bmatrix} - C^+\mu_k\right)' H_k \left(\begin{bmatrix} x_{t,u,k} \\ y_{t,r} \end{bmatrix} - C^+\mu_k\right) \tag{11}$$

Notice that $\mathbf{H}_k$ can be singular (e.g., when the cepstral features have less dimension than the log-spectral features), in which case a k-dependent small fraction of the identity matrix is added to regularize $\mathbf{H}_k$, so a unique solution of (11) is found. Since $\mathbf{H}_k$ is not diagonal, the bounded minimization in (11) can no longer be solved by Equation (2). Instead, it becomes a Constrained Least Square (CLSQ) problem, which does not have an analytical solution. Methods such as the MAP algorithm [24], primal active set methods [31], Multiplicative Updates (MU) [32], and imputation with PROSPECT features [33] have been proposed. But, their computational cost for large vocabulary speech recognizers with tens or hundreds of thousands of Gaussians becomes prohibitive. Below, the MC MDT imputation is proposed to significantly reduce the computational intensity to achieve an MDT recognizer with speed.

4. MC MISSING DATA IMPUTATION

In (11), Gaussian-based imputation is formulated as searching for the optimal clean speech vector within a *feasible* region, i.e., the (continuous) subspace which is spanned by the unreliable components and is bounded by the observation. This process can be approximated by evaluating each Gaussian on a list of feasible clean speech candidates and then selecting the candidate which maximizes the likelihood as the imputed value. This approximation is the basic idea behind the MC MDT imputation. For every Gaussian, the list of candidates is given by the imputation from a small set of CG. The Gaussians in the acoustic model, typically a large number, will be called BGs in the remainder of the article. The optimization for each BG in (11) is then approximated by selecting the $\hat{l}_{t,k}$th clean speech candidate such that:

$$\hat{l}_{t,k} = \arg\max_{l \in \Omega_k} p\left(\tilde{\mathrm{x}}_{t,u,l}, \mathrm{y}_{t,r} \middle| k\right), \text{ i.e. } \hat{\mathrm{x}}_{t,u,k} \cong \tilde{\mathrm{x}}_{t,u,\hat{l}_{t,k}} \qquad (12)$$

where Ω_k represents all the CGs which might generate suitable solutions for Gaussian k, and $\tilde{\mathrm{x}}_{t,u,l}$ is the clean speech estimate of the unreliable speech components obtained from CG l. The construction of Ω_k will be detailed in Section 4.3. Hence, in MC MDT, solving the CLSQ problem of BG k is replaced by L_k likelihood evaluations, where L_k is the cardinality of Ω_k. Whereas solving a large number of BG imputation problems is avoided, the task is shifted to the restricted set of CGs. Solving each of these problems requires a computational effort that is at least an order of magnitude greater than the evaluation of a Gaussian likelihood, so various approaches for the imputation with CGs are discussed below.

4.1. ML-imputation for CG

The imputed value from the CGs can be computed by iterative approaches such as Gradient Descent (GD) [33], MU [32], or MAP [24]. In GD, the gradient for iteration τ is

$$g_{t,k}{}^{\tau} = H_k(x_{t,k}{}^{\tau-1} - C^{+}\mu_k)$$

where each negative component of $\mathbf{g}_{t,k}{}^{\tau}$, for which $\mathbf{x}_{t,k}$ is on the boundary $\mathbf{y}_t$, is zeroed and so is each reliable component of $\mathbf{g}_{t,k}{}^{\tau}$ in order to not violate the constraints. Since the cost function in Equation (10) is quadratic, the optimal step for iteration τ has an analytic expression:

$$step_{t,k}{}^{\tau} = \frac{-(g_{t,k}{}^{\tau})' g_{t,k}{}^{\tau}}{(g_{t,k}{}^{\tau})' H_k g_{t,k}{}^{\tau}} g_{t,k}{}^{\tau} \tag{13}$$

The step direction is maintained, but the step size is reduced such that the boundary constraints are not violated.

$$x_{t,k}{}^{\tau} = x_{t,k}{}^{\tau-1} + step_{t,k}{}^{\tau} \quad x_{t,k}{}^{\tau} \leq y_t$$

To initialize the GD algorithm, the non-diagonal covariance structure is ignored, i.e., it starts from the solution in Equation (2).

We opt for GD rather than MU [32] or MAP [24] because it benefits from several advantages simultaneously: (i) the number of iterations required for practical convergence is smaller [33], (ii) the gradient computation (13) can be carried out from right to left such that only a small number of matrix-vector multiplications and vector operations are required (see Appendix), (iii) only the *constant* transformation matrix **C**, the observation, mean, and variances need to be copied to the cache memory of the CPU while other methods may require a larger memory access bandwidth, (iv) GD does not require square root operations like MU, hence the total number of arithmetic operations per iteration is less than that of MU (as shown in Table 1).

Table 1. The expensive operations in the different methods for Gaussian-based MLE imputation with full covariance matrices

	Full precision matrix in cache	Number of iterations	Likelihood #multiplications	Step calculation #multiplications	Other
MAP [24]	Yes	6	$(D+1)D$	$(D_{t,u}+1)D_{t,u}$	No
MU [32]	Yes	5	$(D+1)D$	$D_{t,u}D_{t,u}+4D_{t,u}$	$D_{t,u}$ √ per step
GD + cepstral	No	2	$2D_mD+D_m+D$	$D_{t,u}(2D_m+3)+D_mD+D_m+D$	No
GD + PROSPECT	No	2	$2(D_c+D)$	$3D_cD_{t,u}+4D_cD+5D+3D_c$	No

D is the dimension of the log spectral features. D_m is the order of the cepstral coefficients in MFCC. $D_{t,u}$ is the number of unreliable components at frame t. D_c is the order of the cepstra in PROSPECT features. Typical values: $D = 22$, $D_m = 13$, $D_c = 4$. $D_{t,u}$ is about 16 on average as measured in [33].

The computational effort is further reduced by using PROSPECT features together with GD, which is proposed in [33].

PROSPECT features are composed of two feature subset. The first are cepstral features of a low order D_c (e.g., $D_c = 4$), which models the rough shape of the spectrum at time t. This cepstral part is given by

$$\mathbf{v}_t^c = \mathbf{C}_c \mathbf{x}_t$$

where $\mathbf{C}_c$ denotes the reduced DCT matrix with orthonormal rows. The remaining details of the signal are captured by

$$\mathbf{v}_t^{\perp} = (\mathbf{I} - \mathbf{C}_c{}'\mathbf{C}_c)\mathbf{x}_t$$

which is termed the projection part because it is the orthogonal projection of $\mathbf{x}_t$ on the orthogonal complement of the subspace spanned by the rows of $\mathbf{C}_c$. The concatenation of the cepstral part and the projection part is referred to as PROjected SPECTral (PROSPECT) features:

$$\mathbf{v}_t = \begin{bmatrix} \mathbf{v}_t^c \\ \mathbf{v}_t^{\perp} \end{bmatrix} = \mathbf{R}\mathbf{x}_t$$

The PROSPECT transformation matrix is

$$\mathbf{R} = \begin{bmatrix} \mathbf{C}_c \\ (I - \mathbf{C}_c{}'\mathbf{C}_c) \end{bmatrix}$$

The likelihood of the kth Gaussian based on the PROSPECT features is formulated as

$$F(\mathbf{v}_t|k) = p(\mathbf{v}_t^c|k)p(\mathbf{v}_t^{\perp}|k)^{\beta} \quad (14)$$

Where

$$p(\mathbf{v}_t^c|k) = \frac{1}{\sqrt{(2\pi)^{D_c}\left|\mathbf{\Sigma}_k^c\right|}} \exp\left(-\frac{1}{2}(\mathbf{v}_t^c - \mathbf{\mu}_k^c)'\mathbf{\Sigma}_k^{c^{-1}}(\mathbf{v}_t^c - \mathbf{\mu}_k^c)\right) \quad (15)$$

and

$$p(\mathbf{v}_t^{\perp}|k) = \frac{1}{\sqrt{(2\pi)^D |\boldsymbol{\Sigma}_k^{\perp}|}} \exp\left(-\frac{1}{2}(\mathbf{v}_t^{\perp} - \boldsymbol{\mu}_k^{\perp})' \boldsymbol{\Sigma}_k^{\perp^{-1}} (\mathbf{v}_t^{\perp} - \boldsymbol{\mu}_k^{\perp})\right) \quad (16)$$

where $\boldsymbol{\mu}_k^c$, $\boldsymbol{\Sigma}_k^c$, $\boldsymbol{\mu}_k^{\perp}$, and $\boldsymbol{\Sigma}_k^{\perp}$ are the means and covariance matrices of cepstral and projection part of PROSPECT Gaussian *k*, respectively. They are all estimated on data using the EM-algorithm and both $\boldsymbol{\Sigma}_k^c$ and $\boldsymbol{\Sigma}_k^{\perp}$ are diagonal. However, a diagonal $\boldsymbol{\Sigma}_k^{\perp}$ implies invalid independence assumptions in the spectral residual $\mathbf{v}_t^{\perp}$. Hence, the stream exponent β in (14) is introduced to reduce the impact of these assumptions. According to [33], a typical value of β is 0.5. Note that $F(\mathbf{v}_t|k)$ is not a strict PDF because it does not integrate to unity due to β, but we will still refer to it as the likelihood of Gaussian *k*. When substituting (15) and (16) in (14), the cost function of Gaussian *k*becomes

$$Q_k = (\mathbf{x}_t - \mathbf{R}'\boldsymbol{\mu}_k)' \left[\mathbf{C}_c'\boldsymbol{\Sigma}_k^{c^{-1}}\mathbf{C}_c + \beta(\mathbf{I} - \mathbf{C}_c'\mathbf{C}_c)\boldsymbol{\Sigma}_k^{\perp^{-1}}(\mathbf{I} - \mathbf{C}_c'\mathbf{C}_c)\right](\mathbf{x}_t - \mathbf{R}'\boldsymbol{\mu}_k) \quad (17)$$

where

$$\boldsymbol{\mu}_k = \begin{bmatrix} \boldsymbol{\mu}_k^c \\ \boldsymbol{\mu}_k^{\perp} \end{bmatrix}$$

The gradient computation and cost function evaluation now involve only multiplication of small matrices and vector additions, which is exploiting the CPU's cache memory more efficiently and reduces the computational effort in comparison to a cepstral (or LDA) model, as witnessed by Table 1. Refer to Appendix for details. The study [33] also shows that the PROSPECT model performs equally well as the cepstral model for a recognizer without MDT. Because of their better efficiency and comparable accuracy, the PROSPECT features are preferred for the CGs and the algorithm selected for minimizing (17) is GD. Since the CGs only serve to generate candidate spectra, there is no need for the CG and the BG to be expressed in the same feature domain. For example, in the experiments of Section 6, the BGs will be trained with the features generated by the Mutual Information-based Discriminant Analysis (MIDA) technique [34].

4.2. Training the CGs

Clustering methods for Gaussians can be categorized as model-based or data-driven. In the former methods, such as the popular *K*-means, the parameters of the CGs are estimated from parameters of the BGs. In the latter methods, parameters of the CGs are estimated from training data. Model-based Gaussian clustering methods are not well suited to create the CGs in MC MDT, because they would involve a transformation between the domains in which CGs and BGs are expressed. For instance, MIDA CGs can be first evaluated using MIDA BGs and then converted into PROSPECT CGs. But this conversion involves a lossy transformation and hence performance cannot be guaranteed. Therefore, approaches driven by data are selected in this study.

In order to obtain the CGs from training data, a compact HMM is trained. The compact model shares its structure with the backend model containing the BGs in the sense that it uses the same phonetic decision tree (PDT) [35], but it has only M Gaussians which are shared among leaves of the PDT. Hence, every HMM state s will have an associated set of CGs as well as a set of BGs, denoted by $G_{CG}(s)$ and $G_{BG}(s)$, respectively. Typically, M is a few hundred and $M << K$, where K is the total number of BGs. These M Gaussians are used as the CGs and can be trained for any feature representation. The parameters to be trained are the PROSPECT means and covariance matrices of the CGs as well as the mixture weights $P_{CG}(m|s)$. Before training the compact model, a state level segmentation is made using the Viterbi algorithm with the backend model, i.e., the segmentation specifies the alignment between the states and the frames of the training data. M BGs are randomly selected to initialize the CGs. However, since BGs and CGs may be expressed on different feature sets, a particular initialization of the CGs is required. Hereto, the M retained BGs are considered as a GMM with uniform weights. The posterior probabilities of the M BGs are calculated on the MIDA representation and are used in the first iteration of the EM algorithm, i.e., the BG posteriors are used to softly assign training samples to the CGs to initialize the mean, covariance and mixture weights. Subsequently, a standard EM training without altering the segmentation is performed using PROSPECT features. Consequently, each tied state is now modeled by a GMM with up to M components trained on PROSPECT features. Finally, every BG can be assigned to multiple CGs to form a soft clustering, as explained below.

4.3. Association between CGs and BGs

The association between the CGs and the BGs is based on the same segmentation used in Section 4.2. In this step, the likelihood of all the BGs belonging to state s at training frame t is calculated along the Viterbi path. The likelihood of the PROSPECT CGs belonging to s is calculated for the same frames. Then CG m^t$\hat{m}_t$ and BG k^t$\hat{k}_t$ are found by

$$\hat{m}_t = \arg\max_{m \in G_{CC}(s)} P_{CG}(m|s) F(\mathbf{R}\mathbf{y}_t|m)$$

and

$$\hat{k}_t = \arg\max_{k \in G_{BG}(s)} P_{BG}(k|s) p(\mathbf{E}\mathbf{y}_t|k)$$

where $F(\mathbf{R}\mathbf{y}_t|m)$ is calculated by Equation (14). **E** represents the linear transformation of the backend features. For every training frame of speech t, entry $(\hat{m}_t, \hat{k}_t)$ of the association matrix $\mathbf{\Phi}$ (as shown in Figure 2) is incremented by 1. After all training data are processed, the set Ω_k in Equation (12) is defined from the k th column of $\mathbf{\Phi}$ as those entries that are larger than the product of a pruning threshold θ_Φ and the maximum of the k th column. Moreover, if Ω_k contains more than L_{max} elements, only the L_{max} largest $\mathbf{\Phi}$-values are retained. The entries of $\mathbf{\Phi}$ that are not in Ω_k are subsequently set to zero.

The probability how often CG m is associated with any BGs is formulated by

$$P(m) = \frac{\sum_{k=1}^{K} \delta_{mk}}{\sum_{i=1}^{M} \sum_{k=1}^{K} \delta_{ik}} \qquad \delta_{mk} = \begin{cases} 1 \text{ if } \mathbf{\Phi}_{mk} > 0 \\ 0 \text{ if } \mathbf{\Phi}_{mk} = 0 \end{cases} \tag{18}$$

and is used as the prior probability of a CG below.

4.4. Application of MC MDT in the recognizer

Figure 2 illustrates the process of calculating the likelihoods of the BGs. Since the CGs and the CG-BG association table are now available, it is also convenient to apply Gaussian selection together with the MC MDT. The motivation of Gaussian selection is that only a small (frame dependent) portion of Gaussians dominate the likelihoods of the HMM states, and are therefore worth evaluating. However, since the likelihood computation in an MDT system involves the imputation of the unknown data, many conventional methods do not apply readily. The proposed approach proceeds as follows. The recognizer first evaluates all the PROSPECT CGs using GD. Only the BGs assigned (as determined by Ω_k) to sufficiently likely CGs will be calculated, while the others will be ignored. The prior probabilities (18) and the resulting likelihoods of CGs are used to calculate the corresponding posterior probabilities. The posterior probabilities are sorted in descending order and then truncated to the length such that a large fraction p (e.g. $p = 0.95$) of the posterior probability mass is included, i.e., the number of CGs kept is the smallest L_s such that

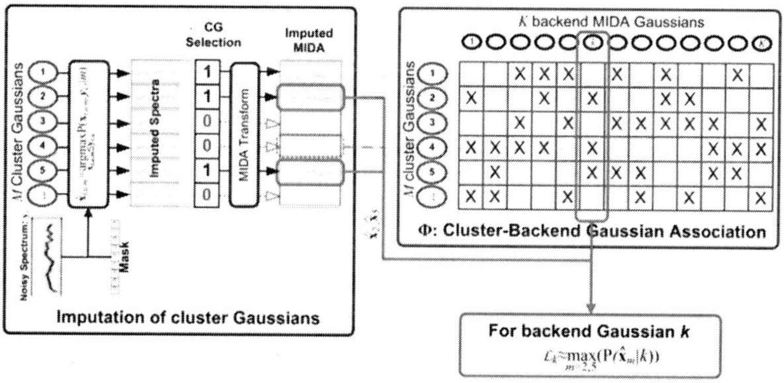

Figure 2. The process of calculating the likelihoods of the BGs in the Gaussian-based MC MDT system. For each of the M CG (left), a clean speech spectrum is imputed using MDT and solutions with high posterior probability (CG selection table) are transformed to the feature representation of the backend (imputed MIDA). BGs (right) are evaluated at the candidates listed in the association table (crosses) and the highest likelihood is retained (bottom).

$$\sum_{m=1}^{L_s} P(m \mid \hat{\mathbf{x}}_{t,u,m}, \mathbf{y}_{t,r}) > p \sum_{i=1}^{M} P(i \mid \hat{\mathbf{x}}_{t,u,i}, \mathbf{y}_{t,r}) \quad (19)$$

where $\hat{\mathbf{x}}_{t,u,m}$ is the imputed value from CG m. The CG are reordered such that

$$P\left(m \left| \hat{\mathrm{x}}_{t,u,m}, \mathrm{y}_{t,r}\right.\right) \geq P\left(m+1 \left| \hat{\mathrm{x}}_{t,u,m+1}, \mathrm{y}_{t,r}\right.\right)$$

and

$$P\left(m \,\middle|\, \hat{\mathbf{x}}_{t,u,m}, \mathbf{y}_{t,r}\right) \cong \frac{p\left(\hat{\mathbf{x}}_{t,u,m}, \mathbf{y}_{t,r} \,\middle|\, m\right)^{\alpha} P(m)}{\sum_{i=1}^{M} p\left(\hat{\mathbf{x}}_{t,u,i}, \mathbf{y}_{t,r} \,\middle|\, i\right)^{\alpha} P(i)} \tag{20}$$

The exponent α is introduced to compensate for unmodeled correlations among the features and will indirectly control the number of selected BGs. A typical value of α is 0.4, which led to a reasonable trade-off between the number of selected BG and recognition accuracy on the development dataset used in [36]. $P(m|\hat{\mathbf{x}}_{t,u,m}, \mathbf{y}_{t,r})$ denotes the posterior probability of CG m based on its imputation. In Figure 2, the CGs labeled with "1" in the CG selection table are selected at frame t. Only the imputed clean spectra resulting from the selected CGs are transformed into the MIDA domain and maintained as possible candidates for BG likelihood evaluation.

When calculating the likelihood of a particular BG k, the MC MDT recognizer looks up the kth column of the CG-BG association table $\mathbf{\Phi}$ to find the candidate list. Notice that some of the associated CGs may have been pruned by criterion (19) and are removed from the list. The recognizer calculates the likelihoods of the BG for the candidates of imputed clean speech and selects the maximum as the likelihood of that BG. If the candidate list is empty, the BG is assigned a likelihood of zero. On average, the number of multiplications involved per BG is reduced to 2L̄ Dm$2\bar{L}D_m$, where L̄ $\bar{L}$ is the average number of CGs associated to a BG and D_m is the dimension of MIDA features. The resulting likelihoods of the BGs are used to calculate the state output PDFs, which are then processed by the decoder.

5. SELECTION OF CG

The MC MDT system can be further sped up by applying Gaussian selection on the CGs. Though $M << K$, the evaluation of a CG is still an order of magnitude more expensive than the evaluation of a BG. Thus, only the likely CGs are selected to impute the candidate clean speech. Existing methods of Gaussian selection can be classified as axis indexing-based methods [37, 38] and VQ-based methods [39, 40]. The former quickly locates the likely regions based on the observation, then selects the Gaussians in the likely regions [38] or removes the Gaussians in the unlikely regions [37]. But in MDT systems, it is not straightforward to determine which regions in the feature space are likely, because some of the components of the observation are missing. On the contrary, VQ-based methods suit the MC MDT system well. Cluster-of-Cluster Gaussians (CCG) in the PROSPECT domain are now established. The MC MDT recognizer will select the CGs based on the likelihoods resulting from the imputation of CCGs, i.e., an additional layer of Gaussian selection is provided. Consequently, it reduces the number of CG CLSQ problems to be solved. Clustering of the CGs is a prerequisite for the VQ-based Gaussian selection. In this study, we apply the soft K-Means algorithm to generate the CCGs. Since the CCGs and the CGs are expressed in the same domain (PROSPECT features in our example), a model-based approach is feasible and preferred here.

5.1. Soft *K*-means clustering

The following pseudo code summarizes the steps to obtain the CCGs. A single cluster is first calculated using all the CGs. The number of CCGs then grows incrementally from 1 to N to avoid suboptimal clustering as much as possible.

1. *1.* Set the number of CG n to 1 and compute a single CCG from all CGs.

2. *2.* While $n < N$

2a. Find CCG j^$\hat{J}$ with the maximum mean WSKLD

2b. Split CCG j^$\hat{J}$ into two and increment n

2c. For iteration τ from 1 to T

2c-1. For CCG i, i from 1 to n

2c-1-1. For CG m, m from 1 to M

Calculate the weight by which CG m updates CCG i, $\hat{g}(i, m)$

2c-1-2. Given $\hat{g}$(i, m), update $\boldsymbol{\mu}_i$, $\boldsymbol{\Sigma}_i$ iteratively

The distance metric between Gaussians and the computation of the CCGs from its member CGs are two crucial components for every step listed in the above pseudo code. The distance metric is Weighted Kullback-Leibler Divergence (WSKLD) in step 2a and is explained in Section 5.2. The parameter estimation algorithms in steps 1, 2c-1-1, and 2-c-1-2 are described in Section 5.3. Step 2b is described in Section 5.4.

5.2. Distance metric between PROSPECT Gaussians

The symmetric Kullback-Leibler Divergence (SKLD) is commonly used to measure the distance between CCG n and CG m:

$$\mathrm{SKLD}(n, m) = \frac{1}{2}\mathrm{trace}\left((\Sigma_n^{-1} + \Sigma_m^{-1})(\mu_n - \mu_m)(\mu_n - \mu_m)' + \Sigma_n^{-1}\Sigma_m + \Sigma_n\Sigma_m^{-1} -\right.$$

The application of SKLD to (14) requires some care: the stream exponent β in the likelihood model for PROSPECT features makes it an improper distribution, requiring renormalization such that it integrates to unity. Second, it was found that SKLD overweighs differences in the projection part of the PROSPECT Gaussians. Therefore, in [41], further simplifications were proposed and experimentally verified leading to the WSKLD as a clustering metric for multi-stream features:

$$\mathrm{WSKLD}(n, m) = \sum_{j=1}^{N_{strm}} \beta_j\, \mathrm{SKLD}_j(n, m)$$

where β_j is the exponent of stream j, SKLD_j is the symmetric KLD computed on the features of stream j only and N_{strm} is the total number of streams. In this study, N_{strm} is 6 because the PROSPECT features contain static, velocity and acceleration stream of both cepstral and projection parts.

5.3. Parameter estimation of CCGs

Following the K-Means algorithm in [42], the cost function to be minimized for clustering is

$$Q_{K-Means} = \sum_{m=1}^{M}\left(\sum_{n=1}^{N} g(n,m)\mathrm{WSKLD}(n, m) + \gamma \sum_{n=1}^{N} g(n,m)\log\frac{1}{g(n, m)}\right) \tag{21}$$

where γ controls the stiffness of the clustering and $g(n, m)$ are unknown clustering weights. The parameters to be updated iteratively are

$$[\hat{\mu}_n, \hat{\Sigma}_n, \hat{g}(n, m)] = \underset{\mu_n, \Sigma_n \sum_{n=1}^{N} g(n,m)=1}{\arg\min} (Q_{K-Means})$$

In each iteration, the first step is to obtain the optimal weight by which CG m affects CCG n as

$$\hat{g}(n,m) = \frac{\exp(-\text{WSKLD}(n,m)/\gamma)}{\sum_{i=1}^{N} \exp(-\text{WSKLD}(i,m)/\gamma)}$$

The second step is to find the optimal values of mean and covariance of each CG given the weights. The estimation of means and covariance matrices of the CCGs is based on the approach in [43], where a method for finding the centroid of a set of Gaussians is derived. The centroid is the CCG that minimizes the sum of the WSKLD to all CGs. Here, we extend the results of [43] by modifying the cost function to (21). The mean of a CCG is thereby estimated as

$$\hat{\mu}_n = \left[\sum_{m=1}^{M} \hat{g}(n,m)(\Sigma_m^{-1} + \Sigma_n^{-1})\right]^{-1} \left[\sum_{m=1}^{M} \hat{g}(n,m)(\Sigma_m^{-1} + \Sigma_n^{-1})\mu_m\right] \quad (22)$$

Matrix **Z** is constructed to facilitate the re-estimation of the covariance matrix of the CCGs

$$Z = \begin{bmatrix} 0 & A_1 \\ A_2 & 0 \end{bmatrix}$$

where

$$\mathbf{A}_1 = \sum_{m=1}^{M} \hat{g}(n,m)\,[(\mu_m - \hat{\mu}_n)(\mu_m - \hat{\mu}_n)' + \Sigma_m]$$

and

$$\mathbf{A}_2 = \sum_{m=1}^{M} \hat{g}(n,m)\Sigma_m^{-1}$$

By construction, **Z** has D_P positive and D_P symmetrically negative eigenvalues, where D_P is the dimension of PROSPECT features. A $2D_P$-by-D_P matrix **V** is constructed whose columns are the D_P eigenvectors corresponding to the positive eigenvalues **V** is partitioned in its upper halve **U** and lower halve **W**:

$$\mathbf{V} = \begin{bmatrix} \mathbf{U} \\ \mathbf{W} \end{bmatrix}$$

$$\hat{\Sigma}_n = \mathbf{U}\mathbf{W}^{-1} \quad (23)$$

Like in [43], $\Sigma\hat{}n\hat{\boldsymbol{\Sigma}}_n$ is constrained to be diagonal during clustering. It can be seen from Equations (22) and (23) that the procedure of estimating the CCGs given the weights $\hat{g}(n,m)$ is iterative. The calculation of the mean depends on the previously calculated covariance and vice versa. The exit criterion is the convergence of the cost function defined in Equation (21).

In step 1 of the pseudo code from Section 5.1, a single CCG is initialized by averaging the means and covariance matrices of the entire set of CGs. The parameters of the single CCG are then updated using Equations (22) and (23) for several iterations. Splitting a CCG and re-estimation of all CCGs are carried out iteratively till *N* CCGs are obtained, as explained below.

5.4. Splitting a CCG

In each iteration, the CCG with the maximum within-cluster mean WSKLD is found

$$\hat{j} = \arg\max_{j=1..n} \frac{\sum_{m=1}^{M} \hat{g}(j,m)\mathrm{WSKLD}(j,m)}{\sum_{m=1}^{M} \hat{g}(j,m)}$$

Principal component analysis is applied on the covariance matrix $\Sigma j\hat{}\Sigma_{\hat{j}}$ to find the first principal eigenvector $\boldsymbol{e}_1$ and eigenvalue, λ_1. If the number of CCGs in the current iteration is *n*, CCG $j\hat{}\hat{j}$ is split into two Gaussians with the means and covariance matrices:

$$\mu_{n+1} \leftarrow \mu_{\hat{j}} + \xi\sqrt{\lambda_1}\mathrm{e}_1$$

$$\mu_{\hat{j}} \leftarrow \mu_{\hat{j}} - \xi\sqrt{\lambda_1}\mathrm{e}_1$$

$$\Sigma_{n+1} = \Sigma_{j} = \Sigma_{\hat{j}}$$

where ξ is the disturbing rate. The WSKLDs of all the *M* CGs to the newly created CCGs is then calculated. Each weight $\hat{g}(j\hat{},m)\hat{g}(\hat{j},m)$ is also split into two according to the WSKLDs:

$$\hat{g}(n+1,m) \leftarrow \frac{\exp(-\text{WSKLD}(n+1,m)/\gamma)\hat{g}(\hat{j},m)}{\exp(-\text{WSKLD}(n+1,m)/\gamma)+\exp(-\text{WSKLD}(\hat{j},m)/\gamma)}$$

$$\hat{g}(\hat{j},m) \leftarrow \hat{g}(\hat{j},m) - \hat{g}(n+1,m)$$

The parameters of CCG $\hat{j}$ and CCG $n+1$ are then re-estimated using Equations (22) and (23) with fixed number (e.g., 3) of iterations. The means and covariance matrices of CCG 1 to $n+1$ are subsequently updated until convergence of the global cost function (21).

Finally, when n reaches N, an N by M CCG-CG table of exponentiated negative WSKLD is calculated. This table plays the same role as the association table in Section 4.3. The same schemes as in Section 4.3 are used to truncate the table. Also, the same schemes as in Section 4.4 are used to select likely CGs, thus avoiding solving CLSQ problems whose solutions are unlikely to survive pruning criterion (19).

6. EXPERIMENTS

To show the effectiveness of the proposed approaches, a large vocabulary speech recognizer was modified accordingly and experiments on the noisy dictation task AURORA-4 were run. In Section 6.1, we describe the training and test datasets and further details on the required acoustic models. Section 6.2 explains various components of the MDT recognizer. Section 6.3 outlines two baseline systems: first, a non-MDT system serving as the *speed* baseline for our MC MDT experiments and second a backend MDT system serving as the *accuracy* baseline for our MC MDT experiments. In Section 6.4, some MC MDT variants are first analyzed and subsequently compared with the cluster-based reconstruction described in Section 6.5. Section 6.6 evaluates MC MDT systems where the CGs are expressed in either the cepstral domain or the log-spectral domain. All testing results are summarized in Tables 2, 3, 4, and 5.

Table 2. WER of the MC MDT experiments on test set 1-7 (Close-talking microphone)

	WER (%)							
	1. Clean	2. Car	3. Babble	4. Restau.	5. Street	6. Airport	7. Train	Average
1. No MDT	6.82	12.98	32.62	40.95	38.50	32.51	38.37	28.96 ± 0.5
2. BE PROSPECT MDT	6.33	10.89	20.14	28.38	25.42	20.57	25.14	19.55 ± 0.4
3. GB GD MC MDT	6.28	10.95	20.08	29.76	24.98	20.18	25.28	19.64 ± 0.4
4. GB MAP MC MDT	6.00	10.31	20.90	29.12	24.86	19.73	25.89	19.55 ± 0.4
5. GB GD MC MDT + CGS	6.16	10.93	20.36	29.48	25.72	19.91	25.13	19.53 ± 0.4
6. GD CLBR	6.18	11.96	22.90	31.22	26.60	21.74	29.03	21.38 ± 0.4
7. MAP CLBR	6.28	11.81	21.69	31.44	27.63	21.74	28.51	21.30 ± 0.4
8. SB MC MDT	6.67	11.25	20.25	28.90	24.49	19.67	25.20	19.49 ± 0.4
9. Spectral MC MDT	6.41	10.46	21.63	29.68	25.89	20.66	25.85	20.08 ± 0.4
10. Cepstral MC MDT	6.44	11.04	19.90	29.46	25.61	19.86	26.53	19.83 ± 0.4

GB, Gaussian-based; SB, State-based; CGS, CG selection; CLBR, cluster-based reconstruction; BE, Backend.

Table 3. WER of the MC MDT experiments on test set 8-14 (Far-talking microphone)

	WER (%)							
	8. Clean	9. Car	10. Babble	11. Restau	12. Street	13. Airport	14. Train	Average
1. No MDT	21.35	30.51	47.71	53.26	55.52	46.95	55.41	44.39 ± 0.5
2. BE PROSPECT MDT	15.93	23.02	36.39	41.29	42.14	34.65	41.32	33.54 ± 0.5
3. GB GD MC MDT	15.93	23.63	37.15	42.27	41.43	35.29	40.91	33.80 ± 0.5
4. GB MAP MC MDT	15.51	23.58	37.17	42.13	41.99	35.00	41.55	33.84 ± 0.5
5. GB GD MC MDT + CGS	15.86	23.96	37.43	42.49	41.58	35.15	40.83	33.90 ± 0.5
6. GD CLBR	19.39	27.93	40.54	45.75	48.14	38.88	45.45	38.01 ± 0.5
7. MAP CLBR	17.86	27.54	43.96	48.10	48.10	39.73	46.98	38.90 ± 0.5
8. SB MC MDT	15.88	23.01	37.23	41.93	41.39	34.99	41.71	33.73 ± 0.5
9. Spectral MC MDT	15.77	24.42	38.74	44.57	42.42	36.17	42.54	34.95 ± 0.5
10. Cepstral MC MDT	16.05	23.04	36.57	42.37	41.74	35.07	41.84	33.62 ± 0.5

GB, Gaussian-based; SB, State-based; CGS, CG selection; CLBR, cluster-based reconstruction; BE, Backend.

Table 4. CPU time breakdown over test set 2-7

	CPU time (ms/frame)					BG calculated (%)
	Mask estimation	BG Calculation	CG Evaluation	Beam Search	Total	
1. No MDT	0.0	3.5	0.2[a]	24.4	28.1	27
2. BE PROSPECT MDT	1.1	133.5	0.0	18.5	153.1	100
3. GB GD MC MDT	1.1	2.8	4.3	20.0	28.2	11
4. GB MAP MC MDT	1.1	3.3	7.6	22.2	34.2	13
5. GB GD MC MDT+CGS	1.1	2.4	1.2	19.1	23.8	9
6. GD CLBR	1.1	1.3	4.3	19.3	26.0	11
7. MAP CLBR	1.1	1.2	10.6[b]	18.5	31.4	9
8. SB MC MDT	1.1	30.2	4.6	20.1	56.0	11
9. Spectral MC MDT	1.1	10.4	0.5	23.7	35.7	38
10.Cepstral MC MDT	1.1	2.8	7.0	19.0	29.9	10.5

[a]In the case of No MDT, the time for CG evaluation is replaced by FRoG. [b]In cluster-based reconstruction with MAP, the time of CG evaluation includes the calculation of the likelihood for 500 PROSPECT CGs, which is equivalent to evaluation of 1000 MIDA Gaussians.

GB, Gaussian-based; SB, State-based; CGS, CG selection; CLBR, Cluster-based reconstruction; BE, Backend.

Table 5. CPU time breakdown for the clean condition (test set 1)

	CPU time (ms/frame)					BG calculated (%)
	Mask estimation	BG calculation	CG evaluation	Beam search	Total	
1. No MDT	0.0	1.9	0.2[a]	5.8	7.9	14
2. BE PROSPECT MDT	1.1	58.9	0.0	5.8	65.8	100
3. GB GD MC MDT	1.1	1.7	3.4	4.8	11.0	5
4. GB MAP MC MDT	1.1	2.2	6.2	6.6	16.1	6
5. GB GD MC MDT + CGS	1.1	1.7	0.7	5.6	9.1	4
6. GD CLBR	1.1	0.8	3.4	5.9	11.2	5
7. MAP CLBR	1.1	0.8	6.9[b]	7.2	16.0	5
8. SB MC MDT	1.1	16.9	3.8	6.0	27.8	5
9. Spectral MC MDT	1.1	6.5	0.5	6.5	14.6	21
10. Cepstral MC MDT	1.1	1.7	4.4	5.2	12.4	5

[a]In the case of No MDT, the time for CG evaluation is replaced by FRoG. [b]In cluster-based reconstruction with MAP, the time of CG evaluation include the calculation of likelihood for 500 PROSPECT CGs, which is equivalent to evaluation of 1000 MIDA Gaussians.

GB, Gaussian-based; SB, State-based; CGS, CG selection; CLBR, Cluster-based reconstruction; BE, Backend.

6.1. Data and models

6.1.1. AURORA-4

Speech recognition experiments were conducted on the AURORA-4 database [44], a large vocabulary task that is derived from the WSJ0 Wall Street Journal 5k-word dictation corpus. A bigram language model for a 5k-word closed vocabulary is provided by Lincoln Laboratory.

For training, only clean-condition data sampled at 16 kHz were used, consisting of 7,138 utterances from 83 speakers, which amounts to 14 h of speech data. All recordings are made with the close talking microphone and no noise is added.

The test database is composed of 330 read sentences (5,353 words) from 8 different speakers. Fourteen different versions of this set are created. The first dataset is clean and is recorded with the same close-talk microphone as used while recording the training data. It is artificially corrupted by adding six types of noise to establish datasets 2-7: car (set 2), babble (set 3), restaurant (set 4), street (set 5), airport (set 6), and train (set 7). Set 8 is recorded with far-talk microphones. Test sets 9-14 are created by artificially adding the same six types of noise as used for generating sets 2-7. Each test set contains 330 utterances and has an SNR that ranges from 5 to 15 dB.

6.1.2. Training backend acoustic model

The design of the front-end as well as the backend acoustic model is based on prior study [23, 33, 37] which obtained competitive accuracies on clean speech and good robustness in an MDT configuration.

The signal power spectrum is calculated with a 32-ms Hamming window and a 10-ms window shift and is integrated using a 22-channel MEL-scaled triangular filter bank with lowest frequency centered at 140 Hz to increase the robustness to low-frequency noises. Since all frequencies above 7 kHz of the AURORA-4 data are filtered out, the last band is centered at 5800 Hz. The 22 log-spectral coefficients are mean-normalized and the first- and second-order time derivatives are appended to result in 66-dimensional spectral features.

To train the backend acoustic model, the normalized spectral features are transformed into 39-dimensional MIDA features, which are improved LDA features leading to decorrelation and diagonalization of the mixture components [34]. It has only half the dimension of PROSPECT features (see Section 6.1.3), hence leading to a significant effort reduction in the likelihood calculation of the BGs and showing better accuracy than MFCC.

The acoustic model uses cross-word and context-dependent triphones. The HMM for each triphone contains three states. A PDT defines 4091 tied states, or senones, which in their turn share 21,037 BGs. The output probability of each state is a mixture of 190 BGs on average and each Gaussian is shared among 45 different tied states.

6.1.3. Training CGs and CCGs

The compact acoustic model containing the CGs is trained with the same training data by following the training procedure outlined in Section 4.2. Here, the state-level segmentation of the training data is obtained by forced alignment using the backend MIDA model of Section 6.1.2. The normalized static log-spectral features and the dynamic features are transformed into PROSPECT features with $D_c = 4$, i.e., for each stream in the features, four cepstral coefficients are kept, and $D = 22$ projection coefficients are appended. Consequently, the PROSPECT features including delta's have 78 dimensions. An earlier experiment on AURORA-4 showed that MC MDT with 500 to 900 CGs yields a reasonable tradeoff between recognition time and accuracy. Therefore, we use 500 CGs in the following experiments. The association table $\mathbf{\Phi}$ is built on the same training data. The maximum number of CGs associated with a particular BG, L_{max}, is 5. An earlier experiment on the Flemish Speecon and SpeechDat Car data [36] showed that increasing L_{max} beyond 5 only leads to more computation without increasing the recognition accuracy. The average number of CGs associated with a particular BG, $\bar{\mathrm{L}}$ $\bar{L}$, is 3.6.

Fifty CCGs are obtained by clustering the 500 CGs using the procedure from Section 5. The maximum number of CCGs associated with a CG is 5 and the average number is 3.6. In previous experiments on Gaussian clustering, we have found a γ of 0.3 in Equation (21) to be a good choice, which we have maintained in these experiments.

6.1.4. Training spectral CGs for the cluster-based reconstruction with MAP

In order to accomplish the experiments of the MAP cluster-based reconstruction for comparison, a mixture of 500 Gaussians with full covariance is trained as well on the spectral data using EM on the same segmentation. As proposed in [24], the initial iterations use a diagonal covariance model that serves to make the posterior probability calculation (6) feasible. Only in the last EM-iteration, the full covariance matrices are estimated for application in Equation (5).

6.1.5. Training backend PROSPECT model

In order to show the speed improvement of MC MDT over a full MDT system [45], i.e., where the CLSQ problem (11) is solved per Gaussian with GD, an acoustic model with Gaussians estimated on PROSPECT features is required. The model has 21,037 PROSPECT Gaussians which are obtained by Single Pass Retraining (SPR) [46] of the acoustic model with MIDA features. The inputs of the SPR are the MIDA features, PROSPECT features, and the MIDA model described above. The MIDA model is used to compute the posterior probabilities of every Gaussian over the training data, which are subsequently combined with the PROSPECT feature observations to estimate their GMM weights, means and diagonal covariance matrices.

6.2. Recognizer

6.2.1. Handling convolutional noise

Besides additive noise, the MDT recognizer also handles convolutional noise by the channel compensation technique described in [23], which maximizes the likelihood of the recognized speech on the backend model. To make the implementation tractable, only the contribution of the single Gaussian that gives the largest contribution to the state likelihood (the *dominating* BG) is taken into account. However, unlike in [23], the current approach computes only approximate solution for BGs which is expressed in a different feature domain. Therefore, each dominating BG is replaced by the PROSPECT CG with the largest **Φ**-value so the maximum likelihood channel estimation of [23] can be readily applied. The channel estimate is subtracted from the observed log-spectra and hence the CCG, CG, and BG models are all compensated for convolutional distortions.

6.2.2. *Mask estimation*

The missing data detector used is the method described in [23] which integrates harmonicity and SNR with a speech model based on vector quantization. At each frame, the best match between a harmonic decomposition of noisy speech and a codebook describing the harmonic decomposition of clean speech is found. VQ mask estimation requires a speech and silence codebook which are trained with a randomly selected subset of the clean training data in Section 6.1.1. The codebook contains 520 codewords which are updated using the channel estimation of Section 6.2.1 during recognition.

6.2.3. *Test configuration*

The decoding consists of a time-synchronous beam search algorithm as described in [47]. The recognizer was launched on a PC installed with Dual Core AMD Opteron 280 2.4 GHz processors with a cache size of 1 MB. Only one processor core is activated. The MDT imputation is only applied to the static stream, while the first- and second-order time derivatives are uncompensated. The Word Error Rates (WER) are calculated for all the experiments. Meanwhile, the CPU time is measured. Tables 2 and 3 list the WERs of the experiments over the 14 types of environmental noises. Tables 4 and 5 contain the timing measurements for the BG and CG evaluation, for beam search as well as the end-to-end timing information (column "TOTAL") of the recognizer under noisy and clean condition, respectively. The timing measurements are achieved by starting and stopping (precise) timers frame-synchronously at the entry and exit of each of the different processing steps: front-end processing, CG imputation, candidate evaluation for all BGs, and beam search. The total time is then obtained by dividing the accumulated timings by the number of processed frames over several utterances.

6.3. Baselines

6.3.1. Recognition without MDT

The system that does not make use of MDT is provided as a baseline in terms of recognition time such that we can measure the computational cost of the robustness obtained from the MDT systems. The acoustic model is the backend HMM containing 21,037 MIDA Gaussians described in Section 6.1.2. An axis indexing-based Gaussian selection method, Fast Removal of Gaussians (FRoG) [37] is used. The testing results are shown in the first rows of Tables 2, 3, 4 and -5. The default FRoG Gaussian pruning setting works well on clean speech and results in only about 5% of Gaussians being evaluated. However, we noticed a performance degradation due to Gaussian pruning on noisy speech. Therefore, the FRoG Gaussian pruning settings were adjusted on the noisy test data such that the accuracy was not degraded more than 2% compared to no pruning, requiring 27% of Gaussians to be kept. Notice that this procedure yields an optimistic speed estimate for this baseline, as tuning on an independent development set would require some safety margin as well. Notice that this non-MDT system produces higher WER than the MDT systems under the clean condition (test set 1), as shown in Table 2. This is mainly due to the non-MDT system using spectral mean normalization to reduce the channel effects, while the MDT systems use the more sophisticated MLE-based channel update as described in Section 6.2.1.

6.3.2. Backend PROSPECT imputation

This setup is the most refined previously published version of our MDT system [23] and serves as a baseline in term of recognition accuracy such that we can measure the accuracy cost of the proposed speed improvements. Two iterations of GD are found to be enough for the convergence in terms of recognition accuracy, hence are applied for all the 21,037 PROSPECT Gaussians. This system runs at 15 times real time in noisy condition and 6.6 times real time in clean condition as shown in row 2 of Tables 4 and 5, respectively. However, the accuracy benefits of MDT can be clearly seen in contrast to the non-MDT system in Tables 2 and 3.

6.4. MC MDT

6.4.1. Gaussian-based MC MDT with GD

The Gaussian-based MC MDT system is an instance of the concepts outlined in Section 4. Two iterations of GD are applied for all the 500 CGs. The posterior probability-based BG selection described in Section 4.4 is applied. α was tuned with an isolated word-recognition experiment of MC-MDT on the Speecon and the SpeechDat Car databases used in [36], which we hence regard as development data for this article. The tuning experiment shows that a good trade-off between accuracy and BG evaluation effort is obtained at $\alpha = 0.4$, but that it does not critically affect the recognition accuracy.

Compared to the backend PROSPECT MDT system, i.e., row 2 versus row 3 in Tables 2, 3, 4, and 5, the Gaussian-based MC MDT yields a comparable WER, while it uses less than 20% of the CPU time over the entire test set.

It is remarkable that the Gaussian-based MC MDT works as fast as the non-MDT recognizer with the same backend acoustic model under noisy conditions (row 1 versus row 3 of Table 4). The MC MDT spends time in evaluating CGs, but its decoding time is reduced by 4 ms per frame. Faster decoding on corrupted data is actually a common benefit from MDT imputation as shown in Table 4. In non-MDT systems, the mismatch between data and model results in a lower likelihood for the ground truth hypothesis and also causes many hypotheses to yield a similar score, so pruning is not effective and the decoder slows down. In the MDT system, noise addition also slows the recognizer down, but through a different mechanism. Thanks to the imputation process in MDT systems, the likelihood of the ground truth hypothesis will not deteriorate. The likelihood of alternative hypotheses will also increase, but because they do not fit the data well, their imputation benefit is not that strong. Apparently, a significant likelihood gap is maintained among the hypothesis, causing pruning in MDT systems to be more effective than in non-MDT systems. The effort spent in evaluating CGs is recovered in the search.

The increase in the likelihood of alternative hypotheses in the MDT system under noisy conditions also causes the MC MDT system with GD to run about 2.5 times slower than under clean conditions (row 3 of Table 4 versus row 3 of Table 5). As the data get noisier, the imputation becomes less constrained, since the number of unreliable components increases and the bounds outlined in Section 2.1 become less strict. Hence, the dynamic range of the BG likelihoods will decrease, such that the hypothesis likelihoods will show smaller differences, causing pruning to be less effective. Additionally, the system is slowed down with increasing noise levels because more spectro-temporal regions are labeled as unreliable and the complexity of imputation for CGs and CCGs increases.

Some common advantages of MDT are revealed by the results shown in Tables 2 and 3. All the experiments with MDT produce lower WERs than the non-MDT system over the corresponding noise types, as well as in the clean condition. Especially for the non-stationary noise types, namely, set 3-7 and 10-14, the benefit from MDT is more significant.

Though MDT systems show an advantage in both the close-talk and the far-talk test sets, the performance is greatly degraded in the latter condition, because the channel compensation technique of Section 6.2.1 is restricted to the estimation of a log-spectral offset vector, which can only compensate for convolutional effects with a short impulse response. However, the fact that the backend PROSPECT MDT and the MC MDT system perform equally on this test set confirms that the modification to estimate the channel on CGs rather than on BGs (see Section 6.2.1) works.

6.4.2. Gaussian-based MC MDT with MAP

This experiment is conducted to compare GD with MAP as a solver for the imputation problems. The full precision matrix of the CGs in Equation (17), as required for MAP, is pre-calculated. The same BG selection as in the previous section is applied. Six iterations are found to be enough for the convergence in terms of WER, and therefore applied for the CGs. Comparing row 3 and 4 of Tables 2 and 3 reveals that the MAP solver performs equally robust as the MC MDT using GD. But as shown in Tables 4 and 5, it is slower, especially in evaluating CGs due to more iterations and copying full precision matrices from the main memory to the cache memory of the CPU.

6.4.3. Gaussian-based MC MDT with CG selection

The CG selection introduced in Section 5 is added to the Gaussian-based MC MDT system in Section 6.4.1. In addition to the 50 PROSPECT imputation operations for the CCGs, about 106 PROSPECT imputation operations for the CGs are observed per frame of 10 ms. Therefore, the number of CLSQ problems solved is less than one-third of that of MC MDT without CG selection. Two iterations of GD are applied on the imputation of CCGs. The implementation of Gaussian-based MC MDT plus CG selection does not harm the recognition accuracy but consumes less CPU time in comparison with the Gaussian-based MC MDT system (compare row 3 with 5 in Tables 2, 3, 4, and 5).

6.4.4. State-based MC MDT

The imputed values of the Gaussian-based MC MDT described in Section 6.4.1 can also be used to perform a state-based MC MDT, where the imputation for state *s* is the linear combination of the imputed values from the BGs included in the GMM of that state.

$$\hat{\mathbf{x}}_{t,u,s} = \sum_{k \in G_{BC}(s)} P\left(k \,\middle|\, \hat{\mathbf{x}}_{t,u,k}, \mathbf{y}_{t,r}, s\right) \hat{\mathbf{x}}_{t,u,k} \tag{24}$$

where $G_{BG}(s)$ represents all the Gaussians belonging to the GMM of state *s*, and

$$P\left(k \,\middle|\, \hat{\mathbf{x}}_{t,u,k}, \mathbf{y}_{t,r}, s\right) = \frac{p\left(\hat{\mathbf{x}}_{t,u,k}, \mathbf{y}_{t,r} \,\middle|\, k\right) P(k|s)}{\sum_{j \in G_{BC}(s)} p\left(\hat{\mathbf{x}}_{t,u,j}, \mathbf{y}_{t,r} \,\middle|\, j\right) P(j|s)} \tag{25}$$

The BG selection from Section 4.4 is also activated for this experiment, so only the selected BGs are actually involved in the imputation formulae. Each BG is shared among about 45 states and is therefore evaluated at multiple imputed spectra from its owner states. Hence, for this state-based MC MDT experiment, every selected BG is evaluated at 45 states-based imputed spectra as x^t,u,s$\hat{\mathbf{x}}_{t,u,s}$ in Equation (24). The MC-based likelihood estimation of each BG is still performed at 3.6 (average number of CGs assigned to each BG) candidate spectra. These likelihood evaluations lead to a computationally expensive implementation. State-based MC MDT yields WERs fairly close to those obtained in other MC MDT experiments, but with a significantly higher computational cost, as shown in the 8th rows in Tables 2, 3, 4, and 5.

6.5. Cluster-based reconstruction

6.5.1. Cluster-based reconstruction with MAP

This experiment is an instance of the concept formulated by Equations (4), (5), and (6). Each of the 500 full-covariance spectral CGs is used to impute clean speech with six iterations of the MAP imputation. The corresponding diagonal-covariance CGs are used to calculate the definite integrals in

Equation (6). To compensate for unmodeled correlations, the integrals are exponentiated with 0.3, a value that is tuned on the test set for best accuracy. The global clean spectrum is then reconstructed using Equation (4). Since the likelihoods of the 500 CGs are already calculated, they are used to select BGs as explained in Section 4.4. Despite the test set optimization, the cluster-based reconstruction with MAP imputation is still less robust than the MC MDT systems when comparing row 7 with rows 3, 4, 5, and 8 in Tables 2and 3. The use of a more accurate speech model provided by the BGs seems to pay off.

6.5.2. Cluster-based reconstruction with GD

This system approximates the previous one by combining the imputed spectra obtained from the PROSPECT CGs like in Equation (4), but takes a different approach to compute the posterior probabilities of the CGs. These posteriors are calculated by renormalizing the likelihoods of the imputed clean spectra. The likelihoods also serve for BG selection as explained in Section 4.4. To compensate for unmodeled correlations, the likelihoods are exponentiated with 0.3, a value that is also tuned on the test set for best accuracy. We did not observe a significant accuracy gain beyond the 500 PROSPECT CGs used to report the results in the tables. The approximations outlined above do not harm the robustness as shown by a comparison between the rows 6 and 7 of Tables 2 and 3, but this implementation is faster because GD imputation is more efficient than MAP and the computation of the posterior probabilities are simplified. Again, despite the test set optimization applied for this cluster-based reconstruction method, MC MDT outperforms it as well.

6.6. Imputation using log-spectral and cepstral CGs

Using a PROSPECT feature representation for the CGs in MC MDT experiments is an implementation choice motivated by speed considerations (see Section 4.1). The CGs can also be trained with other features, e.g., cepstra or log-spectra. To accomplish the comparison of the MC MDT system using CGs in these domains, same number, namely 500 of cepstral CGs and log-spectral CGs are trained using the same data-driven approach as described in Section 6.1.3.

6.6.1. Cepstral imputation

The dimension of the cepstral CGs is 39: 13 static cepstral coefficients, 13 first-and second-order time derivatives. The average number of CGs per BG is 3.6, the same as for PROSPECT CGs. During recognition, the imputation is performed by Multiplicative Updates (MU) [32] with five iterations, an algorithm capable of handling rank-deficient precision matrices, such as $\mathbf{H}_k$ in Equation (11). The testing results are shown in row 10 of Tables 2, 3, 4, and 5. The WER and the percentage of selected BGs obtained by using cepstral CGs are comparable with using PROSPECT CGs. Observe that cepstral CGs introduce time-consuming imputation of MU, which slows down the imputation of CGs by 30-60%.

6.6.2. Spectral imputation

The spectral imputation method described by Equation (2) is tempting for its simplicity. It is worth investigating whether it yields a list of candidate spectra of sufficient quality. The dimension of the log-spectral CGs is 66: 22 static log-spectral coefficients and their first- and second-order time derivatives. The average number of CGs per BG is increased to 5. The test results are shown in row 9 of Tables 2, 3, 4, and 5. While it saves time in CG imputation, the method looses both accuracy and efficiency compared to PROSPECT CG imputation. BG selection is also less effective and more BGs need to be activated to guarantee a reasonable accuracy. Finally, spectral CGs are not able to provide channel estimates (as in Section 6.2.1) as PROSPECT CGs can. This claim is motivated by an experiment (not reported in this article) where the log-spectral CGs provide the candidates of clean speech and trigger the BG selection, while PROSPECT CGs are used for channel estimation, which improved the recognition accuracy by 3.58% relative on test sets 8-14.

7. CONCLUSIONS AND FUTURE WORK

We have proposed several effective optimizations to a large vocabulary speech recognizer that is based on MDT. The outcome is a recognizer that runs equally fast as the uncompensated system, has identical performance on clean data, has the same robustness as our latest published missing data system [23] and shows competitive performance on the AURORA-4 task.

We first formulated the missing data paradigm such that it can be applied to an acoustic model that requires no compromises on accuracy and uses standard feature representations, i.e., a formulation that covers cepstral as well as LDA-features as they are commonly used in today's speech recognizers. This formulation exploits the most accurate speech model that the recognizer disposes of: the backend HMM. The computational load was significantly reduced by the proposed MC approach to solve the CLSQ problems with sufficient accuracy for practical purposes. Here, candidates are obtained from exact solutions on a smaller set of CG, followed by selection of the most likely candidate. The posterior probabilities of the CG were exploited to construct a Gaussian selection algorithm that saves more computation by excluding Gaussians that are unlikely to make a significant contribution to the state likelihoods. Finally, the CGs were structured hierarchically with a model-based Gaussian clustering algorithm to achieve further speed gains.

The proposed method was compared to cluster-based imputation, an MDT that enhances the feature vector based on a GMM speech model, a technique that is also suitable for large vocabulary tasks. Our experiments reveal that it is beneficial to accuracy to exploit the more accurate backend model instead.

The optimizations show that no modeling compromises are required to apply MDT to large vocabulary recognition and that, on noisy data, any additional computational cost in likelihood calculation is easily recovered by a reduction in the search effort. These benefits make the missing data formalism very suitable to tackle various robustness issues beyond the additive noise effects considered in this article. With a suitable missing data detector, the solutions described in this article open pathways to also efficiently cover reverberated speech and exploit multiple microphones to implement directional hearing.

Appendix: Computational complexity of maximized likelihood per Gaussian

This section reveals how the numbers of multiplication involved in each approach in Table 1 are obtained. The complexity is quantified as the number of multiplications or divisions.

MAP

The iterative method of the MAP algorithm in [24] includes the following steps:

1. *a.* Initialize $\mathbf{x}_{t,u}$ using the component-wise minimization: $\mathbf{x}_{t,u}(i) = \min[\boldsymbol{\mu}_{t,u}(i), \mathbf{y}_{t,u}(i)]$ as in Equation (2).

2. *b.* For each i of the unreliable sub vector $\mathbf{x}_{t,u}$, calculate the conditional mean

$$\bar{\mathbf{x}}_{t,u,k}(i) = E(\mathbf{x}_{t,u,k}(i) | \mathbf{x}_{t,u,k}(1) \ldots \mathbf{x}_{t,u,k}(i-1),\ \mathbf{x}_{t,u,k}(i+1) \ldots \mathbf{x}_{t,u,k}(D-D_{t,u}),\ \mathbf{y}_{t,r})$$

where $D_{t,u}$ is the number of unreliable components in the spectrum at time t.

And constrain

x̄ t,u,k(i)←min(yt,u,k(i),x̄ t,u,k(i)) $\bar{\mathbf{x}}_{t,u,k}(i) \leftarrow \min(\mathbf{y}_{t,u,k}(i), \bar{\mathbf{x}}_{t,u,k}(i))$

1. *c.* Repeat step b for several iterations and calculate the likelihood $p(\mathbf{x}_{t,u,k}, \mathbf{y}_{t,r}|k)$

Raj et al. provide a standard solution for the conditional mean in step b:

$$\bar{\mathbf{x}}_{t,u,k} = \boldsymbol{\mu}_{t,u,k} + \boldsymbol{\Sigma}_{t,u,r,k}(\boldsymbol{\Sigma}_{t,r,r,k})^{-1}(\mathbf{y}_{t,r} - \boldsymbol{\mu}_{t,r,k})$$

where $\boldsymbol{\mu}_{t,u,k}$ is the mean of unreliable sub-vector. $\boldsymbol{\Sigma}_k$ is the covariance of Gaussian k. $\boldsymbol{\Sigma}_{t,u,r,k}$ contains only the rows with indices corresponding to the unreliable components and columns with the reliable indices in $\boldsymbol{\Sigma}_{t,k}$.

The conditional mean can also be formulated as

$$\bar{\mathbf{x}}_{t,u,k} = \boldsymbol{\mu}_{t,u,k} - (\mathbf{H}_{t,u,u,k})^{-1}\mathbf{H}_{t,u,r,k}(\mathbf{y}_{t,r} - \boldsymbol{\mu}_{t,r,k})$$

where $\mathbf{H}_k = \boldsymbol{\Sigma}_k^{-1}$ and $\mathbf{H}_{t,u,u,k}$ is a $D_{t,u}$ by $D_{t,u}$ sub-matrix of $\mathbf{H}_k$ containing only the rows and columns corresponding to the unreliable components in the feature vector. $\mathbf{H}_{t,u,r,k}$ is a $D_{t,u}$ by D-$D_{t,u}$ sub-matrix of $\mathbf{H}_k$ containing only the rows corresponding to the indices of unreliable components in the feature and the columns with reliable indices.

In step b, only 1 dimension is free and updated per operation as:

$$\bar{\mathbf{x}}_{t,u,k}(i) = \boldsymbol{\mu}_{t,u,k}(i) - \frac{\sum_{j \neq i, \mathbf{x}(j) \in \mathbf{x}_{t,u,k}} \mathbf{H}_k(i,j)(\mathbf{x}_t(j) - \boldsymbol{\mu}_k(j)) + \sum_{\mathbf{y}(m) \in \mathbf{y}_{t,r}} \mathbf{H}_k(i,m)(\mathbf{y}_t(m) - \boldsymbol{\mu}_k(m))}{\mathbf{H}_k(i,i)}$$

The second part of the summation in the numerator is constant and can be calculated at the first iteration. Hence, the MAP algorithm involves $(D_{t,u} + 1) \times D_{t,u}$ multiplications per iteration where the dimension of $\bar{\mathbf{x}}_{t,u,k}$ is $D_{t,u}$. In the above equation, $\mathbf{x}_t(j)$ is the jth component of the latest updated unreliable component.

Besides updating the clean speech in each iteration, the likelihood of the CG is also required for BG selection, which involves $(D + 1)D$ multiplications. Each iteration of MAP is very efficient, but as shown by the experimental result, MAP needs six iterations to reach convergence in terms of WER. Furthermore, as described in Section 4.1, the full precision matrix has to be handled in the CPU cache memory. Hence, MAP is slower than GD + PROSPECT.

Multiplicative updates

As outlined in [32, 33], the step calculation of the i th unreliable component for Gaussian k is given by

$$\mathbf{x}_u(i) \leftarrow \mathbf{x}_u(i)\frac{\mathbf{b}(i)+\sqrt{\mathbf{b}(i)^2+4[\mathbf{H}_{t,u,u,k}^{+}(\mathbf{x}_{t,u,k}-\boldsymbol{\mu}_{t,u,k})]_i[\mathbf{H}_{t,u,u,k}^{-}(\mathbf{x}_{t,u,k}-\boldsymbol{\mu}_{t,u,k})]_i}}{2[\mathbf{H}_{t,u,u,k}^{+}(\mathbf{x}-\boldsymbol{\mu}_{t,u,k})]_i}$$

$\mathbf{H}_{t,u,u,k}^{+}$($\mathbf{H}_{t,u,u,k}^{-}$) is obtained from $\mathbf{H}_{t,u,u,k}$ by setting all negative (positive) entries to zero. $\mathbf{H}_{t,u,u,k}^{+}(\mathbf{x}_{t,u,k}-\boldsymbol{\mu}_{t,u,k})$ together with $\mathbf{H}_{t,u,u,k}^{-}(\mathbf{x}_{t,u,k}-\boldsymbol{\mu}_{t,u,k})$ involve $D_{t,u} \times D_{t,u}$ multiplication operations.

$\mathbf{b} = \mathbf{H}_{t,u,r,k}(\mathbf{y}_{t,r}-\boldsymbol{\mu}_{r,k}) + \mathbf{H}_{t,u,u,k}(\mathbf{x}_{t,u,k}-\boldsymbol{\mu}_{t,u,k})$ so its first term can be calculated prior to iteration. The second term is already calculated while calculating $\mathbf{H}_{t,u,u,k}^{+}(\mathbf{x}_{t,u,k}-\boldsymbol{\mu}_{t,u,k})$ and $\mathbf{H}_{t,u,u,k}^{-}(\mathbf{x}_{t,u,k}-\boldsymbol{\mu}_{t,u,k})$. The square, multiplication (2 ×) and division in the above equation involves $4 \times D_{t,u}$ multiplications per iteration. In addition, $D_{t,u}$ computationally expensive square root operations are also involved in each iteration. The calculation of the likelihood involves $(D+1)D$ multiplications, the same as MAP. MU shares the same drawback with MAP that it has to handle the full precision matrix whenever it is called. As proved by the experiments, MU needs five iterations for convergence of the WER.

Gradient descent + cepstral Gaussians

To calculate the likelihood and gradient of a Cepstral Gaussian with diagonal covariance given a frame of unreliable spectrum, the precision matrix of the Gaussian must be either pre-calculated or calculated on-line. The pre-calculation implies that the system has to handle the $D \times D$precision matrix which leads to frequent data exchange between CPU and main memory. To calculate the gradient on-line, the precision matrix must be represented in the log-spectral domain as

$$\mathbf{H}_k\left(\begin{bmatrix}\mathbf{y}_{t,r}\\ \mathbf{x}_{t,u}\end{bmatrix}-\boldsymbol{\mu}_k\right)=\mathbf{C}'\boldsymbol{\Sigma}_k^{-1}\mathbf{C}\left(\begin{bmatrix}\mathbf{y}_{t,r}\\ \mathbf{x}_{t,u}\end{bmatrix}-\boldsymbol{\mu}_k\right) \tag{26}$$

where $\mathbf{H}_k$ is the precision matrix of Gaussian k, and it is transformed from the inverse diagonal covariance matrix $\boldsymbol{\Sigma}_k^{-1}$ by applying the transpose of

DCT matrix **C**. Let $\mathbf{C}_r$ be the D_m by $D - D_{t,u}$ sub matrix of **C**, containing the columns with the reliable indices, and $\mathbf{C}_u$ contains the remaining elements. Equation (26) can be represented as

$$C'\Sigma_k^{-1}C\left(\begin{bmatrix} y_{t,r} \\ x_{t,u} \end{bmatrix} - \mu_k\right) = \begin{bmatrix} C_r' \\ C_u' \end{bmatrix}\Sigma_k^{-1}\left[C_r\ C_u\right]\left(\begin{bmatrix} y_{t,r} \\ x_{t,u} \end{bmatrix} - \mu_k\right)$$

$$= C'\Sigma_k^{-1}C_r\left(y_{t,r} - \mu_{t,r,k}\right) + \begin{bmatrix} C_u'\Sigma_k^{-1}C_u\left(x_{t,u} - \mu_{t,u,k}\right) \\ C'_r\Sigma_k^{-1}C_u\left(x_{t,u} - \mu_{t,u,k}\right) \end{bmatrix}$$

$\mathbf{C}'\boldsymbol{\Sigma}_k^{-1}\mathbf{C}_r\left(\mathbf{y}_{t,r} - \boldsymbol{\mu}_{t,r,k}\right)$ is constant for every iteration and is part of the calculation of the likelihood. $\mathbf{C}'\boldsymbol{\Sigma}_k^{-1}\mathbf{C}_u\left(\mathbf{x}_{t,u} - \boldsymbol{\mu}_{t,u,k}\right)$ involves $D_{t,u}(2D_m + 1)$ multiplications for the unreliable component of the gradient. A small fraction of the gradient needs to be added to the gradient to cope with the singularity of $\mathbf{H}_k$ as mentioned in Equation (11). Hence, another $D_{t,u}$ multiplications are needed. The calculation of step size and step scale in Equation (13) involve $D_m D + D_m + D + D_{t,u}$ multiplications. The calculation of likelihood contains $2D_m D + D_m + D$ multiplications.

Gradient descent + PROSPECT features

The cost function for a Gaussian trained with PROSPECT features is shown in Equation (17). The calculation of gradient $\mathbf{g}_{t,k}$ can be decomposed to the projection part and cepstral part. The following quantities must be calculated.

$\mathbf{C}_c\left(\mathbf{x}_t - \mathbf{R}'\boldsymbol{\mu}_k\right)$: $\mathbf{R}'\boldsymbol{\mu}_k$ is the spectral mean of Gaussian k which is pre-calculated from the PROSPECT mean using the inverse PROSPECT transform **R**. $D_c D_{t,u}$ multiplication are involved for the unreliable components every iteration. Additionally $D_c(D - D_{t,u})$ multiplications are required to calculate the reliable components before the first iteration.

$\mathbf{C}_c'\mathbf{C}_c\left(\mathbf{x}_t - \mathbf{R}'\boldsymbol{\mu}_k\right)$: Based on the calculation of $\mathbf{C}_c\left(\mathbf{x}_t - \mathbf{R}'\boldsymbol{\mu}_k\right)$, $D_c D$ multiplications are involved.

$\boldsymbol{\Sigma}_k^{\perp^{-1}}\left(\mathbf{I} - \mathbf{C}_c'\mathbf{C}_c\right)\left(\mathbf{x}_t - \mathbf{R}'\boldsymbol{\mu}_k\right)$: includes another D multiplications.

$\mathbf{C}_c\boldsymbol{\Sigma}_k^{\perp^{-1}}\left(\mathbf{I} - \mathbf{C}_c'\mathbf{C}_c\right)\left(\mathbf{x}_t - \mathbf{R}'\boldsymbol{\mu}_k\right)$: includes another $D_c D$ multiplications.

$\mathbf{C}_c'\mathbf{C}_c\boldsymbol{\Sigma}_k^{\perp^{-1}}\left(\mathbf{I} - \mathbf{C}_c'\mathbf{C}_c\right)\left(\mathbf{x}_t - \mathbf{R}'\boldsymbol{\mu}_k\right)$: requires $D_c D_{t,u}$ multiplications per iteration.

The cepstral part $\mathbf{C}_c'\mathbf{\Sigma}_k^{c^{-1}}\mathbf{C}_c(\mathbf{x}_t - \mathbf{R}'\mu_k)$: Based on the calculation of $\mathbf{C}_c(\mathbf{x}_t - \mathbf{R}'\mu_k)$, $D_c + D_c D_{t,u}$ multiplications per iteration are involved.

Given the obtained gradient $\mathbf{g}_{t,k}$, the step size involves the following quantities as in Equation (13):

$\mathbf{g}_{t,k}'\mathbf{g}_{t,k}$: D multiplications.

$\mathbf{C}_c\mathbf{g}_{t,k}$: $D_c D$ multiplications.

$\mathbf{g}_{t,k}'\mathbf{C}_c'\mathbf{\Sigma}_k^{c^{-1}}\mathbf{C}_c\mathbf{g}_{t,k}$: $2D_c$ multiplications.

$(\mathbf{I}-\mathbf{C}_c'\mathbf{C}_c)\mathbf{g}_{t,k}$: $D_c D$ multiplications given $\mathbf{C}_c\mathbf{g}_{t,k}$.

$\mathbf{g}_{t,k}'(\mathbf{I}-\mathbf{C}_c'\mathbf{C}_c)\mathbf{\Sigma}_k^{\perp^{-1}}(\mathbf{I}-\mathbf{C}_c'\mathbf{C}_c)\mathbf{g}_{t,k}$: $2D$ multiplications

Another D multiplications are required for scaling the gradient as explained in the previous section.

Besides the iterations, the initial likelihood involves $2(D + D_c)$ multiplications.

With the typical values of D, D_m, D_c and $D_{t,u}$ in Table 1 the number of multiplications involved in MAP is 2138 per Gaussian, while it is 2106 for MU. But MU needs 80 square root operations per Gaussian. The number of multiplications involved in GD with cepstral Gaussian is 2177. This number is reduced to 1416 when using PROSPECT features.

ACKNOWLEDGEMENTS

This study was financed by the MIDAS project of the Nederlandse Taalunie under the STEVIN programme. Thanks to Kris Demuynck for various implementations and the anonymous reviewers for suggesting additional interesting comparisons and analyses.

REFERENCES

1. ETSI standard doc., Speech processing, transmission and quality aspects (STQ); distributed speech recognition; advanced frontend feature extraction algorithm; compression algorithms *ETSI, Tech Rep ES 202 050 v1.1.3* 2003.

2. Flores JAN, Young SJ: Continuous speech recognition in noise using spectral subtraction and HMM adaptation. In *Proceedings of ICASSP*. Adelaide, South Australia, Australia; 1994:409-412.

3. Droppo J, Deng L, Acero A: Evaluation of the SPLICE algorithm on the Aurora2 database. In *Proceedings of Eurospeech*. Aalborg, Denmark; 2001:217-220.

4. Moreno PJ, Raj B, Stern RMJ: A vector Taylor series approach for environment-independent speech recognition. In *Proceedings of ICASSP*. Atlanta, Georgia, USA; 1996:733-736.

5. Gales M: Model-based techniques for noise robust speech recognition. PhD thesis. University of Cambridge; 1995.

6. Leggetter CJ, Woodland PC: Maximum likelihood linear regression for speaker adaptation of continuous density hidden Markov models. *Comput Speech Lang* 1995, 9(2):171-185. 10.1006/csla.1995.0010

7. Gauvain JL, Lee CH: Maximum a posteriori estimation for multivariate Gaussian mixture observations of Markov chains. *IEEE Trans Speech Audio Process* 1994, 2(2):291-298. 10.1109/89.279278

8. Bregman AS: *Auditory Scene Analysis*. MIT Press, Cambridge; 1990.

9. Van Segbroeck M, Van hamme H: Vector quantization based mask estimation for missing data ASR. In *Proceedings of Interspeech*. Antwerp, Belgium; 2007:910-913.

10. Barker J, Cooke M, Green P: Robust ASR based on clean speech models: an evaluation of missing data. In *Proceedings of Eurospeech*. Aalborg, Denmark; 2001:213-216.

11. Cooke M: A glimpsing model of speech perception in noise. *J Acoust Soc Am* 2006, 119(3):1562-1573. 10.1121/1.2166600

12. Barker JP, Cooke MP, Ellis DPW: Decoding speech in the presence of other sources. *Speech Commun* 2005, 45(1):5-25. 10.1016/j.specom.2004.05.002

13. Srinivasan S, Wang D: Transforming binary uncertainties for robust speech recognition. *IEEE Trans Audio Speech Lang Process* 2007, 15(7):2130-2140.

14. Srinivasan S, Wang D: Robust speech recognition by integrating speech separation and hypothesis testing. *Speech Commun* 2010, 52(1):72-81. 10.1016/j.specom.2009.08.008

15. Cooke M, Green P, Josifovski L: A Vizinho, Robust automatic speech recognition with missing and unreliable acoustic data. *Speech Commun* 2001, 34(3):267-285. 10.1016/S0167-6393(00)00034-0

16. Lippmann RP, Carlson BA: Using missing feature theory to actively select features for robust speech recognition with interruptions, filtering and noise. In *Proceedings of Eurospeech*. Rhodes, Greece; 1997:37-40.

17. Seltzer ML, Raj B, Stern RM: A Bayesian classifier for spectrographic mask estimation for missing feature speech recognition. *Speech Commun* 2004, 43(4):379-393. 10.1016/j.specom.2004.03.006

18. Cooke M, Morris A, Green P: Missing data techniques for robust speech recognition. In *Proceedings of ICASSP*. Munich, Germany; 1997:863-866.

19. Renevey P, Drygajlo A: Detection of reliable features for speech recognition in noisy conditions using a statistical criterion. In *Proceedings of CRAC Workshop*. Aalborg, Denmark; 2001:71-74.

20. Srinivasan S, Shao Y, Jin Z, Wang D: A computational auditory scene analysis system for robust speech recognition. In *Proceedings of Interspeech*. Pittsburg, Pennsylvania, USA; 2006:73-76.

21. Cerisara C, Demange S, Haton J-P: On noise masking for automatic missing data speech recognition: a survey and discussion. *Comput Speech Lang* 2007, 21(3):443-457. 10.1016/j.csl.2006.08.001

22. Coy A, Barker J: Soft harmonic masks for recognising speech in the presence of a competing speaker. In *Proceedings of Interspeech*. Lisbon, Portugal; 2005:2641-2644.

23. Van Segbroeck M, Van hamme H: Advances in missing feature techniques for robust large vocabulary continuous speech recognition.*IEEE Trans Audio Speech Lang Process* 2011, 19(1):123-137.

24. Raj B, Seltzer ML, Stern RM: Reconstruction of missing features for robust speech recognition. *Speech Commun* 2004, 43(4):275-296. 10.1016/j.specom.2004.03.007

25. Van hamme H: Robust speech recognition using cepstral domain missing data techniques and noisy masks. In *Proceedings of ICASSP.Volume 1*. Montreal, Quebec, Canada; 2004:213-216.

26. Cerisara C: Towards missing data recognition with cepstral features. In *Proceedings of Eurospeech*. Geneva, Switzerland; 2003:3057-3060.

27. Häkkinen J, Haverinen H: On the use of missing feature theory with cepstral features. In *Proceedings of CRAC Workshop*. Aalborg, Denmark; 2001.

28. Faubel F, McDonough J, Klakow D: Bounded conditional mean imputation with Gaussian mixture models: a reconstruction approach to partly occluded features. In *Proceedings of ICASSP*. Taipei, Taiwan; 2009:3869-3872.

29. Haeb-Umbach R, Ney H: Linear discriminant analysis for improved large vocabulary continuous speech recognition. In *Proceedings of ICASSP*. San Francisco, California, USA; 1992:13-16.

30. Kumar N, Andreou AG: A generalization of linear discriminant analysis in maximum likelihood framework. In *Tech Rep JHU-CLSP Technical Report No. 16*. Johns Hopkins University; 1996.

31. Fletcher R: *Practical Methods of Optimization*. John Wiley & Sons, Chichester; 1980.

32. Saul LK, Sha F, Lee DD: Statistical signal processing with non-negativity constraints. In *Proceedings of Eurospeech*. Geneva, Switzerland; 2003:1001-1004.

33. Van hamme H: Prospect features and their application to missing data techniques for robust speech recognition. In *Proceedings of Interspeech*. Jeju, Korea; 2004:101-104.

34. Duchateau J, Demuynck K, Van Compernolle D, Wambacq P: Class definition in discriminant feature analysis. In *Proceeding of Eurospeech*. Aalborg, Denmark; 2001:1621-1624.

35. Young SJ, Odell JJ, Woodland PC: Tree-based state tying for high accuracy acoustic modelling. In *Proceedings of Workshop on Human Language Technology*. Plainsboro, New Jerey, USA; 1994:307-312.

36. Iskra D, Grosskopf B, Marasek K, van den Heuvel H, Diehl F, Kiessling A: SPEECON--Speech Databases for Consumer Devices: Database Specification and Validation. In *Proceedings of LREC*. Las Palmas, Spain; 2002:329-333.

37. Demuynck K: Extracting, modeling and combining information in speech recognition. *PhD thesis*. K.U., Leuven, ESAT; 2001.

38. Fritsch J, Rogina I: The bucket box intersection (BBI) algorithm for fast approximate evaluation of diagonal mixture Gaussians. In*Proceeding of ICASSP. Volume 2.* Atlanta, Georgia, USA; 1996:273-276.

39. Bocchieri E: Vector quantization for efficient computation of continuous density likelihoods. In *Proceeding of ICASSP. Volume 2.* Minneapolis, Minnesota, USA; 1993:692-695.

40. Watanabe T, Shinoda K, Takagi K, Iso KI: High speed speech recognition using tree-structured probability density function. In *Proceeding of ICASSP. Volume 1.* Detroit, Michigan, USA; 1995:556-559.

41. Wang Y, Van hamme H: Speed improvements in a missing data-based speech recognizer by Gaussian selection. In *Proceedings of NAG-DAGA.* Rotterdam, Netherlands; 2009:423-426.

42. Mackay DJ: *Information Theory, Inference, and Learning Algorithms.* Cambridge University Press, Cambridge, UK; 2003.

43. Myrvoll TA, Soong FK: Optimal clustering of multivariate normal distributions using divergence and its application to HMM adaptation. In*Proceedings of ICASSP.* Hong Kong; 2003:552-555.

44. Parihar N, Picone J: Analysis of the aurora large vocabulary evaluations. In *Proceedings of Eurospeech.* Geneva, Switzerland; 2003:337-340.

45. Gemmeke JF, Van Segbroeck M, Wang Y, Cranen B, Van hamme H: Automatic speech recognition using missing data techniques: handling of real-world data. In *Robust Speech Recognition of Uncertain or Missing Data.* Edited by: Haeb-Umbach R, Kolossa D. Berlin-Heidelberg (Germany), Springer Verlag; 2011:157-186.

46. Young S, Kershaw D, Odell J, Ollason D, Valtchev V, Woodland P:*The HTK Book.* [http://htk.eng.cam.ac.uk/docs/docs.shtml]

47. SPRAAK: Speech Processing, Recognition and Automatic Annotation Kit.[http://www.spraak.org/]

2

CHAPTER

Sparse Coding of the Modulation Spectrum for Noise-Robust Automatic Speech Recognition

Sara Ahmadi, Seyed Mohammad Ahadi, Bert Cranen and Lou Boves

[1]*Amirkabir University of Technology, Hafez 424, 15875-4413 Tehran, Iran.*

[2]*Centre for Language Studies, Radboud University Nijmegen, Erasmusplein 1, 6525HT Nijmegen, Netherlands.*

ABSTRACT

The full modulation spectrum is a high-dimensional representation of one-dimensional audio signals. Most previous research in automatic speech recognition converted this very rich representation into the equivalent of a sequence of short-time power spectra, mainly to simplify the computation of the posterior probability that a frame of an unknown speech signal is related to a specific state. In this paper we use the raw output of a modulation spectrum analyser in combination with sparse coding as a means for obtaining state posterior probabilities. The modulation spectrum analyser uses 15 gammatone filters. The Hilbert envelope of the output of these filters is then processed by nine modulation frequency filters, with bandwidths up to 16 Hz. Experiments using the AURORA-2 task show that the novel approach is promising. We found that the representation of medium-term dynamics in the modulation spectrum analyser must be improved. We also found that we should move towards sparse classification, by modifying the cost function in sparse coding such that the class(es) represented by the exemplars weigh in, in addition to the accuracy with which unknown observations are reconstructed. This creates two challenges: (1) developing a method for dictionary learning that takes the class occupancy of exemplars into account and (2) developing a method for learning a mapping from exemplar activations to state posterior probabilities that keeps the generalization to unseen conditions that is one of the strongest advantages of sparse coding.

Keywords: Sparse coding/compressive sensing Sparse classification Modulation spectrum Noise robust automatic speech recognition

1. INTRODUCTION

Nobody will seriously disagree with the statement that most of the information in acoustic signals is encoded in the way in which the signal properties change over time and that instantaneous characteristics, such as the shape or the envelope of the short-time spectrum, are less important - though surely not unimportant. The dynamic changes over time in the envelope of the short-time spectrum are captured in the modulation spectrum [1]-[3]. This makes the modulation spectrum a fundamentally more informative representation of audio signals than a sequence of short-time spectra. Still, most approaches in speech technology, whether it is speech recognition, speech synthesis, speaker recognition, or speech coding, seem to rely on impoverished representations of the modulation spectrum in the form of a sequence of short-time spectra, possibly extended with explicit information about the dynamic changes in the form of delta and delta-delta coefficients. For speech (and audio) coding, the reliance on sequences of short-time spectra can be explained by the fact that many applications (first and foremost telephony) cannot tolerate delays in the order of 250 ms, while full use of modulation spectra might incur delays up to a second. What is more, coders can rely on the human auditory system to extract and utilize the dynamic changes that are still retained in the output of the coders. If coders are used in environments and applications in which delay is not an issue (music recording, broadcast transmission), we do see a more elaborate use of information linked to modulation spectra [4]-[6]. Here too, the focus is on reducing bit rates by capitalizing on the properties of the human auditory system. We are not aware of approaches to speech synthesis - where delay is not an issue - that aim to harness advantages offered by the modulation spectrum. Information about the temporal dynamics of speech signal by means of shifted delta cepstra has proven beneficial for automatic language and speaker recognition [7].

In this paper we are concerned with the use of modulation spectra for automatic speech recognition (ASR), specifically noise-robust speech recognition. In this application domain, we cannot rely on the intervention of the human auditory system. On the contrary, it is now necessary to automatically extract the information encoded in the modulation spectrum that humans would use to understand the message.

The seminal research by [1] showed that modulation frequencies >16 Hz contribute very little to speech intelligibility. In [8] it was shown that attenuating modulation frequencies <1 Hz does not affect intelligibility either. Very low modulation frequencies are related to stationary channel characteristics or stationary noise, rather than to the dynamically changing speech signal carried by the channel. The upper limit of the band with linguistically relevant modulation frequencies is related to the maximum speed with which the articulators can move. This insight gave rise to the introduction of RASTA filtering in [9] and [10]. RASTA filtering is best conceived of as a form of post-processing applied on the output of otherwise conventional representations of the speech signal derived from short-time spectra. This puts RASTA filtering in the same category as, for example, Mel-frequency spectra and Mel-frequency cepstral coefficients: engineering approaches designed to efficiently approximate representations manifested in psycho-acoustic experiments [11]. Subsequent developments towards harnessing the modulation spectrum in ASR have followed pretty much the same path, characterized by some form of additional processing applied to sequences of short-time spectral (or cepstral) features. Perhaps somewhat surprisingly, none of these developments have given rise to substantial improvements of recognition performance relative to other engineering tricks that do not take guidance from knowledge about the auditory system.

All existing ASR systems are characterized by an architecture that consists of a front end and a back end. The back end always comes in the form of a state network, in which words are discrete units, made up of a directed graph of subword units (usually phones), each of which is in turn represented as a sequence of states. Recognizing an utterance amounts to searching the path in a finite-state machine that has the maximum likelihood, given an acoustic signal. The link between a continuous audio signal and the discrete state machine is established by converting the acoustic signal into a sequence of likelihoods that a short segment of the signal corresponds to one of the low-level states. The task of the front end is to convert the signal into a sequence of state likelihood estimates, usually at a 100-Hz rate, which should be more than adequate to capture the fastest possible articulation movements.

Speech coding or speech synthesis with a 100-Hz frame rate using short-time spectra yields perfectly intelligible and natural-sounding results. Therefore, it was only natural to assume that a sequence of short-time spectra at the same frame rate would be a good input representation for an ASR system. However, already in the early seventies, it was shown by Jean-Silvain Liénard [12] that it was necessary to augment the static spectrum representation by so-called delta and delta-delta coefficients that represent the speed and acceleration of the change of the spectral envelope over time and that were popularized by [13]. For reasonably clean speech, this approach appears to be adequate.

Under acoustically adverse conditions, the recognition performance of ASR systems degrades much more rapidly than human performance [14]. Convolutional noise can be effectively handled by RASTA-like processing. Distortions due to reverberation have a direct impact on the modulation spectrum, and they also cause substantial difficulties for human listeners [15],[16]. Therefore, much research in noise-robust ASR has focused on speech recognition in additive noise. Speech recognition in noise basically must solve two problems simultaneously: (1) one needs to determine which acoustic properties of the signal belong to the target speech and which are due to the background noise (the source separation problem), and (2) those parts of the acoustic representations of the speech signal which are not entirely obscured by the noise must be processed to decode the linguistic message (speech decoding problem).

For a recent review of the range of approaches that has been taken towards noise-robust ASR, we refer to [17]. Here, we focus on one set of approaches, guided by the finding that humans have less trouble recognizing speech in noise, which seems to suggest that humans are either better in source separation or in latching on to the speech information that is not obscured by the noise (or in both). This suggests that there is something in the auditory processing system that makes it possible to deal with additive noise. Indeed, it has been suggested that replacing the conventional short-time spectral analysis based on the fast Fourier transform by the output of a principled auditory model should improve robustness against noise. However, up to now, the results of research along this line have failed to live up to the promise [18]. We believe that this is at least in part caused by the fact that in previous research, the output of an auditory model was converted to the equivalent of the energy in one-third octave filters, necessary for interfacing with a conventional ASR back end, but without trying to capture the continuity constraints imposed by the articulatory system. In this conversion most of the additional information carried by the modulation spectrum is lost.

In this paper we explore the use of a modulation spectrum front end that is based on time-domain filtering that does not require collapsing the output to the equivalent of one-third octave filters, but which still makes it possible to estimate the posterior probability of the states in a finite-state machine. In brief, we first filter the speech signal with 15 gammatone filters (roughly equivalent to one-third octave filters) and we process the Hilbert envelope of the output of the gammatone filters with nine modulation spectrum filters [19]. The 135-dimensional (135-D) output of this system can be sampled at any rate that is an integer fraction of the sampling frequency of the input speech signal. For the conversion of the 135-D output to posterior probability estimates of a set of states, we use the sparse coding (SC) approach proposed by [20]. Sparse coding is best conceived of as an exemplar-based approach [21] in which unknown inputs are coded as positive (weighted) sums of items in an exemplar dictionary.

We use the well-known AURORA-2 task [22] as the platform for developing our modulation spectrum approach to noise-robust ASR. We will use the 'standard' back end for this task, i.e. a Viterbi decoder that finds the best path in a lattice spanned by the 179 states that result from representing 11 digit words by 16 states each, plus 3 states for representing non-speech. We expect that the effect of the additive noise is limited to a subset of the 135 output channels of the modulation spectrum analyser.

The major goal of this paper is to introduce a novel approach to noise-robust ASR. The approach that we propose is novel in two respects: we use the 'raw' output of modulation frequency filters and we use Sparse Classification to derive state posterior probabilities from samples of the output of the modulation spectrum filters. We deliberately use unadorned implementations of both the modulation spectrum analyser and the sparse coder, because we see a need for identifying what are the most important issues that are involved with a fundamentally different approach to representing speech signals and with converting the representations to state posterior estimates. In doing so we are fully aware of the risk that - for the moment - we will end up with word error rates (WERs) that are well above what is considered state-of-the-art [23]. Understanding the issues that affect the performance of our system most will allow us to propose a road map towards our final goal that combines advanced insight in what it is that makes human speech recognition so very robust against noise with improved procedures for automatic noise-robust speech recognition.

Our approach combines two novelties, *viz.* the features and the state posterior probability estimation. To make it possible to disentangle the contributions and implications of the two novelties, we will also conduct experiments in which we use conventional multi-layered perceptrons (MLPs) to derive state posterior probability estimates from the outputs of the modulation spectrum analyser. In section 2, we will compare the sparse classification approach with the results obtained with the MLP for estimating state posterior probabilities. This will allow us to assess the advantages of the modulation spectrum analyser, as well as the contribution of the sparse classification approach.

2. METHOD

2.1 Sparse classification front end

The approach to noise-robust ASR that we propose in this paper was inspired by [20] and [24], which introduced *sparse classification* (SCl) as a technique for estimating the posterior probabilities of the lowest-level states in an ASR system. The starting point of their approach was a representation of noisy speech signals as overlapping sequences of up to 30 speech frames that together cover up to 300 ms intervals of the signals. Individual frames were represented as Mel-frequency energy spectra, because that representation conforms to the additivity requirement imposed by the sparse classification approach. SC is an exemplar-based approach. Handling clean speech requires the construction of an exemplar dictionary that contains stretches of speech signals of the same length as the (overlapping) stretches that must be coded. The exemplars must be chosen such that they represent arbitrary utterances. For noisy speech a second exemplar dictionary must be created, which contains equally long exemplars of the additive noises. Speech is coded by finding a small number of speech and noise exemplars which, added together with positive weights, accurately approximate an interval of the original signal. The algorithms that find the best exemplars and their weights are called *solvers*; all solvers allow imposing a maximum on the number of exemplars that are returned with a weight >0 so that it is guaranteed that the result is sparse. Different families of solvers are available, but some require that all coefficients in the representations of the signals and the exemplars are non-negative numbers. Least angle regression [25], implemented by means of a version of the *Lasso* solver, can operate with representations that contain positive and negative numbers.

The SC approach sketched above is interesting for two reasons. Sequences of short-time spectra implicitly represent a substantial part of the information in the modulation spectrum. That is certainly true if the sequences cover up to 300-ms signal intervals. In addition, in [26] it was shown that it is possible to convert the weights assigned to the exemplars in a SC system to the estimates of state probabilities, provided that the frames in the exemplars are assigned to states. The latter can be accomplished by means of a forced alignment of the database from which the exemplars are selected with the states that correspond to a phonetic transcription. In actual practice, the state labels are obtained by means of a forced alignment using a conventional hidden Markov model (HMM) recognizer.

The success of the SC approach in [20],[24] for noise-robust speech recognition is attributed to the fact that the speech exemplars are characterized by peaks in the spectral energy that exhibit substantial continuity over time; the human articulatory system can only produce signals that contain few clear discontinuities (such as the release of stop consonants), while many noise types lack such continuity. Therefore, it is reasonable to expect that the modulation spectra of speech and noise are rather different, even if the short-time spectra may be very similar.

In this paper we use the modulation spectrum directly to exploit the continuity constraints imposed by the speech production system. Since the modulation spectrum captures information about the continuity of the speech signal in the low-frequency bands, there is no need for a representation that stacks a large number of subsequent time frames. Therefore, our exemplar dictionary can be created by selecting individual frames of the modulation spectrum in a database of labelled speech. As in [20],[24], we will convert the weights assigned to the exemplars when coding unknown speech signals into estimates of the probability that a frame in the unknown signal corresponds to one of the states.

In [20],[24] the conversion of exemplar weights into state probabilities involved an averaging procedure. A frame in an unknown speech signal was included in as many solutions of the solver as there were frames in an exemplar. In each position of a sliding window, an unknown frame is associated with the states in the exemplars chosen in that position. While individual window positions return a small number of exemplars and therefore a small number of possible states, the eventual set of state probabilities assigned to a frame is not very sparse. With the single-frame exemplars in the approach presented here, no such averaging is necessary or possible. The potential downside of relying on a single set of exemplars to estimate state probabilities is that it may yield overly sparse state probability vectors.

2.2 Data

In order to provide a proof of concept that our approach is viable, we used a part of the AURORA-2 database [22]. This database consists of speech recordings taken from the TIDIGITS corpus for which participants read sequences of digits (only using the words 'zero' to 'nine' and 'oh') with one up to seven digits per utterance. These recordings were then artificially noisified by adding different types of noise to the clean recordings at different signal-to-noise ratios. In this paper we focus on the results obtained for test set *A*, i.e. the test set that is corrupted using the same noise types that occur in the multi-condition training set. We re-used a previously made state-level segmentation of the signals obtained by means of a forced alignment with a conventional HMM-based ASR system. These labels were also used to estimate the prior probabilities of the 179 states.

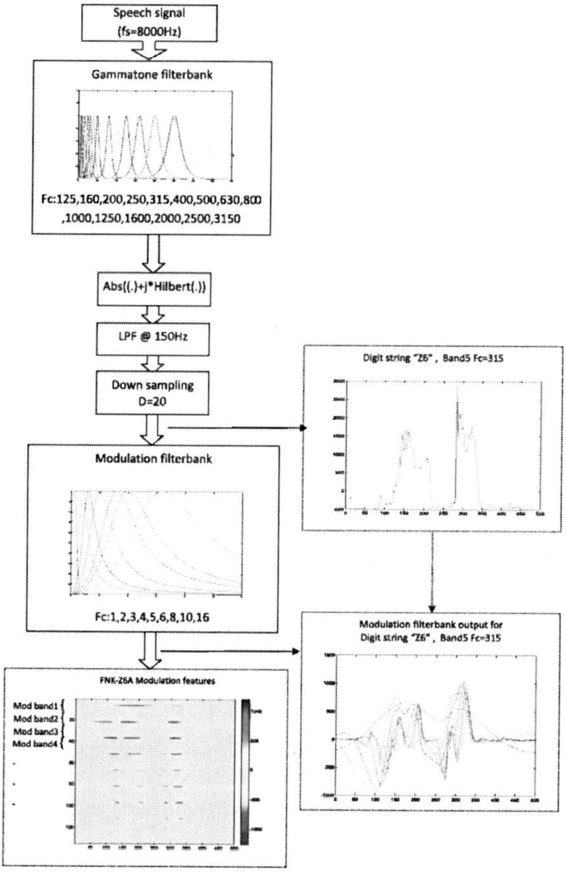

Figure 1. Feature extraction. The magnitude envelope of each of the 15 gammatone filters is decomposed into nine different modulation frequency bands. Thus, the speech is represented by 9×15=135-D feature vectors which are computed every 2.5 ms.

2.3 Feature extraction

The feature extraction process that we employ is illustrated in Figure 1. First, the (noisy) speech signal (sampling frequency F_s=8 kHz) is analysed by a *gammatone filterbank* consisting of 15 band-pass filters with centre frequencies (F_c) spaced at one-third octave. More specifically, F_c = 125, 160, 200, 250, 315, 400, 500, 630, 800, 1,000, 1,250, 1,600, 2,000, 2,500, and 3,150 Hz, respectively. The amplitude response of an *n* th-order gammatone filter with centre frequency F_c is defined by

$$g(t) = a \cdot t^{n-1} \cdot \cos(2\pi F_c t + \phi) \cdot e^{-2\pi bt}. \tag{1}$$

With b=1.0183×(24.7+F_c/9.265) and n=4, this yields band-pass filters with equivalent rectangular bandwidth equal to 1 [27]. Subsequently, the time envelope $e_i(t)$ of the i th filter output, x_i, is computed as the magnitude of the analytic signal

$$e_i(t) = \sqrt{x_i^2 + \hat{x}_i^2}, \tag{2}$$

with $\hat{x}_i$ the Hilbert transform of x_i. We assume that the time envelopes of the outputs of the gammatone filters are a sufficiently complete representation of the input speech signal. The frequency response of the gammatone filterbank is shown in the upper part at the left-hand side of Figure 1.

The Hilbert envelopes were low-pass filtered with a fifth-order Butterworth filter (*cf.* (3)) with cut-off frequency at 150 Hz and down-sampled to 400 Hz. The down-sampled time envelopes from the 15 gammatone filters are fed into another filterbank consisting of nine modulation filters. This so-called modulation filterbank is similar to the EPSM-filterbank as presented by [28]. In our implementation of the modulation filterbank, we used one-third-order Butterworth low-pass filter with a cut-off frequency of 1 Hz, and eight band-pass filters with centre frequencies of 2,3,4,5,6,8,10, and 16 Hz[a].

The frequency response of an *n* th-order low-pass filter with gain *a* and cut-off frequency F_c is specified by [29]

$$H(f) = \frac{a}{1.0 + \left(\frac{f}{F_c}\right)^{2n}} \tag{3}$$

The complex-valued frequency response of a band-pass modulation filter with gain a, centre frequency F_c and quality factor Q=1 is specified by

$$H(f) = \frac{a}{1.0 + jQ.\left(\frac{f}{F_c} - \frac{F_c}{f}\right)} \tag{4}$$

As an example, the upper panel at the right-hand side in Figure 1 shows the time envelope of the output of the gammatone filter with centre frequency at 315 Hz for the digit sequence 'zero six'. The frequency response of the complete filterbank, i.e. the sum of the responses of the nine individual filters, is shown in Figure 2. Due to the spacing of the centre frequency of the filters and the overlap of their transfer functions, we effectively give more weight to the modulation frequencies that are dominant in speech [30].

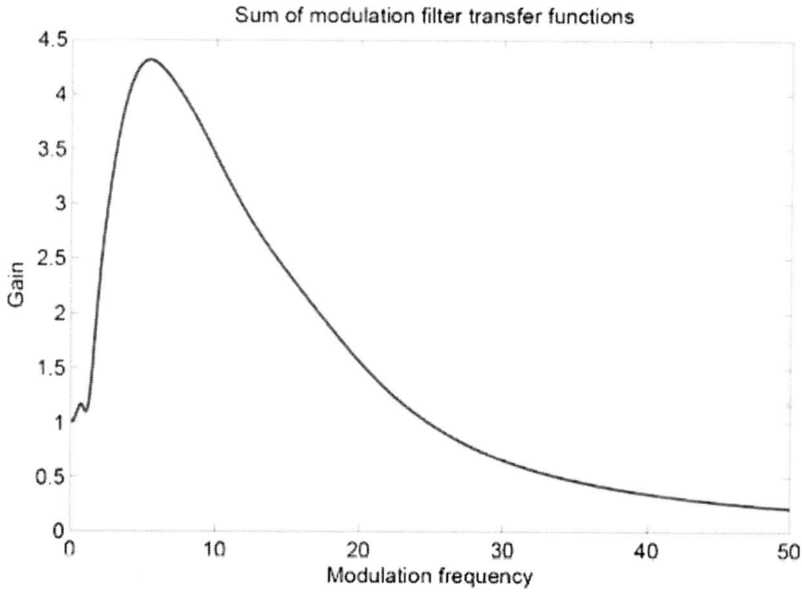

Figure 2. Sum of modulation transfer functions. The sum of the transfer functions of all modulation frequency filters gives a stronger weight to the frequencies that are known to be important for speech recognition [30].

The modulation frequency filterbank is implemented as a set of frequency domain filters. To obtain a frequency resolution of 0.1 Hz with the Hilbert envelopes sampled at 400 Hz, the calculations were based on Fourier transforms consisting of 4,001 frequency samples. For that purpose we computed the complex-valued frequency response of the filters at 4,001 frequency points. An example of the ensemble of waveforms that results from the combination of the gammatone and modulation filterbank analysis for the digit sequence 'zero six' is shown in the lower panel on the right-hand side of Figure 1. The amplitudes of the 9×15=135 signals as a function of time are shown in the bottom panel at the left-hand side of Figure 1. The top band represents the lowest modulation frequencies (0 to 1 Hz) and the bottom band the highest (modulation filter with centre frequency F_c=16 Hz).

We experimented with two different implementations of the modulation frequency filterbank, one in which we kept the phase response of the filters and the other in which we ignored the phase response and only retained the magnitude of the transfer functions. The results are illustrated in Figure 3 for clean speech and for the 5-dB signal-to-noise ratio (SNR) condition. From the second and third rows in that figure, it can be inferred that the linear phase implementation renders sudden changes in the Hilbert envelope as synchronized events in all modulation bands, while the full-phase implementation appears to smear these changes over wider time intervals. The (visual) effect is especially apparent in the right column, where the noisy speech is depicted. However, preliminary experiments indicated that the information captured in the 'visually noisy' full-phase representation could be harnessed by the recognition system: the full-phase implementation yields a performance increase in the order of 20% at the lower SNR levels compared with the performance of the linear phase implementation. However, the linear phase implementation works slightly better in clean and high SNR conditions (yielding ≈1% higher accuracies). This confirms the results of previous experiments in [31]. Therefore, all results in this paper are based on the full-phase implementation.

Another unsurprising observation that can be made from Figure 3 is that the non-negative Hilbert envelopes are turned into signals that have both positive and negative amplitude values. This will limit the options in choosing a solver in the SC approach to computing state posterior probabilities.

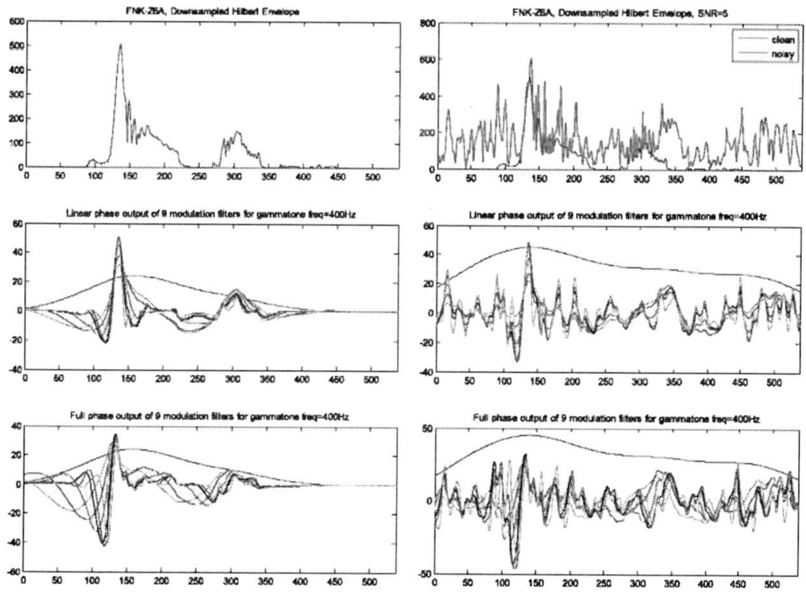

Figure 3. Full and linear phase features comparison. Top: spectrum envelope of 6th gammatone band for a sample utterance for clean (left) and 5-dB SNR (right). Middle: output of linear phase modulation filterbank. Bottom: output of full-phase modulation filterbank.

Figure 4 provides an extended view of the result of a modulation spectrum analysis of the utterance 'zero six'. The nine heat map representations in the lower left-hand part of Figure 1 are re-drawn in such a way that it is possible to see the similarities and differences between the modulation bands. The top panel in Figure 4 shows the output amplitude of the low-pass filter of the modulation filter bank. Subsequent panels show the amplitude of the outputs of the higher modulation band filters. It can be seen that overall, the amplitude decreases with increasing band number.

Speech and background noise tend to cover the same frequency regions in the short-time spectrum. Therefore, speech and noise will be mixed in the outputs of the 15 gammatone filters. The modulation filterbank decomposes each of the 15 time envelopes into a set of nine time-domain signals that correspond to different modulation frequencies. Generally speaking, the outputs of the lowest modulation frequencies are more associated with events demarcating syllable nuclei, while the higher modulation frequencies represent shorter-term events. We want to take advantage of the fact that it is unlikely that speech and noise sound sources with frequency components in the same gammatone filter also happen to overlap completely in the modulation frequency domain. Stationary noise would not affect the output of the higher modulation frequency filters, while pulsatile noise should not affect the lowest modulation frequency filters. Therefore, we expect that many of the naturally occurring noise sources will show temporal variations at different rates than speech.

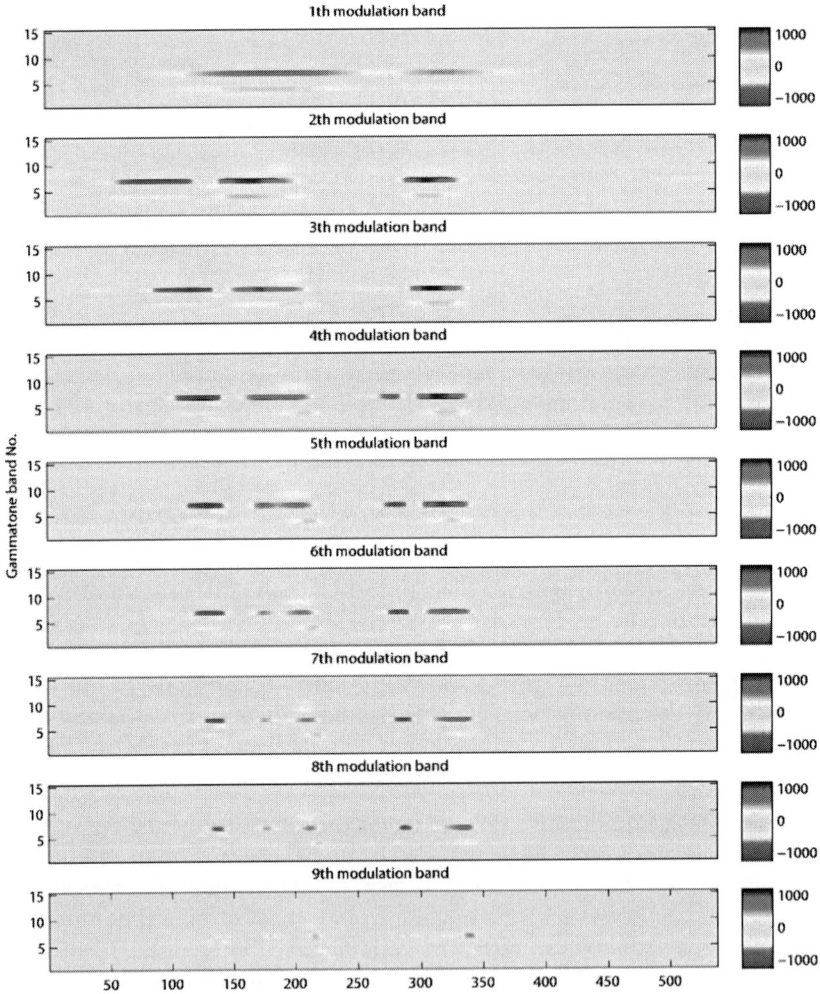

Figure 4. An extended view of the result of a modulation spectrum analysis of the utterance ‘zero six’.

Although the modulation spectrum features capture short- and medium-time spectral dynamics, the information is encoded in a manner that might not be optimal for automatic pattern recognition purposes. Therefore, we decided to also create a feature set that encodes the temporal dynamics more explicitly. To that end we concatenated 29 frames (at a rate of one frame per 2.5 ms), corresponding to 29×2.5=72.5 ms; to keep the number of features within reasonable limits, we performed dimensionality reduction by means of linear discriminant analysis (LDA), with the 179 state labels as categories. The reference category was the state label of the middle frame of a 29-frame sequence. The LDA transformation matrix was learned using the exemplar dictionary (*cf.*, section 2). The dimension of the feature vectors was reduced the 135, the same number as with single-frame features. To be able to investigate the effect of the LDA transform, we also applied an LDA transform to the original single-frame features. Here, the dimension of the transformed feature vector was limited to 135 (nine modulation bands in 15 gammatone filters).

2.4 Composition of exemplar dictionary

To construct the speech exemplar dictionary, we first encoded the clean train set of AURORA-2 with the modulation spectrum analysis system, using a frame rate of 400 Hz. Then, we quasi-randomly selected two frames from each utterance. To make sure that we had a reasonably uniform coverage of all states and both genders, 2×179 counters were used (one for each state of each gender). The counters were initialized at 48. For each selected exemplar, the corresponding counter was decremented by 1. Exemplars of a gender-state combination were no longer added to the dictionary if the counter became zero. A simple implementation of this search strategy yielded a set of 17,148 exemplars, in which some states missed one or two exemplars. It appeared that 36 exemplars had a Pearson correlation coefficient of >0.999 with at least one other exemplar. Therefore, the effective size of the dictionary is 17,091.

We also encoded the four noises in the multi-condition training set of AURORA-2 with the modulation spectrum analysis system. From the output, we randomly selected 13,300 frames as noise exemplars, with an equal number of exemplars for the four noise types.

When using LDA-transformed concatenated features, a new equally large set of exemplars was created by selecting sequences of 29 consecutive frames, using the same procedures as for selecting single-frame exemplars. In a similar vein, 29-frame noise exemplars were selected that were reduced to 135-D features using the same transformation matrix as for the speech exemplars.

2.5 The sparse classification algorithm

The use of sparse classification requires that it must be possible to approximate an unknown observation with a (positive) weighted sum of a number of exemplars. Since all operations in the modulation spectrum analysis system are linear and since the noisy signals were constructed by simply adding clean speech and noise, we are confident that the modulation spectrum representation does not violate additivity to such an extent that SC is rendered impossible. The same argument holds for the LDA-transformed features. Since linear transformations do not violate additivity, we assume that the transformed exemplars can be used in the same way as the original ones.

As can be seen in Figures 1 and 3, the output of the modulation filters contains both positive and negative numbers. Therefore, we need to use the Lasso procedure for solving the sparse coding problem, which can operate with positive and negative numbers [25]. We are not aware of other solvers that offer the same freedom. Lasso uses the Euclidean distance as the divergence measure to evaluate the similarity of vectors. This raises the question whether the Euclidean distance is a suitable measure for comparing modulation spectrum vectors. We verified this by computing the distributions of the Euclidean distance between neighbouring frames and frames taken at random time distances of >20 frames in a set of 100 randomly selected utterances. As can be seen from Figure 5, the distributions of the distances between neighbouring and distant frames hardly overlap. Therefore, we believe that it is safe to assume that the Euclidean distance measure is adequate.

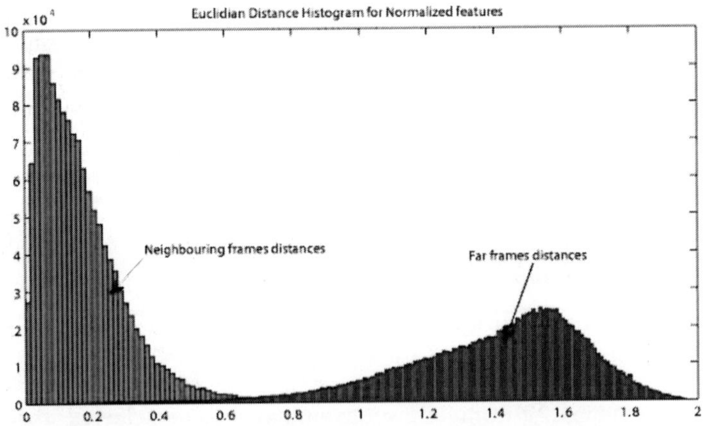

Figure 5. Distributions of the Euclidean distance between neighbouring (red) and distant (blue) *135* -D feature vectors.

Using the Euclidean distance in a straightforward manner implies that vector elements that have a large variance or large absolute values will dominate the result. Preliminary experiments showed that the modulation spectra suffer from this effect. It appeared that the difference between /u/ in *two* and /i/ in *three*, which is mainly represented by different energy levels in the 2,000-Hz region, was often very small because of the absolute values of the output of the modulation filters in the gammatone filters with centre frequencies of 2,000 and 2,500 Hz which were very much smaller than the values in the gammatone filters with centre frequencies up to 400 Hz. This effect can be remedied by using a proper normalization of the vector elements. After some experiments, we decided to equalize the variance in the gammatone bands. For this purpose we first computed the variance in all 135 modulation bands in the set of speech exemplars. Then, we averaged the variance over the nine modulation bands in each gammatone filter. The resulting averages were used to normalize the outputs of the modulation filters. The effect of this procedure on the representation of the output of the modulation filters is shown in Figure 6. This procedure reduced the number of /u/ - /i/ confusions by almost a factor of 3.

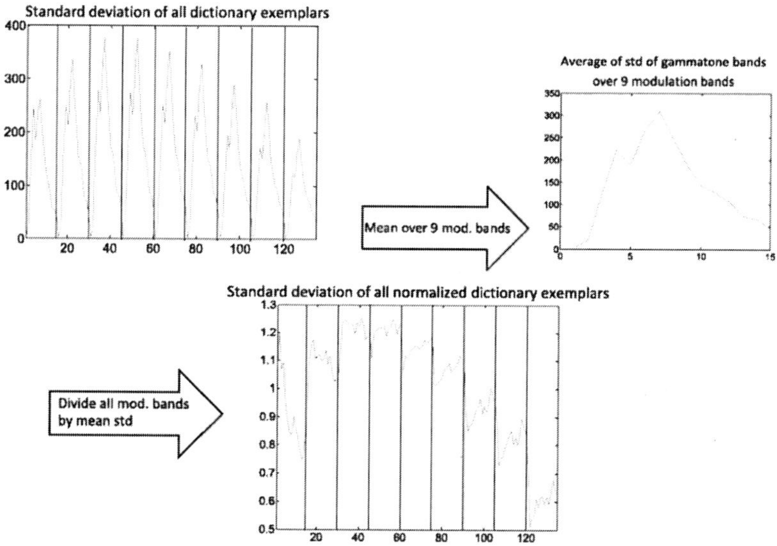

Figure 6. Normalization of the modulation filter outputs. Upper left: standard deviation of all 135 elements in the speech exemplars. Upper right: standard deviation in the gammatone filters averaged over all nine modulation filters. Lower panel: standard deviation of all 135 elements in the speech exemplars after normalization.

2.5.1 Obtaining state posterior estimates

The weights assigned to the exemplars by the Lasso solver must be converted to estimates of the probability that a frame corresponds to one of the 179 states. In the sparse classification system of [20], weights of up to 30 window positions were averaged. In our SC system, we do not have a sliding window with heavy overlap between subsequent positions. We decided to use the weights of the exemplars that approximate individual frames to derive the state posterior probability estimates. In doing so, we simply added the weights of all exemplars corresponding to a given state. The average number of non-zero elements in the activation vector varied between 15.1 for clean speech and 6.5 at −5-dB SNR. Therefore, we may face overly sparse and potentially somewhat noisy state probability estimates. This is illustrated in Figure 7a for the digit sequence '3 6 7' in the 5-dB SNR condition. The traces of state probability estimates are not continuous (do not traverse all 16 states of a word) and they include activations of other states, some of which are acoustically similar to the states that correspond to the digit sequence.

2.6 Recognition based on combinations of individual modulation bands

Substantial previous research has investigated the possibility to combat additive noise by fusing the outputs of a number of parallel recognizers, each operating on a separate frequency band (*cf.*, [32] for a comprehensive review). The general idea underlying this approach is that additive noise will only affect some frequency bands so that other bands should suffer less. The same idea has also been proposed for different modulation bands [33]. In this paper we also explore the possibility that additive noise does not affect all modulation bands to the same extent. Therefore, we will compare recognition accuracies obtained when estimating state likelihoods using a single set of exemplars represented by 135-D feature vectors and the fusion of the state likelihoods estimated from the 135-D system and nine sets of exemplars (one for each modulation band) represented as 15-D feature vectors (for the 15 gammatone filters). The optimal weights for the nine sets of estimates will be obtained using a genetic algorithm with a small set of held-out training utterances. Also, combining state posterior probability estimates from ten decoders might help to make the resulting probability vectors less sparse.

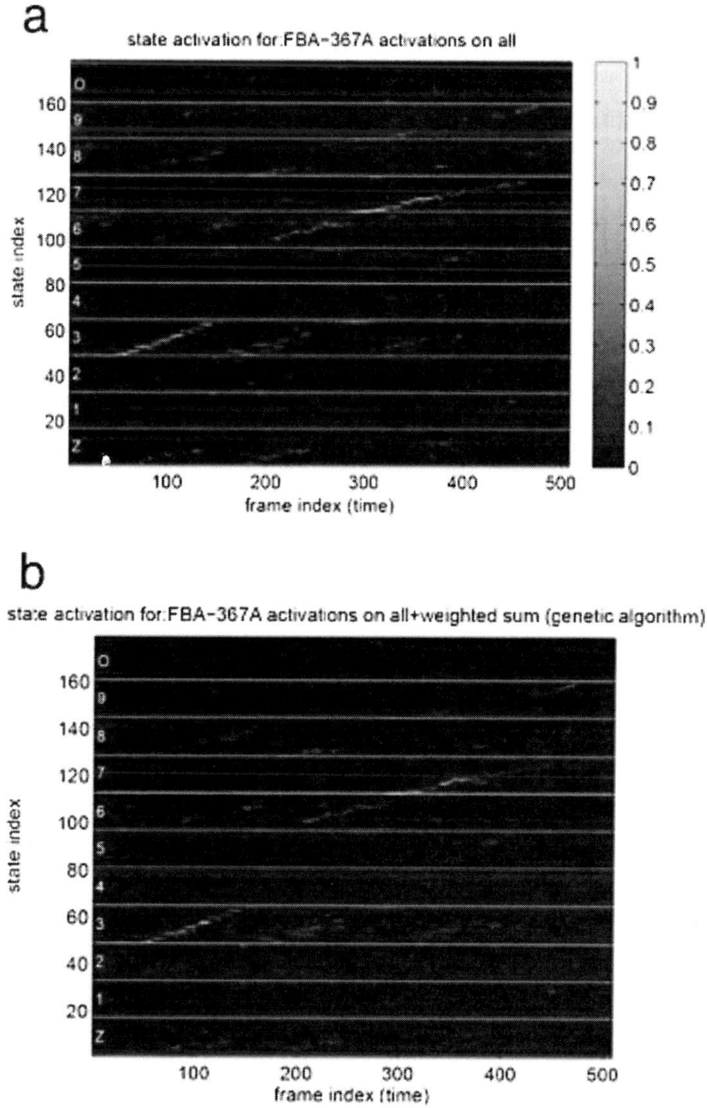

Figure 7. State probability traces for the digit sequence '3 6 7' at 5-dB SNR. (a) Traces obtained by using the activation weights of the full modulation spectrum exemplars only. The Viterbi decoder returns the incorrect sequence '3 3 7'. **(b)** Traces obtained from fusing the probability estimates obtained with the full modulation spectrum and the probability estimates obtained from nine modulation bands (weights obtained with a genetic algorithm). The Viterbi decoder now returns the correct sequence '3 6 7'.

2.7 State posteriors estimated by means of an MLP

In order to tease apart the contributions of the modulation frequency features and the sparse coding, we also conducted experiments in which we used a MLP for estimating the posterior probabilities of the 179 states in the AURORA-2 task. For this purpose we trained a number of networks by means of the QuickNet software package [34]. We trained networks on clean data only, as well as on the full set of utterances in the multi-condition training set. Analogously to [35], we used 90% of the training set, i.e. 7,596 utterances for training the MLP and the remaining 844 utterances for the cross-validation. To enable a fair comparison, we trained two networks, both operating on single frames. The first network used frames consisting of 135 features; the second network used 'static' modulation frequency features extended with delta and delta-delta features estimated over a time interval of 90 ms, making for 405 input features. The delta and delta-delta features were obtained by fitting a linear regression on the sequence of feature values that span the 90-ms intervals. Actually, the 90-ms interval corresponds to the time interval covered by the perceptual linear prediction (PLP) features used in [35]. There too, the static PLP features were extended by delta and delta-delta features, making for 9×39=351 input nodes.

3. RESULTS

The recognition accuracies obtained with the 135-D modulation spectrum features are presented in the top part of Tables 1 and 2 for the SC-based system. The second and third rows of Table 2 show the results for the MLP-based system. Both tables also contain results obtained previously with conventional Mel-spectrum or PLP features. Note that the results in Table 1 pertain to a single-noise condition of test set A (subway noise), while Table 2 shows the accuracies averaged over all four noise types in test set A. In experimenting with the AURORA-2 task, it is a pervasive finding that the results depend strongly on the word insertion penalty (WIP) that is used in the Viterbi back end. A WIP that yields the lowest WER in the clean condition invariably gives a very high WER in the noisiest conditions. In this paper we set aside a small development set, on which we searched the WIP that gave the best results in the conditions with SNR ≤5 dB; in these conditions the best performance was obtained with the same WIP value. Inevitably, this means that we will end up with relatively bad results in the cleanest conditions. Unfortunately, there is no generally accepted strategy for selecting the 'optimal' WIP. Since different authors make different (and not always explicit) decisions, detailed comparisons with results reported in the literature are difficult. For this paper this is less of an issue, since we are not aiming at outperforming previously published results.

Table 1. Accuracy for five systems on noise type 1 (subway noise) of test set A

	Clean	20 dB	15 dB	10 dB	5 dB	0 dB	−5 dB
Sys1 (single frame)	90.51	91.00	89.53	87.69	83.76	76.76	65.31
Sys2 (single frame) (LDA transformed)	89.19	89.62	87.57	83.54	76.51	62.57	36.91
Sys3 (29 frames) (LDA transformed)	87.50	88.70	87.41	85.42	77.62	59.41	27.85
Sys4 (9 bands - GA)	89.71	90.57	89.28	87.41	84.13	77.71	63.83
Sparse coding [24] 5-frame exemplars	93.12	90.18	87.22	82.62	72.64	56.31	34.57
Sparse coding [24] 30-frame exemplars	93.21	91.86	91.53	89.62	87.47	80.01	61.61

Sys1, 135-D vectors; Sys2, LDA-transformed 135-D vectors of Sys1; Sys3, LDA-transformed 29 × 135-D vectors of 29 consecutive frames; Sys4, Sys1 plus nine recognizers operating on 15-D vectors, weights obtained from a genetic algorithm. Recognition results for noise type 1 using the sparse coding approach [20,24] using 5 and 30 frame windows are included for comparison in the bottom part.

Table 2. Accuracies averaged over all noise types in test set A

	Clean	20 dB	15 dB	10 dB	5 dB	0 dB	−5 dB
Modulation features sparse coding 1-frame exemplar (Sys1)	90.62	90.87	89.90	88.17	84.46	76.83	59.65
Modulation features MLP 135 input nodes multi-condition	96.93	96.66	95.84	94.07	87.14	68.05	35.46
Modulation features + Δ + ΔΔ MLP 405 input nodes multi-condition	97.71	97.36	96.74	95.08	89.79	70.58	34.55
PLP + Δ and ΔΔ MLP 351 input nodes [35] multi-condition	99.08	98.89	98.45	96.89	91.80	72.80	35.67
Mel features sparse coding [24] 5-frame exemplars	93.43	90.94	89.06	84.57	75.91	58.20	32.57
Mel features sparse coding [24] 30-frame exemplars	93.68	92.53	92.02	90.78	88.01	78.93	57.11

Accuracies (averaged over all noise types in test set A) obtained with Sys1 (SC system operating on 135-D modulation spectrum features), MLP classifiers (on same features without and with Δs and ΔΔs), MLP classifier on PLP features with Δs and ΔΔs [35], SC classifier on Mel spectra [24] using 5- and 30-frame windows, respectively.

3.1 Analysing the features

To better understand the modulation spectrum features, we carried out a clustering analysis on the exemplars in the dictionary, using k-means clustering. We created 512 clusters using the scikit-learn software package

[36]. We then analysed the way in which clusters correspond to states. The results of the analysis of the raw features are shown in Figure 8a. The horizontal axis in the figure corresponds to the 179 states, and the vertical axis to cluster numbers. The figure shows the association between clusters and states. It can be seen that the exemplar clusters do associate to states, but there is a substantial amount of 'confusions'. Figure 8b shows the result of the same clustering of the exemplars after applying an LDA transform to the exemplars, keeping all 135 dimensions. It can be seen that the LDA-transformed exemplars result in clusters that are substantially purer. Figure 8c shows the results of the same clustering on the 135-D features obtained from the LDA transform of sequences of 29 subsequent frames. Now, the cluster purity has increased further.

Although cluster purity does not guarantee high recognition performance, from Tables 1 and 2 it can be seen that the modulation spectrum features appear to capture substantial information that can be exploited by two very different classifiers.

3.2 Results obtained with the SC system

Table 1 summarizes the recognition accuracies obtained with six different systems, all of which used the SC approach to estimate state posterior probabilities. Four of these systems use the newly proposed modulation spectrum features, while the remaining two describe the results using Mel-spectrum features as obtained in research done by Gemmeke [24].

From the first three rows of Table 1, it can be seen that estimating state posterior probabilities from a single frame of a modulation spectrum analysis by converting the exemplar weights obtained with the sparse classification system already yields quite promising results. Indeed, from a comparison with the results obtained with the original SC system using five-frame stacks in [24], it appears that the modulation spectrum features outperform stacks of five Mel-spectrum features in all but one condition. The conspicuous exception is the clean condition, where the performance of *Sys1* is somewhat disappointing. Our Sys1 performs worse than the system in [24] that used 30-frame exemplars. From the first and second rows, it can be inferred that transforming the features such that the discrimination between the 179 states is optimized is harmful for all conditions. Apparently, the transform learned on the basis of 17.148 exemplars does not generalize sufficiently to the bulk of the feature frames. In section 2 we will propose an alternative perspective that puts part of the blame on the interaction between LDA and SC.

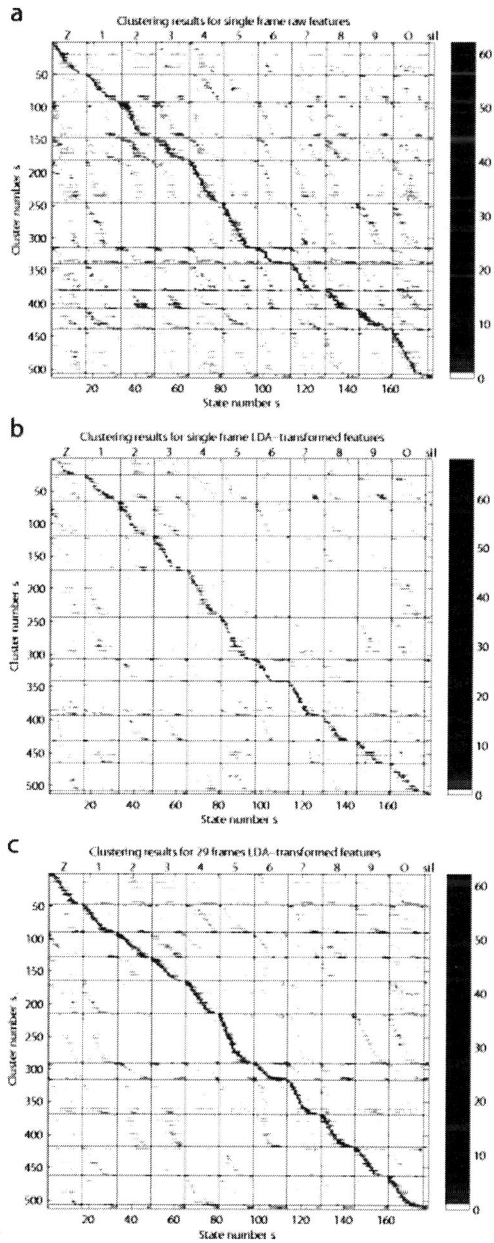

Figure 8. Clustering results. (a) Single-frame raw features. **(b)** Single-frame LDA-transformed features. **(c)** The 29-frame LDA-transformed features.

3.2.1 The representation of the temporal dynamics

In [20],[24] the recognition performance in AURORA-2 was compared for exemplar lengths of 5,10,20,30 frames. For clean speech, the optimal exemplar length was around ten frames and the performance dropped for longer exemplars; at SNR =-5 dB, increasing exemplar length kept improving the recognition performance and the optimal length found was the longest that was tried (i.e. 30). Longer windows correspond with capturing the effects of lower modulation frequencies. The trade-off between clean and very noisy signals suggests that emphasizing long-term continuity helps in reducing the effect of noises that are not characterized by continuity, but using 300-ms exemplars may not be optimal for covering shorter-term variation in the digits. From the two bottom rows in Table 1, it can be seen that going from 5-frame stacks to 30-frame stacks improved the performance for the noisiest conditions very substantially. From the second and third rows in that table, it appears that the performance gain in our system that used 29-frame features (covering 72.5 ms) is nowhere near as large. However, due to the problems with the generalizability of the LDA transform that we already encountered in *Sys2*, it is not yet possible to draw conclusions from this finding.

A potentially important side effect of using exemplars consisting of 30 subsequent frames in [20],[24] was that the conversion of state activations to state posterior probabilities involved averaging over 30 frame positions. This diminishes the risk that a 'true' state is not activated at all. Our system approximates a feature frame as just one sum of exemplars. If an exemplar of a 'wrong' state happens to match best with the feature frame, the Lasso procedure may fill the gap between that exemplar and the feature frame with completely unrelated exemplars. This can cause gaps in the traces in the state probability lattice that represent the digits. This effect is illustrated in Figure 7a, which shows the state activations over time of the digit sequence '3 6 7' at 5-dB SNR for the state probabilities in Sys1. The initial fricative consonants / *θ*/ and /s/ and the vowels /i/ and /I/ in the digits '3' and '6' are acoustically very similar. For the second digit in the utterance, this results in somewhat grainy, discontinuous, and largely parallel traces in the probability lattice for the digits '3' and '6'. Both traces more or less traverse the sequence of all 16 required states. The best path according to the Viterbi decoder corresponds to the sequence '3 3 7', which is obviously incorrect.

3.2.2 Results based on fusing nine modulation bands

In *Sys1, Sys2,* and *Sys3,* we capitalize on the assumption that the sparse classification procedure can harness the differences between speech and noise in the modulation spectra without being given any specific information. In [32] it was shown that it is beneficial to 'help' a speech recognition system in handling additive noise by fusing the results of independent recognition operations on non-overlapping parts of the spectrum. The success of the multi-band approach is founded in the finding that additive noise does not affect all parts of the spectrum equally severely. Recognition on sub-bands can profit from superior results in sub-bands that are only marginally affected by the noise. Using modulation spectrum features, we aim to exploit the different temporal characteristics of speech and noise, which are expected to have different effects in different modulation bands. Therefore, we conducted an experiment to investigate whether combining the output of nine independent recognizers, each operating on a different modulation frequency band, will improve recognition accuracy. In each modulation frequency band, we have the output of all 15 gammatone filters; therefore, each modulation band 'hears' the full 4-kHz spectrum. The experiment was conducted using the part of test set *A* that is corrupted by subway noise.

In our experiments we opted for fusion at the state posterior probability level: We constructed a single-state probability lattice for each utterance by means of a weighted sum of the state posteriors obtained from the individual SC systems. In all cases we fused the probability estimates of Sys1, which operates with 135-D exemplars with nine sets of state posteriors from SC classifiers that each operate on 15-D exemplars. Sys1 was always given a weight equal to 1. The weights for the nine modulation band classifiers were obtained using a genetic algorithm that optimized the weights on a small development set. The weights and WIP that yielded the best results in the SNR conditions ≤5 dB were applied to all SNR conditions. The set of weights is shown in Table 3.

Table 3. Weights obtained for combining the 15 gammatone filterbands in the multi-stream analysis

F_c (Hz)	0	2	3	4	5	6	8	10	16
GA	−0.0172	−0.0921	0.0001	−0.0103	−0.223	−0.0336	−0.0072	−0.0625	0.201

GA, weights obtained with a genetic algorithm.

From row 4 (*Sys4*) in Table 1, it can be seen that fusing the state likelihood estimates from the nine individual modulation filters with the state likelihoods from the full modulation spectrum deteriorates the recognition accuracy for all but two SNRs. From Table 3 it appears that the Genetic Algorithm returns very small weights for all nine modulation bands. This strongly suggests that the individual modulation bands are not able to highlight specific information that is less easily seen in the complete modulation spectrum.

A potentially very important concomitant advantage of fusing the probability estimates from the 135-D system and the nine 15-D systems is that the fusion process may make the probability vectors less sparse, thereby reducing the risk that wrong states are being promoted. This is illustrated in Figure 7b, where it can be seen that the state probability traces obtained from the fusion of the full 135-D system and the weighted sub-band systems suffer less from competing 'ghost traces' of acoustically similar competitors that traverse all 16 states of the wrong digit: Due to the lack of consensus between the multiple classifiers, the trace for the wrong digit '3', which is clearly visible in Figure 7a, has become less clear and more 'cloud-like' in Figure 7b. As a consequence, the digit string is now recognized correctly as '3 6 7'. However, from the results in Table 1, it is clear that on average the impact of making the probability vectors less sparse by means of fusing modulation frequency sub-bands is negligible.

3.3 Results obtained with MLPs

We trained four MLP systems for computing state posterior probabilities on the basis of the modulation spectrum features, two using only clean speech and two using the multi-condition training data. We increased the number of hidden nodes, starting with 200 hidden nodes up to 1,500 nodes. In all cases the eventual recognition accuracy kept increasing, although the rate of increase dropped substantially. Additional experiments showed that further increasing the number of hidden nodes no longer yields improved recognition results. For each number of hidden nodes, we also searched for the WIP that would provide optimal results for the cross-validation set (*cf.* section 2). We found that the optimal accuracy in the different SNR conditions was obtained for quite different values of the WIP. Training on multi-condition data had a slight negative effect on the recognition accuracy in the clean condition, compared to training on clean data only. However, as could be expected, the MLPs trained on clean data did not generalize to noisy data.

Table 2 shows the results obtained with SC systems operating on modulation spectrum and Mel-spectrum features and the MLP-based systems trained with multi-condition data. It can be seen that adding Δ and $\Delta\Delta$ features to the 'static' modulation spectrum features increases performance somewhat, but by no means to the extent that adding Δ and $\Delta\Delta$ features improves performance with Mel-spectrum or PLP features [12],[13].

The two systems that used modulation spectrum features perform much worse on clean speech than the MLP based system that used nine adjacent 10-ms PLP $+\Delta+\Delta\Delta$ features [37]. This suggests that the modulation spectrum features fail to capture part of the dynamic information that is represented by the speed and acceleration features derived from PLPs. Interestingly, that information is not restored by adding the regression coefficients obtained with stacks of modulation frequency features. In the noisier conditions, the networks trained with modulation frequency features derived from the multi-condition training data approximate the performance of the stacks of nine extended PLP features.

4. DISCUSSION

In this paper we introduced a basic implementation of a noise-robust ASR system that uses the modulation spectrum, instead of the short-time spectrum to represent noisy speech signals, and sparse classification to derive state probability estimates from time samples of the modulation spectrum. Our approach differs from previous attempts to deploy sparse classification for noise-robust ASR. The first difference is the use of the modulation spectrum and the second is that the exemplars in our system are constituted by individual frames, rather than by (long) sequences of adjacent frames in [20],[24], which needed such sequences to effectively cover essential information about continuity over time that comes for free in the modulation spectrum, where individual frames capture information about the dynamic changes in the short-time spectrum. Our unadorned implementation yielded recognition accuracies that are slightly below the best results in [20],[24], but especially the fact that our system yielded higher accuracies in the −5-dB SNR condition than their systems with exemplars with a length of 50 ms corroborates our belief that we are on a promising track towards a novel approach to noise-robust ASR. Although all results are based on a combination of feature extraction and posterior state probability estimation, we will discuss the features and the estimators separately - to the extent possible.

4.1 The features

In designing the modulation spectrum analysis system, a number of decisions had to be made about implementation details. Although we are confident that all our decisions were reasonable (and supported by data from the literature), we cannot claim that they were optimal. Most data in the literature on modulation spectra are based on perception experiments with human subjects, but more often than not these experiments use auditory stimuli that are very different from speech. While the results of those experiments surely provide guidance for ASR, it may well be that the automatic processing aimed at extracting the discriminative information is so different from what humans do that some of our decisions are sub-optimal. Our gammatone filterbank contains 15 one-third octave filters, which have a higher resolution in the frequencies <500 Hz than the Mel filterbank that is used in most ASR systems. However, initial experiments in which we compared our one-third octave filterbank with a filterbank consisting of 23 Mel-spaced gammatone filters, spanning the frequency range of 64 to 3,340 Hz did not show a significant advantage of the latter over the former. From the speech technology's point of view, this may seem surprising because the narrow-band filters of the one-third octave filterbank in the low frequencies may cause interactions with fundamental frequency, while the relatively broad filters in the higher frequencies cannot resolve formants. But from an auditory system's point of view, there is no such surprise, since one-third octave filters are compatible with most, if not all, outcomes of psycho-acoustic experiments. This is also true for experiments that focused on speech intelligibility [1].

For the modulation filterbank, it also holds that the design is partly based on the results of perception experiments [19]. Our modulation frequency analyser contained filters with centre frequencies ranging from 0 to 16 Hz. From [30] it appears that the modulation frequency range of interest for ASR is limited to the 2- to 16-Hz region. Therefore, here too we must ask whether our design is optimal for ASR. It might be that the spacing of the modulation filters in the frequency band that is most important for human speech intelligibility is not optimal for automatic processing. However, as with the gammatone filters, it is not evident why a different spacing should be preferred. It might be necessary to treat modulation frequencies ≤1 Hz, which are more likely to correspond to the characteristics of the transmission channel, different than modulation frequencies that might be related to articulation. One might think that the very low modulation frequencies would best be discarded completely in the AURORA-2 task, where transmission channel characteristics do not play a role. However, experiments in which we did just that yielded substantially worse results. Arguably, the lowest modulation frequencies help in distinguishing time intervals that contain speech from time intervals that contain only silence or background noise. We decided to not include modulation filters with centre frequencies >16 Hz. This implies that we ignore almost all information related to the periodicity that characterizes many speech sounds. However, it is well known that the presence of periodicity is a powerful indicator of the presence of speech in noisy signals and also, in case the background noise consists of speech from one or more interfering speakers, a powerful means to separate the target speech from the background speech. In future experiments we will investigate the possibility of adding explicit information about the harmonicity of the signals to the feature set.

The experiments with the MLP classifiers for obtaining state posterior probabilities from the modulation spectrum features confirm that the modulation spectrum features capture most of the information that is relevant for speech decoding. Still, the WERs obtained with the MLPs were always inferior to the results obtained with stacks of nine conventional PLP features that include Δ and $\Delta\Delta$ features, especially in the cleanest SNR conditions. Although the modulation spectrum features are performing quite well in noisy conditions, in cleaner conditions their performance is worse than the classical PLP features. Adding Δ s and $\Delta\Delta$ s, computed as linear regressions over 90 ms windows, to the modulation spectrum features does not improve performance nearly as much as adding speed and acceleration to MFCC or PLP features. This suggests that our modulation spectrum features are suboptimal with respect to describing the medium-term dynamics of the speech signal. The time windows associated with the modulation frequency filters with the lowest centre frequencies is larger than 500 ms. As a consequence, time derivatives computed over a window of 90 ms for these slowly varying filter outputs is not likely to carry much additional information. We suspect that the features in the lowest modulation bands play too heavy a role. If we want to optimally exploit the redundancy in the different modulation frequency channels when part of them gets obscured by noise, information about relevant speech events (such as word or syllable onsets and offsets) should ideally be represented equally well by their temporal dynamics in all channels.

Perhaps the most striking difference between the auditory model used in this paper and the model proposed in [38] is the absence of the adaptation/compression network between the gammatone filters and the modulation frequency filters. Preliminary experiments in which we applied tenth root compression to the output of the modulation filters (rather than the gammatone filters) already showed a substantial beneficial effect. The additional high-pass filtering that is performed in the compression/adaptation network (which should only be applied to the output of the gammatone filters) is expected to have a further beneficial effect in that it implements the medium-term dynamics that we seem to be missing at the moment. Including the adaptation stage is also expected to enhance the different dynamic characteristics of speech and many noise types in the modulation frequency bands. If this expectation holds, the absence of a proper adaptation network might explain the failure of the nine band fusion system.

4.2 The classifiers

Visual inspection of traces of state activations as a function of time obtained with the SC system suggested that the similarity between adjacent feature vectors was much higher than the similarity between adjacent state activation vectors. Figure 9 shows scatter plots of the relation between the similarity between adjacent feature vectors and the corresponding state probability vectors. It can be seen that the Pearson correlation coefficient between adjacent feature frames is very high, which is what one would expect, given the high sampling rate. It is also evident, and expected, that the variance increases as the SNR decreases. However, the behaviour of the state probability vectors is quite different. While for part of the adjacent vectors it holds that they are very similar (the pairs with a similarity close to one, represented by the points in the upper right-hand corner of the panels), it can be seen that there is a substantial proportion of adjacent state probability vectors that are almost orthogonal. We believe that this discrepancy is related to the difference between sparse coding (reconstruction of an observed modulation spectrum in terms of a linear combination of exemplars), what it is that the Lasso solver does, and sparse classification (estimating the probability of the HMM state underlying the observed modulation spectrum), which is our final goal. The frames that represent an unknown (noisy) speech signals are all decoded individually; for each frame the Lasso procedure starts from scratch. If occasionally a speech atom related to a wrong state or an atom from the noise dictionary happens to match best with an input frame, this can have a very large impact on the resulting state activation vector. Lasso can turn a close similarity between an input frame and exemplars related to the true state at the feature level into a close-to-zero probability of the 'correct' state in the probability vector because an exemplar related to another state (or noise) happened to match slightly better.

The substantial deterioration of the recognition performance with LDA-transformed features came as a surprise, not in the last place because we have seen that cluster purity increases after LDA transform. The fact that we see a negative effect of the transform already for clean speech suggests that the transformation matrix learned from the exemplar dictionary does not generalize well to the continuous speech data. While the correlation between the raw features in adjacent frames was very close to one in the raw features, the average Pearson correlation coefficient between adjacent frames dropped to about 0.75 after the LDA transform. The LDA

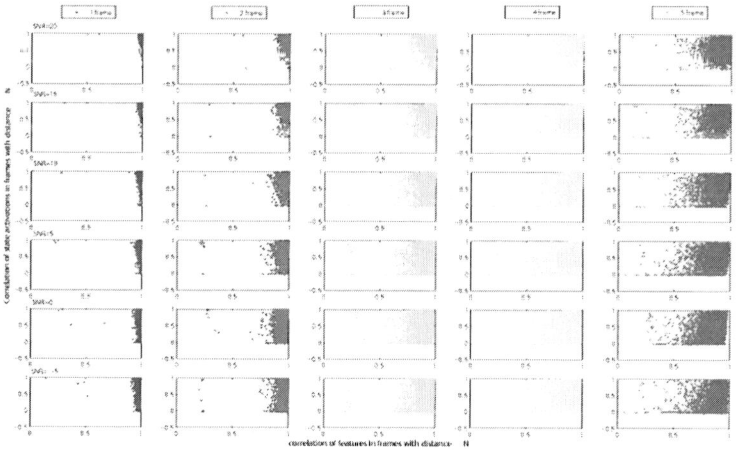

Figure 9. Relationship between the similarity between adjacent time frames and the corresponding adjacent state activation vectors.Correlations are computed using ten randomly selected utterances. Rows, SNR conditions. Columns, time distance between frames.

transformation maximizes the differences among the 179 states, regardless of whether states are actually very similar or not. Distinguishing adjacent states in the digit word 'oh' is equally important as distinguishing the eighth state of oh from the first state of 'seven'. Exaggerating the differences between adjacent frames, because these may relate to different states, is likely to aggravate the risk that Lasso returns high activations for a wrong state because an exemplar assigned to that state happens to fit the frame under analysis best. In addition, the LDA transform affects the relations between the distributions of the features. Because we believe that the feature normalization applied to the raw modulation spectrum features yielded the best performance since it conforms with the mathematics in Lasso, we applied the same normalization to the LDA-transformed features. We did not (yet) check whether a different normalization could improve the results. The comparison between the single-frame LDA-transformed and 29-frame features that are reduced to 135-D features by means of an LDA-transform shows that adding a more explicit representation of the time context only improves the recognition accuracy in the 10- and 5-dB SNR conditions; in all other conditions, the results obtained with single-frame features are better. We believe that this finding is related to the difficulty of representing medium-term speech dynamics in the present form of the modulation spectrum features.

We experimented with LDA in order to be able to explicitly include additional information about temporal dynamics. In the present implementation, with its 400-Hz frame rate, a stack of 29 adjacent frames covers a time interval of 72.5 ms, resulting in 3,915-D feature vectors. However, the 400-Hz frame rate does not seem to be necessary. Preliminary experiments with low-pass filtering the Hilbert envelopes of the outputs of the gammatone filters with a cut-off frequency of 50 Hz and a frame rate of 100 Hz yielded equal WER results. This opens the possibility of covering time spans of about 70 ms by concatenating only nine frames. However, an experiment in which we decoded the clean speech with exemplars consisting of nine subsequent 10-ms frames did not yield accuracies better than what we had obtained with single-frame features. This corroborates our belief that the medium-term dynamics is not sufficiently captured by our modulation spectrum features.

The success of the MLP classifiers that is apparent from Table 2 shows that sparse classification is not the only way for estimating state posterior probabilities from modulation spectrum features. In fact, the MLP classifier yielded consistently better results than the SC classifier in the SNR conditions covered by the training data. However, in the 0- and −5-dB SNR conditions, which are not present in the multi-condition training, the SC classifier yielded better performance. This raises the question whether it is possible to add supervised learning to the design of an SC-based system without sacrificing its superior generalization to unseen conditions.

In [20] and [24] it is mentioned that they failed to improve the performance of their sparse coding systems by machine learning techniques in the construction of the exemplar dictionaries. However, the cause of the failure was not explained. It may well be that the situation with single-frame modulation spectrum exemplars is different from 30-frame Mel-spectrum exemplars so that clever dictionary learning might be beneficial. We have started experiments with fast dictionary learning along the lines set out in [39]. Our first results suggest that there are two quite different issues that must be tackled. The first issue relates to the cost function used in creating the optimal exemplars. Conventional approaches to dictionary learning use the difference between unknown frames and their approximation as a weighted sum of exemplars as the criterion to minimize. While this criterion is obviously valid in sparse *coding* applications, it is not the criterion of choice in sparse*classification*. In the latter application, the exemplars carry information about the states (the classes) that they represent, and this information should enter into the cost function, for example, in the form of the requirement that individual exemplars are promoted for frames that do correspond to a certain state (or set of acoustically similar states).

The second issue is that the mapping from state activations returned by some *solver* to state posterior probabilities is less straightforward than was implemented in [20] and [24] and in this paper. There is a need for including some learning mechanisms that can find the optimal mapping from a complete set of state activations to a set of state posteriors. It is quite possible that there will be interactions between enhanced dictionary learning and learning the mapping from activations to probabilities. The challenge here is to find strategies that do not fall into the trap that we have seen in our experiments with MLPs, *viz.*, that the eventual performance increases in the conditions for which training material was available but at the cost of a diminished generalization to unseen conditions.

An issue that surely needs further investigation in the construction of the dictionary is the selection of the noise exemplars. So far, noise exemplars were extracted quasi-randomly from the four noise types that were used in creating the multi-condition training set in AURORA-2. It is quite likely that the collection of noise exemplars is much more compactly distributed in the feature space than the speech exemplars because the variation in the noise signals is less than in the speech signals. The generalization to other noise types can be improved by sampling the exemplars from a wider range of noises, for example all noise types that are available in the NOISEX CD-ROM [40]. However, we think that the most important issue in the construction of the noise exemplar dictionary is the need for avoiding overlap between noise and speech exemplars. In the Lasso procedure, it is difficult - if not impossible - to enforce a preference for speech atoms over noise atoms. If a noise exemplar that is very similar to a speech exemplar happens to fit best, this may give rise to suppressing relevant speech information. It might be beneficial to not simply discard all noise exemplars activations but rather to include these, along with the activations of the speech exemplars, in a procedure that learns the mapping from activations to state posteriors that optimizes recognition performance. An approach in which all activations are used in estimating the eventual posterior probabilities would be especially important in cases where noise and speech are difficult to distinguish in terms of spectro-temporal properties, such as in babble noise or if the 'noise' consists of competing speakers. These cases will surely require additional processing, for example, aimed at tracking continuity in pitch, in addition to continuity in the modulation spectrum.

5. CONCLUSIONS

In this paper we presented a novel noise-robust ASR system that uses the modulation spectrum in combination with a sparse coding approach for estimating state probabilities. Importantly, in its present implementation, the system does not involve any form of learning/training. The best recognition accuracies obtained with the novel system are slightly below the results that have been obtained with conventional engineering systems. We have also sketched several research lines that hold the promise of improving the results and, at the same time, to advance our knowledge of those aspects of the human auditory system that are most important for ASR. We have shown that the output of a modulation spectrum analyser that does not involve any form of conversion to the equivalent of a short-time power spectrogram is able to exploit the spectro-temporal continuity constraints that are typical for speech and which are a prerequisite for noise robust ASR. However, we also found that the representation of medium-term dynamics in the output of the modulation spectrum analyser must be improved. With respect to the sparse coding approach to estimate state posterior probabilities, we have found that there is a fundamental distinction between sparse coding, where the task is to find the optimal representation of an unknown observation in a very large dimensional space, and sparse classification, where the task is to obtain the best possible estimates of the posterior probability that an unknown observation belongs to a specific class. In this context one challenge for future research is developing a procedure for dictionary learning that uses state posterior probabilities, in addition to or rather than reconstruction error, as the cost function. The second challenge is finding a procedure for learning a mapping from state activations to state posterior probabilities that provides the same excellent generalization to unseen conditions that has been found with sparse coding.

ENDNOTE

[a] The software used for implementing the modulation frequency analyser was adapted from Matlab code that was kindly provided by Søren Jørgensen [41]. Some choices that are somewhat unusual in speech technology, such as the 400-Hz frame rate, were kept.

ACKNOWLEDGEMENTS

Part of this research has been funded with support from the European Commission under contract FP7-PEOPLE-2011-290000 to the Marie Curie ITN *INSPIRE*. We would like to thank Hugo Van hamme and Jort Gemmeke for discussing feature extraction and sparse coding issues and Søren

Jørgensen for making available the Matlab code for implementing the modulation spectrum analyser. Finally, we owe thanks to two anonymous reviewers, whose comments greatly helped to improve the paper.

REFERENCES

1. Drullman R, Festen JM, Plomp R: Effect of temporal envelope smearing on speech reception. *J. Acoust. Soc. Am* 1994, 95: 1053-1064. 10.1121/1.408467
2. H Hermansky, in *Proceedings of IEEE Workshop on Automatic Speech Recognition and Understanding*. The modulation spectrum in the automatic recognition of speech (Santa Barbara, 14–17 December 1997), pp. 140–147.
3. Xiao X, Chng ES, Li H: Normalization of the speech modulation spectra for robust speech recognition. *IEEE Trans. Audio Speech Lang. Process* 2008, 16(8):1662-1674. 10.1109/TASL.2008.2002082
4. JK Thompson, LE Atlas, in *Proceedings IEEE International Conference on Acoustics, Speech, and Signal Processing*, 5. A non-uniform modulation transform for audio coding with increased time resolution (Hong Kong, 6–10 April 2003), pp. 397–400.
5. Paliwal K, Schwerin B, Wójcicki K: Role of modulation magnitude and phase spectrum towards speech intelligibility. *Speech Commun* 2011, 53(3):327-339. 10.1016/j.specom.2010.10.004
6. Pichevar R, Najaf-Zadeh H, Thibault L, Lahdili H: Auditory-inspired sparse representation of audio signals. *Speech Commun* 2011, 53(5):643-657. 10.1016/j.specom.2010.09.008
7. PA Torres-Carrasquillo, E Singer, MA Kohler, RJ Greene, DA Reynolds, JR Deller Jr, in *Proceedings of International Conference on Spoken Language Processing*. Approaches to language identification using gaussian mixture models and shifted delta cepstral features (Denver, 16–20 September 2002), pp. 89–92.
8. Arai T, Pavel M, Hermansky H, Avendano C: Syllable intelligibility for temporally filtered LPC cepstral trajectories. *J. Acoust. Soc. Am* 1999, 105(5):783-791.
9. H Hermansky, N Morgan, A Bayya, P Kohn, in *Proceedings of EUROSPEECH*. Compensation for the effect of the communication

channel in auditory-like analysis of speech RASTA-PLP, (1991), pp. 1367–1370.

10. Hermansky H, Morgan N: RASTA processing of speech. *IEEE Trans. Speech Audio Process* 1994, 2(4):578-589. 10.1109/89.326616

11. Hermansky H: Speech recognition from spectral dynamics. *Sadhana* 2011, 36(5):729-744. 10.1007/s12046-011-0044-2

12. M Mlouka, J Liénard, in *Proceedings of the 2nd Speech Communication Seminar*. Word recognition based either on stationary items or on transitions (Almquist & Wiksell InternationalStockholm, 1974).

13. Furui S: Cepstral analysis technique for automatic speaker verification. *IEEE Trans. Acoust. Speech Signal Process* 1981, 29(2):254-272. 10.1109/TASSP.1981.1163530

14. Lippmann RP: Speech recognition by humans and machines: miles to go before we sleep. *Speech Commun* 1996, 18(3):247-248. 10.1016/0167-6393(96)00018-0

15. Houtgast T, Steeneken HJM: A review of the MTF concept in room acoustics and its use for estimating speech intelligibility in auditoria. *J. Acoust. Soc. Am* 1985, 77: 1069-1077. 10.1121/1.392224

16. Rennies J, Brand T, Kollmeier B: Prediction of the influence of reverberation on binaural speech intelligibility in noise and in quiet. *J. Acoust. Soc. Am* 2011, 130: 2999-3012. 10.1121/1.3641368

17. (T Virtanen, R Singh, B Raj, eds.), *Techniques for Noise Robustness in Automatic Speech Recognition* (Wiley, Hoboken, 2012).

18. Ghitza O: Auditory models and human performance in tasks related to speech coding and speech recognition. *IEEE Trans. Speech Audio Process* 1994, 2(1):115-132. 10.1109/89.260357

19. Jørgensen S, Dau T: Predicting speech intelligibility based on the signal-to-noise envelope power ratio after modulation-frequency selective processing. *J. Acoust. Soc. Am* 2011, 130(3):1475-1487. 10.1121/1.3621502

20. Gemmeke JF, Virtanen T, Hurmalainen A: Exemplar-based sparse representations for noise robust automatic speech recognition. *IEEE Trans. Audio Speech Lang. Process* 2011, 19(7):2067-2080. 10.1109/TASL.2011.2112350

21. A Hurmalainen, K Mahkonen, JF Gemmeke, T Virtanen, in *International Workshop on Machine Listening in Multisource Environments*. Exemplar-based recognition of speech in highly variable noise (Florence, 1 September 2011).

22. HG Hirsch, D Pearce, in *ISCA ITRW ASR2000*. The AURORA experimental framework for the performance evaluation of speech recognition systems under noisy conditions (Paris, 18–20 September 2000), pp. 29–32.

23. Bourlard H, Hermansky H, Morgan N: Towards increasing speech recognition error rates. *Speech Commun* 1996, 18: 205-231. 10.1016/0167-6393(96)00003-9

24. J Gemmeke, *Noise robust ASR: missing data techniques and beyond* (PhD thesis, Radboud University, Nijmegen, 2010).

25. Efron B, Hastie T, Johnstone I, Tibshirani R: Least angle regression. *Ann. Stat* 2004, 32(2):407-499. 10.1214/009053604000000067

26. A Hurmalainen, K Mahkonen, JF Gemmeke, T Virtanen, in *International Workshop on Machine Listening in Multisource Environments*. Exemplar-based recognition of speech in highly variable noise (Florence, 1 September 2011).

27. Glasberg BR, Moore BCJ: Derivation of auditory filter shapes from notched-noise data. *Hear. Res* 1990, 47: 103-138. 10.1016/0378-5955(90)90170-T

28. Ewert SD, Dau T: Characterizing frequency selectivity for envelope fluctuations. *J. Acoust. Soc. Am* 2000, 108(3):1181-1196. 10.1121/1.1288665

29. LR Rabiner, B Gold, *Theory and Application of Digital Signal Processing* (Prentice-Hall, Englewood Cliffs, 1975).

30. Kanadera N, Arai T, Hermansky H, Pavel M: On the relative importance of various components of the modulation spectrum for automatic speech recognition. *Speech Commun* 1999, 28(1):43-55. 10.1016/S0167-6393(99)00002-3

31. N Moritz, J Anemüller, B Kollmeier, in *Proceedings IEEE International Conference on Acoustics, Speech and Signal Processing*. Amplitude modulation spectrogram based features for robust speech recognition in noisy and reverberant environments (Prague, 22–27 May 2011), pp. 5492–5495.

32. Cerisara C, Fohr D: Multi-band automatic speech recognition. *Comput. Speech Lang* 2001, 15: 151-174. 10.1006/csla.2001.0163

33. H Hermansky, P Fousek, in *Proceedings of Interspeech*. Multi-resolution RASTA filtering for TANDEM-based ASR (Lisbon, 4–8 September 2005), pp. 361–364.

34. D Johnson, D Ellis, C Oei, C Wooters, P Faerber, N Morgan, K Asanovic, ICSI Quicknet Software Package (2004). . accessed 1-June-2013.,

35. Y Sun, MM Doss, JF Gemmeke, B Cranen, L ten Bosch, L Boves, in *Proceedings on Interspeech*. Combination of sparse classification and multilayer perceptron for noise-robust ASR (Portland, 9–13 September 2012).

36. Pedregosa F, Varoquaux G, Gramfort A, Michel V, Thirion B, Grisel O, Blondel M, Prettenhofer P, Weiss R, Dubourg V, Vanderplas J, Passos A, Cournapeau D, Brucher M, Perrot M, Duchesnay E: Scikit-learn: machine learning in Python. *J. Mach. Learn. Res*, 12(2011):2825-2830.

37. Y Sun, B Cranen, JF Gemmeke, L Boves, L ten Bosch, MM Doss, in *Proceedings on Interspeech*. Using sparse classification outputs as feature observations for noise-robust ASR (Portland, 9–13 September 2012).

38. Dau T, Püschel D, Kohlrausch A: A quantitative model of the “effective” signal processing in the auditory system. I. model structure. *J. Acoust. Soc. Am* 1996, 99(6):3615-3622. 10.1121/1.414959

39. J Mairal, F Bach, J Ponce, G Sapiro, in *Proceedings of the 26th Annual International Conference on Machine Learning, ICML ‘09*. Online dictionary learning for sparse coding (Montreal, 14–18 May 2009), pp. 689–696.

40. Varga A, Steeneken HJM: Assessment for automatic speech recognition: II NOISEX-92: a database and an experiment to study the effect of additive noise on speech recognition systems. *Speech Commun* 1993, 12(3):247-251. 10.1016/0167-6393(93)90095-3

41. S Jørgensen, T Dau, Modeling speech intelligibility based on the signal-to-noise envelope power ratio. PhD thesis. Department of Electrical Engineering, Technical University of Denmark (2014).

3

CHAPTER

Biomimetic Multi-Resolution Analysis for Robust Speaker Recognition

Sridhar Krishna Nemala, Dmitry N Zotkin, Ramani Duraiswami and Mounya Elhilal

[1]*Department of Electrical and Computer Engineering, Center for Language and Speech Processing, Johns Hopkins University, Baltimore, MD, USA.*

[2]*Institute for Advanced Computer Studies, University of Maryland, College Park, MD, USA*

ABSTRACT

Humans exhibit a remarkable ability to reliably classify sound sources in the environment even in presence of high levels of noise. In contrast, most engineering systems suffer a drastic drop in performance when speech signals are corrupted with channel or background distortions. Our brains are equipped with elaborate machinery for speech analysis and feature extraction, which hold great lessons for improving the performance of automatic speech processing systems under adverse conditions. The work presented here explores a biologically-motivated multi-resolution speaker information representation obtained by performing an intricate yet computationally-efficient analysis of the information-rich spectro-temporal attributes of the speech signal. We evaluate the proposed features in a speaker verification task performed on NIST SRE 2010 data. The biomimetic approach yields significant robustness in presence of non-stationary noise and reverberation, offering a new framework for deriving reliable features for speaker recognition and speech processing.

INTRODUCTION

In addition to the intended message, human voice carries the unique imprint of a speaker. Just like fingerprints and faces, voice prints are biometric markers with tremendous potential for forensic, military, and commercial applications[1]. However, despite enormous advances in computing technology over the last few decades, automatic speaker verification (ASV) systems still rely heavily on training data collected in controlled environments, and most systems face a rapid degradation in performance when operating under previously unseen conditions (e.g. channel mismatch, environmental noise, or reverberation). In contrast, human perception of speech and ability to identify sound sources (including voices) is quite remarkable even at relatively high distortion levels[2]. Consequently, the pursuit of human-like recognition capabilities has spurred great interest in understanding how humans perceive and process speech signals.

One of the intriguing processes taking place in the central auditory system involves ensembles of neurons with variable tuning to spectral profiles of acoustic signals. In addition to the frequency (tonotopic) organization emerging as early as the cochlea, neurons in the central auditory system (specifically in the midbrain and more prominently in the auditory cortex) exhibit tuning to a variety of filter bandwidths and shapes[3]. This elegant neural architecture provides a detailed multi-resolution analysis of the spectral sound profile, which is presumably relevant to speech and speaker recognition. Only few studies so far have attempted to use this cortical representation in speech processing, yielding some improvements for automatic speech recognition at the expense of *substantial computational complexity*[4, 5]. To the best of our knowledge, no similar work was done in ASV.

In the present report, we explore the use of a multi-resolution analysis for robust speaker verification. Our representation is simple, effective, and computationally-efficient. The proposed scheme is carefully optimized to be particularly sensitive to the information-rich spectro-temporal attributes of the signal while maintaining robustness to unseen noise distortions. The choice of model parameters builds on our current knowledge of psychophysical principles of speech perception in noise[6, 7] complemented with a statistical analysis of the dependencies between spectral details of the message and speaker information. We evaluate the proposed features in an ASV system and compare it against one of the best performing systems in NIST 2010 SRE evaluation[8] under detrimental conditions such as white noise, non-stationary additive noise, and reverberation.

The following section describes details of the proposed multi-resolution spectro-temporal model. It is followed by an analysis that motivates the choice of model parameters to maximize speaker information retention. Next, we describe the experimental setup and results. We finish with a discussion of these results and comment on potential extensions towards achieving further noise robustness.

The biomimetic multi-resolution analysis

An overview of the processing chain described in this section is presented in Figure1.

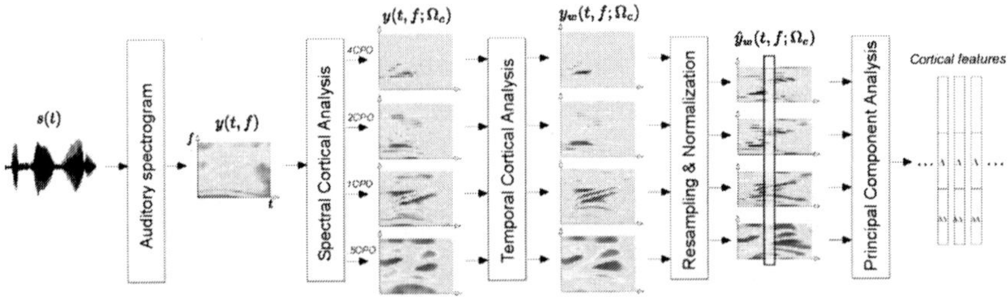

Figure 1. An outline of the cortical features extraction algorithm. A schematic diagram of the algorithm that transforms a speech waveform into a sequence of cortical feature vectors.

Peripheral analysis

The speech signal is processed through a pre-emphasis stage (implemented as a first-order high pass filter with pre-emphasis coefficient 0.97), and a time-frequency auditory spectrogram is generated using a biomimetic sound processing model described in details in[9] and briefly summarized here (Equation 1). First, the signal $s(t)$ undergoes a cochlear frequency analysis modeled by a bank of 128 constant-Q(Q=4) highly asymmetric bandpass filters $h(t;f)$ equally spaced over the span of 51/3 octaves on a logarithmic frequency axis. The filterbank output is a spatiotemporal pattern of cochlea basilar membrane displacements $y_{coch}(t f)$ over 128 channels. Next, a lateral inhibitory network detects discontinuities in the responses across the tonotopic (frequency) axis, resulting in further filterbank frequency selectivity enhancement. This step is modeled as a first-order differentiation operation across the channel array followed by a half-wave rectifier and a short-term integrator. The temporal integration window is given by $\mu(t;\tau)=e^{-t/\tau}u(t)$ with time constant τ=10 ms mimicking the further loss of phase-locking observed in the midbrain. This time constant controls the frame rate of the spectral vectors. Finally, a nonlinear cubic root compression of the spectrum is performed, resulting in an auditory spectrogram $y(t\,f)$:

$$\begin{aligned} y_{\text{coch}}(t,f) &= s(t) \otimes_t h(t;f), \\ y_{\text{lin}}(t,f) &= \max(\partial_t y_{\text{coch}}(t,f), 0), \\ y(t,f) &= \left[y_{\text{lin}}(t,f) \otimes_t \mu(t;\tau) \right]^{1/3}, \end{aligned} \tag{1}$$

where $\otimes_t$ represents convolution with respect to time. The choice of the auditory spectrogram is motivated by its neurophysiological foundation as well as its proven self-normalization and robustness properties (see[10] for full details).

Spectral cortical analysis

The auditory spectrogram is processed further in order to capture the spectral details present in each spectral slice. The processing is based on neurophysiological findings that neurons in the central auditory pathway are tuned not only to frequencies but also to spectral shapes, in particular to peaks of various widths on the log-frequency axis[3, 11, 12]. The spectral width is characterized by a parameter called scale and is measured in cycles per octave, or CPO. Physiological data indicates that auditory cortex neurons are highly scale-selective, thus expanding the cochlear one-dimensional tonotopic axis onto a two-dimensional sheet that explicitly encodes tonotopy as well as spectral shape details (see Figures1 and2).

The cortical analysis is implemented using a bank of modulation filters operating in the Fourier domain. The algorithm processes each data frame individually. The Fourier transform of each spectral slice $y(t_0,f)$ is multiplied by a modulation filter $H_S(\Omega;\Omega_c)$ that is tuned to spectral features of scale Ω_c. The filtering operates on the magnitude of the signal. After filtering, the inverse Fourier transform is performed and the real part is taken as the new filtered slice. This process is then repeated with a number of different Ω_c, yielding a number of filtered spectrograms $y(t,f;\Omega_c)$, each with features of scale Ω_c emphasized (see Figure1). This set of spectrograms constitutes the spectral cortical representation of the sound.

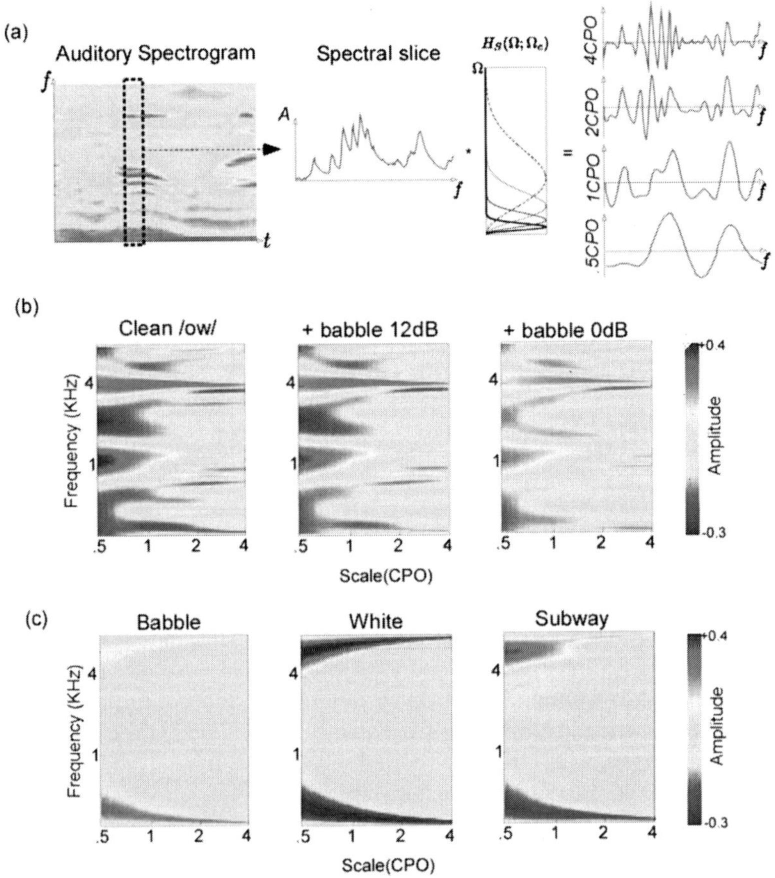

Figure 2. Details of the speech spectral analysis. (a) The speech spectrogram is analyzed separately at each time instant. Each spectrogram slice is filtered through a bandpass filter $H_S(\Omega;\Omega_c)$ parameterized by Ω_c. The $*$ operator signifies the filtering operation. Four such filtering operations yield four views of the same spectral slice; each view highlights different details about the spectrum, notably formant peaks and harmonic structure. **(b)** Cortical features for clean and noisy versions of one phoneme \ow\. The plots show magnitude as a function of frequency and scale. For visualization, the discrete image points have been interpolated in MATLAB using a bicubic interpolation routine. Notice the consistency of formant peaks around 1 and 4 KHz and of harmonic energies at 2 CPO and 4 CPO despite the additive noise distortion. **(c)** Cortical features for different types of additive noise. Note that the patterns exhibited are quite different. Subtle peaks due to harmonicity and formant structure of human speech can be seen in the left panel (babble noise).

The filter $H_S(\Omega;\Omega_c)$ is defined as

$$H_S(\Omega;\Omega_c) = (\Omega/\Omega_c)^2 e^{\left[1-(\Omega/\Omega_c)^2\right]}, \quad 0 \leq \Omega \leq \Omega_{\max}, \tag{2}$$

where $\Omega_{\max}$ is the highest spectral modulation frequency (set at 12 CPO given our spectrogram resolution of 24 channels per octave).

Choice of spectral parameters

The set of scales Ω_c is chosen by dividing the spectral modulation axis into equal energy regions using a training corpus (TIMIT database[13]) as described below. Define the average spectral modulation $\overline{Y}(\Omega) = \langle\langle|Y(\Omega;t_0)|\rangle_T\rangle_\Psi$ as the ensemble mean of the magnitude Fourier transform of the spectral slice $y(t_0f)$ averaged over all times T and over entire speech corpus Ψ. The resulting ensemble profile (shown in Figure3a) is then divided into M equal energy regions Γ_k:

$$\Gamma_k = \int_{\Omega_k}^{\Omega_{k+1}} \overline{Y}(\Omega)d\Omega, \quad \Gamma_k = \Gamma_{k+1}, \quad k = 1,\ldots,M-1, \tag{3}$$

where Ω_k and Ω_{k+1} denote the lower and upper cutoffs for k th band, Ω_1=0, and Ω_M=4.[a] This sampling scheme ensures that the high energy regions are sampled more densely, which has the dual advantage of sampling the given modulation space with a relatively small set of scales and emphasizing high-energy signal components, which are presumably noise-robust. Setting M=5 results in cutoffs at {0.18,0.59,1.34,2.36,4}, which are approximated to the nearest log-scale as Ω_c={0.25,0.5,1.0,2.0,4.0}. Finally, in order to put less emphasis on message-dominant regions of the spectrum, we drop the 0.25 CPO filter, which carries mostly articulatory and formant-specific information relevant to the speech message (analysis presented in the next section). The remaining set of Ω_c={0.5,1.0,2.0,4.0} is found to be a good tradeoff between computational complexity and system performance.

Temporal filtration

In this stage, the spectral cortical features are processed through a bandpass temporal modulation filter to remove information that is believed to be mostly irrelevant. It was shown in[14] that the neurons in the auditory cortex are mostly sensitive to the modulation rates between 0.5 and 12 Hz and that the same modulation range represents the information

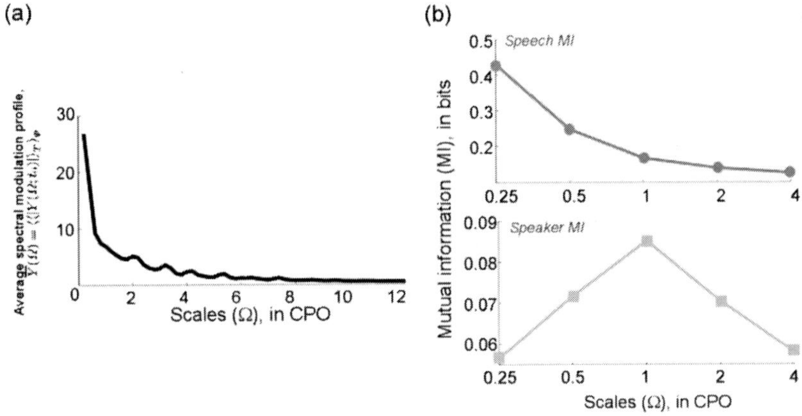

Figure 3. Speech signal spectral analysis. (a) Average spectral modulation profile $\overline{Y}(\Omega) = \langle\langle|Y(\Omega; t_0)|\rangle_T\rangle_\Psi$; **(b)** Top panel: MI between feature representation and speech message as a function of scale. Bottom panel: MI between feature representation and speaker identity as a function of scale.

crucial for speech comprehension[7]. Accordingly, the filtering is performed by multiplying the Fourier transform of the time sequence of each spectral feature by a bandpass filter $H_T(w; w_l w_h)$:

$$H_T(w; w_l, w_h]) = (\alpha w)^2\, e^{[1-(\alpha w)^2]},$$

$$\alpha = \begin{cases} 1/w_l, & 0 \leq w < w_l, \\ 1/w, & w_l \leq w \leq w_h, \\ 1/w_h, & w_h < w \leq w_{\max}, \end{cases} \qquad (4)$$

where w_l=0.5 Hz, w_h=12.0 Hz, $w_{\max}$=1/(2t_f), and t_f=10 ms (the frame length). After filtering in Fourier domain, the inverse Fourier transform is performed and the real part of the output forms the temporally filtered spectral cortical representation of the sound $y_w(tf;\Omega_c)$. This operation is performed on an utterance by utterance basis.

Cortical features

To reduce computational complexity and to allow use of state-of-the-art speaker verification machinery (which generally expects a relatively low-dimensional input), the spectral cortical representation is downsampled in frequency by a factor of 4 (Figure1). The resulting feature representation has a dimensionality of 128 (32 auditory frequency channels multiplied by four scales used for analysis). The features are then normalized to zero mean and unit variance for each utterance, yielding the reduced set of spectro grams $\hat{y}_w(t,f;\Omega_c)$. Principal component analysis is used to further reduce the feature dimensionality to 19. This number is chosen for consistency with the dimensionality of the standard Mel-Frequency Cepstral Coefficients (MFCC) feature set used for speaker recognition. The reduced features, along with their first- and second-order derivatives, form the final 57-dimensional cortical feature vector used for the speaker verification task.

Speech information versus speaker information

The speech signal carries both speech message and speaker identity information in distinct yet overlapping components. Separation of these elements is a non-trivial task in general. In the multi-resolution framework presented above, the broadest filters (0.25 and 0.5 CPO) capture primarily the overall spectral profile and formant peaks, while the others (1, 2, and 4 CPO) reflect narrower spectral details such as harmonics and subharmonic structure. In order to select a set of scales (Ω_c) that are most relevant for the speaker recognition task, we analyze the mutual information (MI) between the feature vector (X), the speech message (Y_1), and the speaker identity (Y_2). The MI is a measure of the statistical dependence between random variables[15] and is defined for two discrete random variables X and Y as

$$I(X;Y_i) = \sum_{x \in X, y \in Y_i} p(x,y) \log_2 \frac{p(x,y)}{p(x)p(y)}. \tag{5}$$

To estimate the MI, the continuous feature vector is quantized by dividing its support into cells of equal volume. To characterize the speech message, phoneme labels from the TIMIT corpus are first divided into four broad phoneme classes. The variable Y_1thus takes four discrete values representing the phoneme categories: vowels, stops, fricatives, and nasals. The average MI (taken as the mean MI across all the frequency bands for a given scale) between the feature vector and the speech message is shown in Figure3b (top) as a function of scale. For the speaker identity MI test, the TIMIT "sa1" speech utterance (*She had your dark suit in greasy wash water all year*) spoken by 100 different subjects is used; thus, Y_2 takes 100 discrete values representing the speaker. The average MI between the feature vector and the speaker identity is shown in Figure3b (bottom), again as a function of scale.[b]

Notice that while the lower scale (0.25 CPO) clearly provides significantly more information about the underlying linguistic message, the MI peak in Figure3c (bottom) is centered at 1 CPO, highlighting the significance of pitch and harmonically-related frequency channels in representing speaker-specific information. In order to put less emphasis on message-carrying features of the speech signal, we drop the 0.25 CPO filter at the feature encoding stage for our ASV system and choose Ω_c={0.5,1.0,2.0,4.0} CPO.[c]

Experiments and results

Recognition setup

Text independent speaker verification experiments are conducted on the NIST 2010 speaker recognition evaluation (SRE) data set[8]. The*extended core* task of the evaluation involves 6.9 million trials broken down into nine common conditions reflecting a variety of channel mismatch scenarios[8] (see Table1).

Table 1. List of conditions for NIST 2010 *extended core* task

Condition	Description
1	Microphone training, same microphone testing
2	Microphone training, different microphone testing
3	Microphone training, telephone testing
4	Microphone training, telephone conversation recorded with room microphone testing
5	NVE telephone training, NVE telephone testing
6	NVE telephone training, HVE telephone testing
7	Microphone training, HVE telephone testing
8	NVE telephone training, LVE telephone testing
9	Microphone training, LVE telephone testing

NVE, LVE, and HVE stand for normal, low, and high vocal effort, respectively.

The front end of the implemented ASV system uses either the 57-dimensional MFCC feature vector or the 57-dimensional cortical feature vector. The MFCC feature vector is computed by invoking RASTAMAT "melfcc" function with 'numcep' parameter set to 20, dropping the first (energy) component of the output, and appending first- and second-order derivatives of the resultant feature vector. The cortical feature vector is obtained as described in the previous sections. For fair comparison between MFCC and cortical features, MFCC was supplemented with mean subtraction, variance normalization, and RASTA filtering[16] applied at the utterance level. Such processing parallels the temporal filtering and normalization performed on cortical features. A combination of ASR output provided by NIST and an in-house energy-based VAD system is used to drop all non-speech frames from input data.

The back-end is a robust state-of-the-art UBM-GMM system[17, 18]. In a UBM-GMM system, each speaker's distribution of feature vectors is modeled as a mixture of Gaussians, forming a Gaussian mixture speaker model (GMSM). In addition, a universal background model (UBM) defines a "generic" speaker. The UBM typically has hundreds of thousands of parameters and is trained on a very large amount of data (hundreds of hours of speech), which should include speech produced by a large number of individual speakers (in our case, the 2048-center diagonal-covariance UBM is trained on NIST SRE 2004, 2005, 2006, and 2008; Fisher; Switchboard-2; and Switchboard-Cellular databases). As the amount of speech available per individual speaker is typically much less than required to train the speaker model from scratch, the GMSM is produced by adapting UBM means so that the resulting model best describes the available speaker data. Finally, given the UBM, the candidate GMSM, and the audio file, the system extracts the feature vectors from the audio file and computes the log-likelihoods of these feature vectors belonging to the GMSM and to the UBM. The difference between these log-likelihoods constitutes the output score for this particular trial.

Our ASV system additionally employs the technique known as joint factor analysis[19, 20]. JFA use enables channel variability compensation by offsetting the channel effects and more robust speaker model estimation by using more informative prior on speaker model distribution. To use JFA in the described framework, an alternative representation of the speaker model—a single vector Z ("supervector")—is formed by concatenaging all GMSM means. JFA is trained in advance on a large annotated collection of audio files to learn the channel subspace (the basis over which Z preferentially varies when the same speaker's voice is presented over different channels) and the speaker subspace (the basis over which Z preferentially varies when different speakers are presented over the same channel). In our system, the dimensionalities of speaker subspace and of channel subspace are 300 and 150, respectively. Then, when processing the previously unseen data, components of inter-speaker differences attributable to speaker/to channel are emphasized/canceled, respectively. This is done by projecting corresponding supervectors into speaker/channel subspaces, using speaker subspace projection of Z to modify GMSM, using channel subspace projection of Z to modify UBM, and performing scoring with these modified GMSM and UBM. Also, as the log-likelihood calculation is expensive, in our system an approximation to it is computed based on an inner product[20] is used.

Finally, the obtained scores are subject to ZT-normalization[21], and the decision threshold minimizing equal error rate (EER) is chosen (separately for each condition).

NOISE CONDITIONS

Every trial in NIST SRE 2010 consists of computing the matching score between a speaker model and an audio file. To evaluate the noise robustness of the proposed cortical features, several distorted versions of these audio files are created by adding different types of noise reflecting a variety of real world scenarios:

- White noise at signal-to-noise ratio (SNR) levels from 24 to 0 dB in 6 dB steps;
- Babble noise (from Aurora database[22]), same SNR levels;
- Subway noise (from Aurora database[22]), same SNR levels;
- Simulated reverberation with $R\,T_{60}$ from 200 to 1,200 ms in steps of 200 ms.

It is important to mention that all training (UBM, JFA, and speaker model training) is done exclusively on clean data, and only the test audio files are corrupted. Note also that the train-test mismatch created by addition of noise/reverberation is superimposed on the train-test mismatch inherent to the SRE 2010 data.

RESULTS

Figure 4 shows the speaker verification performance in terms of EER for the cortical features and for the MFCC features as a function of noise type/strength and trial condition. The results clearly demonstrate that the proposed cortical features provide substantially lower EER than the MFCC as noise level increases, indicating their robustness. The average performance for each noise type and trial condition is shown in Table2. On average (across all conditions and all noise types), the cortical-features-based system yields 15.9% relative EER improvement over the robust state-of-the-art MFCC system. It is worth noting that the proposed approach is outperformed by the MFCC-based approach in only 4 out of the 36 cases. Because the proposed metric incorporates both a biomimetic auditory spectrogram previously shown to exhibit some noise-robustness characteristics[10] as well as multiresolution decomposition, we investigated further the contribution of both components in the reported improvements. We tested the system using the auditory spectrogram alone or an adaptation of the auditory spectrogram described here, coupled with a cepstral transformation. Neither system performed as well as the proposed multiresolution decomposition, hence strengthening the claim that our proposed multiresolution analysis is indeed responsible for the performance improvements shown in Table 2.

Table 2. Average ASV performance (EER, %) as a function of noise type and condition

Cond.	Babble (0–24 dB)		White (0–24 dB)		Subway (0–24 dB)		Reverb (200–1,200 ms)	
	MFCC	Cortical	MFCC	Cortical	MFCC	Cortical	MFCC	Cortical
1	6.43	5.24	12.3	7.93	8.5	6.97	9.39	6.87
2	11.47	9.09	18.06	12.71	14.1	11.55	13.88	9.58
3	7.33	6.31	10.86	8.87	8.89	7.84	16.70	14.96
4	7.86	6.78	14.88	10.87	10.36	8.79	12.66	9.78
5	6.39	5.98	8.52	7.55	7.70	6.89	14.05	10.59
6	10.45	9.95	11.04	10.48	11.12	10.39	20.00	16.14
7	9.62	10.64	13.30	12.67	10.67	12.09	19.21	16.65
8	5.19	5.46	7.19	6.48	6.00	6.04	12.78	9.48
9	6.84	6.00	13.58	11.46	8.94	8.59	9.43	6.84

In some ASV applications, metrics other than EER may be more relevant. For example, in certain biometric speaker verification systems the key requirement is a low false alarm rate. We present our results here in terms of two additional metrics more suitable in such case, namely Miss-10 and quadratic DCF (decision cost function) metrics. These two metrics were used in the NIST 2011 IARPA BEST program SRE[23]. The Miss-10 metric is defined as the false alarm rate P_{FA} obtained when the decision threshold is set such that the miss rate P_{Miss}=10%, and the quadratic DCF is defined as

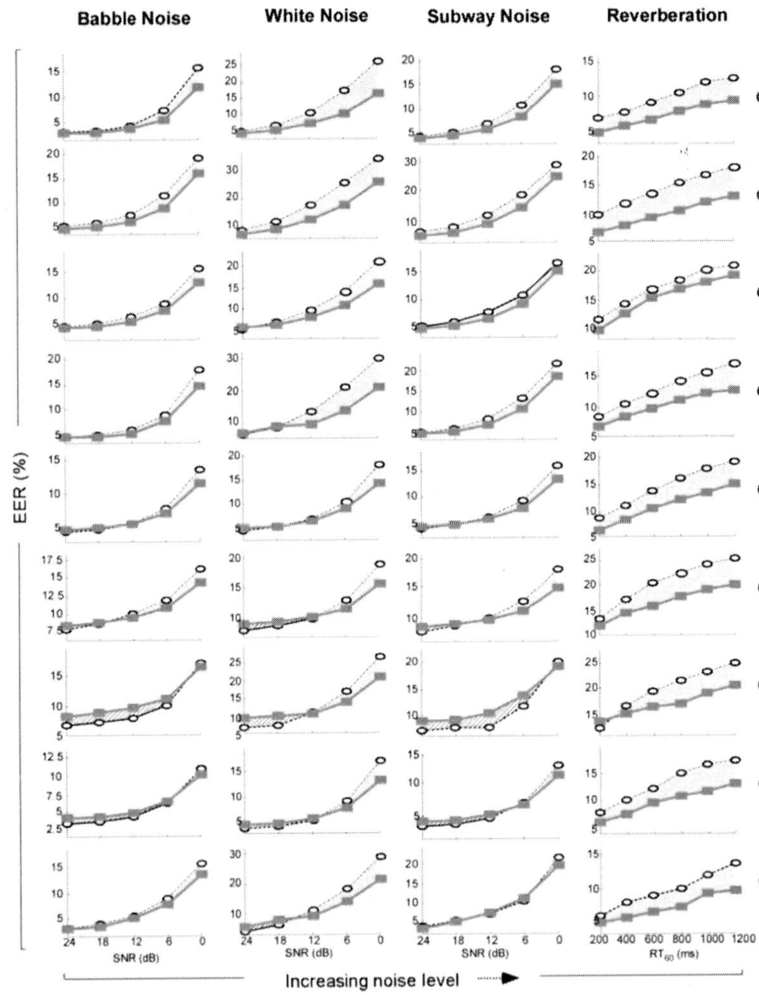

Figure 4. Evaluation results. Performance of the proposed cortical features (red filled squares) and enhanced MFCC features (black open circles) on NIST SRE 2010 "extended core" database as a function of noise level, noise type, and condition. In each subplot, the noise level is shown on X axis and the EER (in percents) is on Y axis. Columns and rows of subplots belong to the same noise type and to the same condition, respectively. Note the Y-axis ranges are not the same in the subplots.

$$\mathrm{DCF} = C_{\mathrm{Miss}} \times P_{\mathrm{Miss}}{}^{2} \times P_{\mathrm{target}} + C_{\mathrm{FA}} \times P_{\mathrm{FA}} \times (1 - P_{\mathrm{target}}) \tag{6}$$

with the parameter values C_{Miss}=100, C_{FA}=10, and P_{target}=0.01.

The average verification performance for each noise type using the Miss-10 and quadratic DCF metrics is shown in Tables3 and4, respectively. As seen from the data, in the low false alarm region the proposed cortical features outperform the robust state-of-the-art MFCC system with even larger margin: 28.8% relative using the Miss-10 metric and 22.6% relative using the quadratic DCF metric.

Table 3. Average ASV performance (Miss-10 metric, %) as a function of noise type and condition

Cond.	Babble (0–24 dB)		White (0–24 dB)		Subway (0–24 dB)		Reverb (200–1,200 ms)	
	MFCC	Cortical	MFCC	Cortical	MFCC	Cortical	MFCC	Cortical
1	5.3	3.2	17.2	7.9	9.4	6.0	9.1	4.6
2	16.6	10.8	31.3	18.1	22.9	16.4	19.8	9.5
3	6.2	4.4	14.0	9.0	9.2	6.9	26.5	21.9
4	8.1	5.7	22.9	13.7	13.0	9.9	16.9	9.9
5	4.9	3.7	9.4	6.7	7.0	5.3	20.3	11.8
6	11.6	10.2	13.6	11.4	13.2	11.2	35.6	25.1
7	11.8	12.5	18.6	16.6	13.0	16.5	34.2	26.6
8	3.2	2.9	7.7	5.0	4.7	3.9	17.0	9.4
9	6.5	5.5	21.4	15.4	11.0	9.9	9.0	4.6

Table 4. Average ASV performance (quadratic DCF metric) as a function of noise type and condition

Cond.	Babble (0–24 dB)		White (0–24 dB)		Subway (0–24 dB)		Reverb (200–1,200 ms)	
	MFCC	Cortical	MFCC	Cortical	MFCC	Cortical	MFCC	Cortical
1	0.129	0.098	0.371	0.211	0.208	0.147	0.219	0.150
2	0.247	0.183	0.506	0.342	0.356	0.266	0.353	0.221
3	0.149	0.116	0.282	0.196	0.199	0.155	0.481	0.403
4	0.176	0.136	0.446	0.287	0.276	0.199	0.317	0.237
5	0.139	0.114	0.186	0.150	0.171	0.136	0.379	0.262
6	0.236	0.230	0.255	0.240	0.245	0.241	0.557	0.457
7	0.231	0.240	0.452	0.362	0.302	0.300	0.543	0.486
8	0.105	0.088	0.154	0.119	0.122	0.105	0.331	0.212
9	0.134	0.105	0.405	0.288	0.218	0.175	0.220	0.145

DISCUSSION AND CONCLUSIONS

In this report, we explore the applicability of a multi-resolution analysis of speech signals to ASV. This framework maps the speech signal onto a rich feature space, highlighting and separating information about the glottal excitation signal, glottal shape, vocal tract geometry, and articulatory configuration (as each of these elements is an underlying factor for features of different width located in different areas on the log-frequency axis; see e.g.[24]). The cortical representation can be viewed as a "local" variant (w.r.t. log-frequency axis) of the analysis provided by MFCC analysis. This analogy stems from the fact that MFCC roughly correspond to spectral features of different widths integrated over the whole frequency range. In this work, both the "global-integration" MFCC approach and the "local" cortical approach are tested in a state-of-the-art ASV system on the NIST SRE 2010 dataset. While both perform comparably in clean condition, the cortical features are substantially more robust on noisy data, including non-stationary distortions as well as reverberation.

One of the intuitions behind the robustness observed in the proposed features is the fact that speech and noise generally exhibit different spectral shapes while occupying an overlapping spectral range. The expansion of the spectral axis with the multi-resolution analysis allows the extrication of some speech components from the masking noise, suppressing the noise components and providing for increased robustness. Furthermore, by highlighting the range between 0.5 and 4 CPO, the model stresses the most speaker-informative regions in the speech spectrum, which in turn map onto a modulation space to which humans are highly sensitive[7]. Such range is also commensurate with neurophysiological tuning observed in mammalian auditory cortex with most neurons concentrated around a spectral tuning of the order of few CPOs[3, 14]. A similar emphasis is put on the temporal dynamics of the signal by underscoring the region between 0.5 and 12 Hz, which defines natural boundaries for speech perception in noise by human listeners[7, 25–28] and mostly coincides with temporal tuning of mammalian cortical neurons[14]. Higher temporal modulation frequencies represent mostly the syllabic and segmental rate of speech[2].

Unlike comparable multi-resolution schemes recently developed[4, 5], the proposed approach does not involve dimension-expanded representations (close to 30,000 dimensions, which inherently require computationally-expensive schemes and therefore have limited applicability). Instead, our model is constrained to lie in a perceptually-relevant spectral modulation space and further uses a careful sampling scheme to encode the information with only four spectral analysis filters. This has the dual advantage of producing a feature space that is both low-dimensional and highly robust.

The careful optimization of model parameters is necessary to strike a balance between simple and efficient computation and noise robustness.

Importantly, in our approach no model components have been customized in any way to deal with a specific noise condition, making it suitable for a wide range of acoustic environments. In addition, the model has been minimally customized for the speaker recognition task and can in fact provide a general framework for a variety of speech processing tasks. Our preliminary results do indeed show great robustness of a similar scheme for automatic speech recognition. It is therefore essential to emphasize that the performance obtained with the cortical features is *solely a property of the features themselves* and is achieved without any noise compensation techniques. Our ongoing efforts are aimed at achieving further improvements by applying the described multi-resolution cortical analysis on enhanced spectral profiles obtained using speech enhancement techniques, which involve estimation of noise characteristics in various forms[29].

ENDNOTES

[a]We constraint the range of spectral modulations to 4 CPO, which covers more than 90% of the entire spectral modulation energy in speech and is most important for speech comprehension[7].

[b]The difference in MI levels between the speech message and speaker identity may be attributed to the observation that the speech signal encodes more information about the underlying linguistic message than about the speaker.

[c]In addition to the MI analysis, we performed an empirical test regarding use of 0.25 CPO filter. An experiment was run on clean data with Ω_c={0.25,0.5,1.0,2.0} CPO and yielded a 3.4% EER—a decrease of performance compared with 2.7% EER for the system that used Ω_c={0.5,1.0,2.0,4.0} CPO.

ACKNOWLEDGEMENTS

This research is partly supported by the IIS-0846112 (NSF), FA9550-09-1-0234 (AFOSR), 1R01AG036424-01 (NIH), N000141010278 (ONR), and by the Office of the Director of National Intelligence (ODNI), the Intelligence Advanced Research Projects Activity (IARPA), through the Army Research

Laboratory (ARL). All statements of fact, opinion, or conclusions contained herein are those of the authors and should not be construed as representing the official views or policies of IARPA, the ODNI, or the U.S. Government.

REFERENCES

1. Beigi H: *Fundamentals of Speaker Recognition*. Springer, Berlin; 2011.
2. Greenberg S, Popper A, Ainsworth W: *Speech Processing in the Auditory System*. Springer, Berlin; 2004.
3. O'Connor K, Yin P, Petkov C, Sutter M: Complex spectral interactions encoded by auditory cortical neurons: relationship between bandwidth and pattern. *Front Syst. Neurosci* 2010, 4: 4-145.
4. Woojay J, Juang B: Speech analysis in a model of the central auditory system. *IEEE Trans. Speech Audio Process* 2007, 15: 1802-1817.
5. Wu Q, Zhang L, Shi G: Robust speech feature extraction based on Gabor filtering and tensor factorization. *Proc. IEEE Intl. Conf. Acoust. Speech Signal Proc., Taipei, Taiwan* 2009, 4649-4652.
6. Elhilali M, Chi T, Shamma SA: A spectro-temporal modulation index (STMI) for assessment of speech intelligibility. *Speech Commun* 2003, 41: 331-348. 10.1016/S0167-6393(02)00134-6
7. Elliott T, Theunissen F: The modulation transfer function for speech intelligibility. *PLoS Comput. Biol* 2009, 5: e1000302. 10.1371/journal.pcbi.1000302
8. NIST 2010 speaker recognition evaluation http://www.nist.gov/speech/tests/sre/2010
9. Yang X, Wang K, Shamma SA: Auditory representations of acoustic signals. *IEEE Trans. Inf. Theory* 1992, 38: 824-839. 10.1109/18.119739Wang K, Shamma SA: Self-normalization noise-robustness in early auditory representations. *IEEE Trans. Speech Audio Process* 1994, 2: 421-435. 10.1109/89.294356
10. Schreiner C, Calhoun B: Spectral envelope coding in cat primary auditory cortex: properties of ripple transfer functions. *J. Aud. Neurosc*1995, 1: 39-61.

11. Versnel H, Kowalski N, Shamma SA: Ripple analysis in ferret primary auditory cortex. iii. topographic distribution of ripplc response parameters. *J. Aud. Neurosc* 1995, 1: 271-286.

12. Garofolo JS, Lamel LF, Fisher WM, Fiscus JG, Pallett DS, Dahlgren NL: *DARPA TIMIT Acoustic Phonetic Continuous Speech Corpus.* vol LDC93S1 Linguistic Data Consortium, Philadelphia; 1993.

13. Miller L, Escabi M, Read H, Schreiner C: Spectrotemporal receptive fields in the lemniscal auditory thalamus and cortex. *J. Neurophysiol* 2002, 87(1):516-527.

14. Cover T, Thomas J: *Elements of Information Theory.* 2nd edition. Wiley-Interscience, New York; 2006.

15. Hermansky H, Morgan N: RASTA processing of speech. *IEEE Trans. Speech Audio Process* 1994, 2(4):382-395.

16. Kinnunen T, Lib H: An overview of text-independent speaker recognition: from features to supervectors. *Speech Commun* 2010, 52: 12-40. 10.1016/j.specom.2009.08.009

17. Garcia-Romero D, *et al.*: The UMD-JHU 2011 speaker recognition system. In *Proc. IEEE Intl. Conf. Acoust. Speech Signal Proc.* Kyoto, Japan; 2012:4229-4232.

18. Kenny P, Boulianne G, Ouellet P, Dumouchel P: Speaker and session variability in gmm-based speaker verification. *IEEE Trans. Audio Speech Lang. Process* 2007, 15: 1448-1460.

19. Garcia-Romero D, Espy-Wilson C: Joint factor analysis for speaker recognition reinterpreted as signal coding using overcomplete dictionaries. In *Proc. Odyssey Speaker and Language Recognition Workshop.* Brno, Czech Republic; 2010:117-124.

20. Auckenthaler R, Carey M, Lloyd-Thomas H: Score normalization for text-independent speaker verification system. *Digit. Signal Proc* 2000, 1(10):42-54.

21. Hirsch H, Pearce D: The Aurora experimental framework for the performance evaluation of speech recognition systems under noisy conditions. In *ISCA ITRW ASR2000.* vol. 4 Beijing, China; 2000:29-32.

22. NIST 2011 speaker recognition evaluation http://www.nist.gov/itl/iad/mig/best.cfm

23. Zotkin D, Chi T, Shamma SA, Duraiswami R: Neuromimetic sound representation for percept detection and manipulation. *EURASIP J. App. Sig. Process* 2005, 2005: 1350-1364. 10.1155/ASP.2005.1350

24. Steeneken H, Houtgast T: A physical method for measuring speech-transmission quality. *J. Acoust. Soc. Am* 1979, 67: 318-326.

25. Drullman R, Festen J, Plomp R: Effect of temporal envelope smearing on speech reception. *J. Acoust. Soc. Am* 1994, 95: 1053-1064. 10.1121/1.408467

26. Arai T, Pavel M, Hermansky H, Avendano C: Syllable intelligibility for temporally filtered lpc cepstral trajectories. *J. Acoust. Soc. Am* 1999, 105: 2783-2791. 10.1121/1.426895

27. Greenberg S, Arai T, Grant K: The Role of Temporal Dynamics in Understanding Spoken Language. In *NATO Science Series: Life and Behavioural Sciences.* IOS Press, Amsterdam; 2006:171-190.

28. Loizou P: *Speech Enhancement: Theory and Practice.* CRC Press, Boca Raton; 2007.

4

CHAPTER

Noisy Training for Deep Neural Networks in Speech Recognition

Shi Yin, Chao Liu, Zhiyong Zhang, Yiye Lin, Dong Wang Javier Tejedor, Thomas Fang Zheng and Yinguo Li

[1]*Center for Speech and Language Technology, Research Institute of Information Technology, Tsinghua University, ROOM 1-303, BLDG FIT, 100084 Beijing, China.*

[2]*Center for Speech and Language Technologies, Division of Technical Innovation and Development, Tsinghua National Laboratory for Information Science and Technology, ROOM 1-303, BLDG FIT, 100084 Beijing, China.*

[3]*Department of Computer Science and Technology, Tsinghua University, ROOM 1-303, BLDG FIT, 100084 Beijing, China.*

[4]*School of Computer Science and Technology, Chongqing University of Posts and Telecommunications, No.2, Chongwen Road, Nan'an District, 400065 Chong Qing, China.*

[5]*Beijing Institute of Technology, No.5 South Zhongguancun Street, Haidian District, 100081 Beijing, China.*

[6]*GEINTRA, University of Alcalá, 28801 Alcalá de Henares, Madrid, Spain.*

ABSTRACT

Deep neural networks (DNNs) have gained remarkable success in speech recognition, partially attributed to the flexibility of DNN models in learning complex patterns of speech signals. This flexibility, however, may lead to serious over-fitting and hence miserable performance degradation in adverse acoustic conditions such as those with high ambient noises. We propose a noisy training approach to tackle this problem: by injecting moderate noises into the training data intentionally and randomly, more generalizable DNN models can be learned. This 'noise injection' technique, although known to the neural computation community already, has not been studied with DNNs which involve a highly complex objective function. The experiments presented in this paper confirm that the noisy training approach works well for the DNN model and can provide substantial performance improvement for DNN-based speech recognition.

Keywords: Speech recognition Deep neural network Noise injection

1 INTRODUCTION

A modern automatic speech recognition (ASR) system involves three components: an acoustic feature extractor to derive representative features for speech signals, an emission model to represent static properties of the speech features, and a transitional model to depict dynamic properties of speech production. Conventionally, the dominant acoustic features in ASR are based on short-time spectral analysis, e.g., Mel frequency cepstral coefficients (MFCC). The emission and transition models are often chosen to be the Gaussian mixture model (GMM) and the hidden Markov model (HMM), respectively.

Deep neural networks (DNNs) have gained brilliant success in many research fields including speech recognition, computer vision (CV), and natural language processing (NLP) [1]. A DNN is a neural network (NN) that involves more than one hidden layer. NNs have been studied in the ASR community for a decade, mainly in two approaches: in the 'hybrid approach', the NN is used to substitute for the GMM to produce frame likelihood [2], and in the 'tandem approach', the NN is used to produce long-context features that are used to substitute for or augment to short-time features, e.g., MFCCs [3].

Although promising, the NN-based approach, either by the hybrid setting or the tandem setting, did not deliver overwhelming superiority over the conventional approaches based on MFCCs and GMMs. The revolution took place in 2010 after the close collaboration between academic and industrial research groups, including the University of Toronto, Microsoft, and IBM [1,4,5]. This research found that very significant performance improvements can be accomplished with the NN-based hybrid approach, with a few novel techniques and design choices: (1) extending NNs to DNNs, i.e., involving a large number of hidden layers (usually 4 to 8); (2) employing appropriate initialization methods, e.g., pre-training with restricted Boltzmann machines (RBMs); and (3) using fine-grained NN targets, e.g., context-dependent states. Since then, numerous experiments have been published to investigate various configurations of the DNN-based acoustic modeling, and all the experiments confirmed that the new model is predominantly superior to the classical architecture based on GMMs [2,4,6–13].

Encouraged by the success of DNNs in the hybrid approach, researchers reevaluated the tandem approach using DNNs and achieved similar performance improvements [3,14–20]. Some comparative studies were conducted for the hybrid and tandem approaches, though no evidence supports that one approach clearly outperforms the other [21,22]. The study of this paper is based on the hybrid approach, though the developed technique can be equally applied to the tandem approach.

The advantage of DNNs in modeling state emission distributions, when compared to the conventional GMM, has been discussed in some previous publications, e.g., [1,2]. Although no full consentience exists, researchers agree on some points, e.g., the DNN is naturally discriminative when trained with an appropriate objective function, and it is a hierarchical model that can learn patterns of speech signals from primitive levels to high levels. Particularly, DNNs involve very flexible and compact structures: they usually consist of a large amount of parameters, and the parameters are highly shared among feature dimensions and task targets (phones or states). This flexibility, on one hand, leads to very strong discriminative models, and on the other hand, may cause serious over-fitting problems, leading to miserable performance reduction if the training and test conditions are mismatched. For example, when the training data are mostly clean and the test data are corrupted by noises, ASR performance usually suffers from a substantial degradation. This over-fitting is particularly serious if the training data are not abundant [23].

A multitude of research has been conducted to improve noise robustness of DNN models. The multi-condition training approach was presented in [24], where DNNs were trained by involving speech data in various channel/noise conditions. This approach is straightforward and usually delivers good performance, though collecting multi-condition data is not always possible. Another direction is to use noise-robust features, e.g., auditory features based on Gammatone filters [23]. The third direction involves various speech enhancement approaches. For example, the vector Taylor series (VTS) was applied to compensate for input features in an adaptive training framework [25]. The authors of [26] investigated several popular speech enhancement approaches and found that the maximum likelihood spectral amplitude estimator (MLSA) is the best spectral restoration method for DNNs trained with clean speech and tested on noisy data. Some other researches involve noise information in DNN inputs and train a 'noise aware' network. For instance, [27] used the VTS as the noise estimator to generate noise-dependent inputs for DNNs.

Another related technique is the denoising auto-encoder (DAE) [28]. In this approach, some noises are randomly selected and intentionally injected to the original clean speech; the noise-corrupted speech data are then fed to an auto-encoder (AE) network where the targets (outputs) are the original clean speech. By this configuration, the AE will learn the denoising function in a non-linear way. Note that this approach is not particular for ASR, but a general denoising technique. The authors of [29] extended this approach by introducing recurrent NN structures and demonstrated that the deep and recurrent auto-encoder can deliver better performance for ASR in most of the noise conditions they examined.

This paper presents a noisy training approach for DNN-based ASR. The idea is simple: by injecting some noises to the input speech data when conducting DNN training, the noise patterns are expected to be learned, and the generalization capability of the resulting network is expected to be improved. Both may improve robustness of DNN-based ASR systems within noisy conditions. Note that part of the work has been published in [30], though this paper presents a full discussion of the technique and reports extensive experiments.

The paper is organized as follows: Section 6 discusses some related work, and Section 6 presents the proposed noisy training approach. The implementation details are presented in Section 6, and the experimental settings and results are presented in Section 6. The entire paper is concluded in Section 6.

2 RELATED WORK

The noisy training approach proposed in this paper was highly motivated by the noise injection theory which has been known for decades in the neural computing community [31–34]. This paper employs this theory and contributes in two aspects: first, we examine the behavior of noise injection in DNN training, a more challenging task involving a huge amount of parameters; second, we study mixture of multiple noises at various levels of signal-to-noise ratios (SNR), which is beyond the conventional noise injection theory that assumes small and Gaussian-like injected noises.

Another work related to this study is the DAE approach [28,29]. Both the DAE and the noisy training approaches corrupt NN inputs by randomly sampled noises. Although the objective of the DAE approach is to recover the original clean signals, the focus of the noisy training approach proposed here is to construct a robust classifier.

Finally, this work is also related to the multi-condition training [24], in the sense that both train DNNs with speech signals in multiple conditions. However, the noisy training obtains multi-conditioned speech data by corrupting clean speech signals, while the multi-condition training uses real-world speech data recorded in multiple noise conditions. More importantly, we hope to set up a theoretical foundation and a practical guideline for training DNNs with noises, instead of just regarding it as a blind noise pattern learner.

3 NOISY TRAINING

The basic process of noisy training for DNNs is as follows: first of all, sample some noise signals from some real-world recordings and then mix these noise signals with the original training data. This operation is also referred to as 'noise injection' or 'noise corruption' in this paper. The noise-corrupted speech data are then used to train DNNs as usual. The rationale of this approach is twofold: firstly, the noise patterns within the introduced noise signals can be learned and thus compensated for in the inference phase, which is straightforward and shares the same idea as the multi-condition training approach; secondly, the perturbation introduced by the injected noise can improve generalization capability of the resulting DNN, which is supported by the noise injection theory. We discuss these two aspects sequentially in this section.

3.1 Noise pattern learning

The impact of injecting noises in training data can be understood as providing some noise-corrupted instances so that they can be learned by the DNN structure and recognized in the inference (test) phase. From this perspective, the DNN and GMM are of no difference, since both can benefit from matched acoustic conditions of training and testing, by either re-training or adaptation.

However, the DNN is more powerful in noise pattern learning than the GMM. Due to its discriminative nature, the DNN model focuses on phone/state boundaries, and the boundaries it learns might be highly complex. Therefore, it is capable of addressing more severe noises and dealing with heterogeneous noise patterns. For example, a DNN may obtain a reasonable phone classification accuracy in a very noisy condition, if the noise does not drastically change the decision boundaries (e.g., with car noise). In addition, noises of different types and at different magnitude levels can be learned simultaneously, as the complex decision boundaries that the DNN classifier may learn provide sufficient freedom to address complicated decisions in heterogeneous acoustic conditions.

In contrast, the GMM is a generative model and focuses on class distributions. The decision boundaries a GMM learns (which are determined by the relative locations of the GMM components of phones/states) are relatively much simpler than those a DNN model learns. Therefore, it is difficult for GMMs to address heterogeneous noises.

The above argument explains some interesting observations in the DNN-based noise training in our experiments. First, learning a particular type of noise does not necessarily lead to performance degradation in another type of noise. In fact, our experiments show that learning a particular noise usually improves performances on other noises, only if the property of the 'unknown' noise is not drastically different from the one that has been learned. This is a clear advantage over GMMs, for which a significant performance reduction is often observed when the noise conditions of training and test data are unmatched.

Moreover, our experiments show that learning multiple types of noises are not only possible, but also complementary. As we will see shortly, learning two noises may lead to better performance than learning any single noise, when the test data are corrupted by either of the two noises. This is also different from GMMs, for which learning multiple noises generally leads to interference among each other.

The power of DNNs in learning noise patterns can be understood in a deeper way, from three perspectives. Firstly, the DNN training is related to feature selection. Due to the discriminative nature, the DNN training can infer the most discriminative part of the noise-corrupted acoustic features. For instance, with the training data corrupted by car noise, the DNN training process will learn that the corruption is mainly on the low-frequency part of the signal, and so the low-frequency components of the speech features are de-emphasized in the car noise condition. Learning the car noise, however, did not seriously impact the decision boundaries in other conditions in our experiments, e.g., with clean speech, probably due to the complicated DNN structure that allows to learn noise-conditioned decision boundaries. Moreover, learning car noise may benefit other noise conditions where the corruption mainly resides in low-frequency components (as the car noise), even though the noise is not involved in the training.

Secondly, the DNN training is related to perceptual classification. Thanks to the multi-layer structure, DNNs learn noise patterns gradually. This means that the noise patterns presented to the DNN inputs are learned together with the speech patterns at low levels, but only at high levels, the noise patterns are recognized and de-emphasized in the decision. This provides a large space for DNNs to learn heterogeneous noise patterns and 'memorize' them in the abundant parameters. This process also simulates the processing procedure of the human brain, where noise patterns are processed and recognized by the peripheral auditory system but are ignored in the final perceptual decision by the central neural system.

Finally, the DNN training is related to the theory of regularization. All admit that a large amount of parameters of DNNs allow great potential to learn complex speech and noise patterns and their class boundaries. If the training is based on clean speech only, however, the flexibility provided by the DNN structure is largely wasted. This is because the phone class boundaries are relatively clear with clean speech, and so the abundant parameters of DNNs tend to learn the nuanced variations of phone implementations, conditioned on a particular type of channel and/or background noise. This is a notorious over-fitting problem. By injecting random noises, the DNN training is enforced to emphasize on the most discriminative patterns of speech signals. In other words, the DNNs trained with noise injection tend to be less sensitive to noise corruptions. This intuition is supported by the noise injection theory as presented in the next section.

3.2 Noise injection theory

It has been known for two decades that imposing noises to the input can improve the generalization capability of neural networks [35]. A bunch of theoretical studies have been presented to understand the implication of this 'noise injection'. Nowadays, it is clear that involving a small magnitude of noise in the input is equivalent to introducing a certain regularization in the objective function, which in turn encourages the network converging to a smoother mapping function [36]. More precisely, with noise injection, the training favors an optimal solution at which the objective function is less sensitive to the change of the input [32]. Further studies showed that noise injection is closely correlated to some other well-known techniques, including sigmoid gain scaling and target smoothing by convolution [37], at least with Gaussian noises and multi-layer perceptrons (MLP) with a single layer. The relationships among regularization, weight decay, and noise injection, on one hand, provide a better understanding for each individual technique, and on the other hand, motivate some novel and efficient robust training algorithms. For example, Bishop showed that noise injection can be approximated by a Tikhonov regularization on the square error cost function [33]. Finally, we note that noise injection can be conducted in different ways, such as perturbation on weights and hidden units [31], though we just consider the noise injection to the input in this paper.

In order to highlight the rationale of noise injection (and so noisy training), we reproduce the formulation and derivation in [32] but migrate the derivation to the case of cross-entropy cost which is usually used in classification problems such as ASR.

First of all, formulate an MLP as a non-linear mapping function fθ:RM⟼RKfθ:RM⟼RK where M is the input dimension and K is the output dimension, and θ encodes all the parameters of the network including weights and biases. Let x∈RMx∈RM denote the input variables, and$\mathbf{y}\in\{0,1\}^K$denote the target labels which follow the 1-of-K encoding scheme. The cross-entropy cost is defined as follows:

$$E(\theta) = -\sum_{n=1}^{N}\sum_{k=1}^{K}\left\{\mathbf{y}^{(n)} ln f_k\left(\mathbf{x}^{(n)}\right)\right\} \tag{1}$$

where n indexes the training samples and k indexes the output units. Consider an identical and independent noise $\mathbf{v}$ whose first and second moments satisfy the following constraints:

$$\mathbb{E}\{\mathbf{v}\} = 0 \quad \mathbb{E}\left\{\mathbf{v}^2\right\} = \epsilon I \tag{2}$$

where I is the M-dimensional identity matrix, and ε is a small positive number. Applying the Taylor series of $l\,n\,f(\mathbf{x})$, the cost function with the noise injection can be derived as follows:

$$\begin{aligned} E_v(\theta) &= -\sum_{n=1}^{N}\sum_{k=1}^{K}\left\{\mathbf{y}_k^{(n)} ln f_k\left(\mathbf{x}^{(n)} + \mathbf{v}^{(n)}\right)\right\} \\ &\approx -\sum_{n=1}^{N}\sum_{k=1}^{K}\left\{\mathbf{y}_k^{(n)} ln f_k\left(\mathbf{x}^{(n)}\right)\right\} \\ &\quad -\sum_{n=1}^{N}\sum_{k=1}^{K}\mathbf{y}_k^{(n)}\left\{\mathbf{v}^{(n)T}\frac{\nabla f_k\left(\mathbf{x}^{(n)}\right)}{f_k\left(\mathbf{x}^{(n)}\right)} + \frac{1}{2}\mathbf{v}^{(n)T}H_k\left(\mathbf{x}^{(n)}\right)\mathbf{v}^{(n)}\right\} \end{aligned}$$

where $H_k(x)$ is defined as follows:

$$H_k(x) = \frac{-1}{f_k(\mathbf{x})}\nabla f_k(\mathbf{x})\nabla f_k(\mathbf{x})^T + \frac{1}{f_k^2(\mathbf{x})}\nabla^2 f_k(\mathbf{x}).$$

Since $\mathbf{v}^{(n)}$ is independent of $\mathbf{x}^{(n)}$ and E{v}=0E{v}=0, the first-order item vanishes and the cost is written as:

$$E_v(\theta) \approx E(\theta) - \frac{\epsilon}{2} \sum_{k=1}^{K} tr\left(\tilde{H}_k\right) \tag{3}$$

where tr denotes the trace operation, and

$$\tilde{H}_k = \sum_{n \in C_k} H_k\left(\mathbf{x}^{(n)}\right)$$

where Ck is the set of indices of the training samples belonging to the kth class.

In order to understand the implication of Equation 3, an auxiliary function can be defined as follows:

$$E(\theta, \mathbf{v}) = -\sum_{n=1}^{N} \sum_{k=1}^{K} \left\{ \mathbf{y}_k^{(n)} \ln f_k\left(\mathbf{x}^{(n)} + \mathbf{v}\right) \right\}$$

where $\mathbf{v}$ is a small change to the input vectors $\{\mathbf{x}^{(n)}\}$. Note that $E(\theta,\mathbf{v})$ differs from $E_v(\theta)$: $\mathbf{v}$ in $E(\theta,\mathbf{v})$ is a fixed value for all $\mathbf{x}^{(n)}$, while $\mathbf{v}^{(n)}$ in $E_v(\theta)$ is a random variable and differs for each training sample. The Laplacian of $E(\theta,\mathbf{v})$ with respect to $\mathbf{v}$ is computed as follows:

$$\begin{aligned} \nabla^2 E(\theta, \mathbf{v}) &= tr\left\{ \frac{\partial^2 E(\theta, \mathbf{v})}{\partial \mathbf{v}^2} \right\} \\ &= -tr\left\{ \sum_{n=1}^{N} \sum_{k=1}^{K} \mathbf{y}_k^{(n)} H_k\left(\mathbf{x}^{(n)} + \mathbf{v}\right) \right\} \\ &= -tr\left\{ \sum_{k=1}^{K} \sum_{n \in C_k} H_k\left(\mathbf{x}^{(n)} + \mathbf{v}\right) \right\}. \end{aligned} \tag{4}$$

By comparing Equations 4 and 3, we get:

$$E_v(\theta) \approx E(\theta) + \frac{\epsilon}{2} \nabla^2 E(\theta, 0). \tag{5}$$

Equation 5 indicates that injecting noises to the input units is equivalent to placing a regularization on the cost function. This regularization is related to the second-order derivatives of the cost function with respect to the input, and its strength is controlled by the magnitude of the injected noise. Since $\nabla^2 E(\theta,0)$ is positive at the optimal solution of θ, the regularized cost function tends to accept solutions with a smaller curvature of the cost. In other words, the new cost function $E_v(\theta)$ is less sensitive to the change on inputs and therefore leads to better generalization capability. Note that this result is identical to the one obtained in [32], where the cost function is the square error.

4 NOISY DEEP LEARNING

From the previous section, the validity of the noisy training approach can be justified in two ways: discriminative noise pattern learning and objective function smoothing. The former provides the ability to learn multiple noise patterns, and the latter encourages a more robust classifier. However, it is still unclear if the noisy training scheme works for the DNN model which involves a large number of parameters and thus tends to exhibit a highly complex cost function. Particularly, the derivation of Equation 5 assumes small noises with diagonal covariances, while in practice we wish to learn complex noise patterns that may be large in magnitude and fully dimensional correlated. Furthermore, the DNN training is easy to fall in a local minimum, and it is not obvious if the random noise injection may lead to fast convergence.

We therefore investigate how the noise training works for DNNs when the injected noises are large in magnitude and heterogeneous in types. In order to simulate noises in practical scenarios, the procedure illustrated in Figure 1 is proposed.

For each speech signal (utterance), we first select a type of noise to corrupt it. Assuming that there are *n* types of noises, we randomly select a noise type following a multinomial distribution:

$v \sim Mult(\mu 1,\mu 2,...,\mu n).v \sim Mult(\mu 1,\mu 2,...,\mu n).$

The parameters $\{\mu_i\}$ are sampled from a Dirichlet distribution:

$(\mu 1,\mu 2,...,\mu n) \sim Dir(\alpha 1,\alpha 2,...,\alpha n)(\mu 1,\mu 2,...,\mu n) \sim Dir(\alpha 1,\alpha 2,...,\alpha n)$

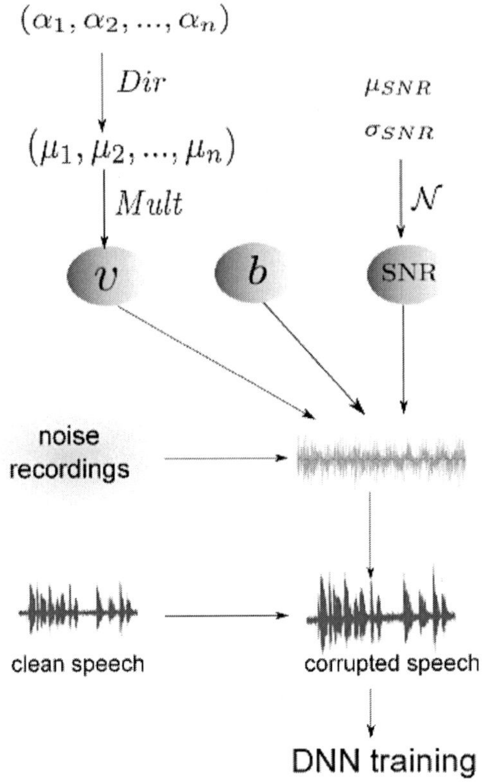

Figure 1. The noise training procedure. 'Dir' denotes the Dirichlet distribution, 'Mult' denotes the multinomial distribution, and '$\mathcal{N}$' denotes the Gaussian distribution. v is a variable that represents the noise type, b represents the starting frame of the selected noise segment, and 'SNR' is the expected SNR of the corrupted speech data.

where the parameters $\{\alpha_i\}$ are manually set to control the base distribution of the noise types. This hierarchical sampling approach (Dirichlet followed by multinomial) simulates the uncertain noise type distributions in different operation scenarios. Note that we allow a special noise type 'no-noise', which means that the speech signal is not corrupted.

Secondly, sample the noise level (i.e., SNR). This sampling follows a Gaussian distribution N(μSNR,σSNR) where μ_{SNR} and σ_{SNR} are the mean and variance, respectively, and are both manually defined. If the noise type is no-noise, then the SNR sampling is not needed.

The next step is to sample an appropriate noise segment according to the noise type. Tnis is achieved following a uniformed distribution, i.e., randomly select a starting point *b* in the noise recording of the required noise type and then excerpt a segment of signal which is of the same length as the speech signal to corrupt. Circular excerption is employed if the length of the noise signal is less than that of the speech signal.

Finally, the selected noise segment is scaled to reach the required SNR level and then is used to corrupt the clean speech signal. The noise-corrupted speech is fed into the DNN input units to conduct model training.

5 EXPERIMENTS

5.1 Databases

The experiments were conducted with the Wall Street Journal (WSJ) database. The setting is largely standard: the training part used the WSJ si284 training dataset, which involves 37,318 utterances or about 80 h of speech signals. The WSJ dev93 dataset (503 utterances) was used as the development set for parameter tuning and cross validation in DNN training. The WSJ eval92 dataset (333 utterances) was used to conduct evaluation.

Note that the WSJ database was recorded in a noise-free condition. In order to simulate noise-corrupted speech signals, the DEMAND noise database (http://parole.loria.fr/DEMAND/) was used to sample noise segments. This database involves 18 types of noises, from which we selected 7 types in this work, including white noise and noises at cafeteria, car, restaurant, train station, bus and park.

5.2 Experimental settings

We used the Kaldi toolkit (http://kaldi.sourceforge.net/) to conduct the training and evaluation and largely followed the WSJ s5 recipe for Graphics Processing Unit (GPU)-based DNN training. Specifically, the training started from a monophone system with the standard 13-dimensional MFCCs plus the first- and second-order derivatives. Cepstral mean normalization (CMN) was employed to reduce the channel effect. A triphone system was then constructed based on the alignments derived from the monophone system, and a linear discriminant analysis (LDA) transform was employed to select the most discriminative dimensions from a large context (five frames to the left and right, respectively). A further refined system was then constructed by applying a maximum likelihood linear transform (MLLT) upon the LDA feature, which intended to reduce the correlation among feature dimensions so that the diagonal assumption of the Gaussians is satisfied. This MLLT+LDA system involves 351 phones and 3,447 Gaussian mixtures and was used to generate state alignments.

The DNN system was then trained utilizing the alignments provided by the MLLT+LDA GMM system. The feature used was 40-dimensional filter banks. A symmetric 11-frame window was applied to concatenate neighboring frames, and an LDA transform was used to reduce the feature dimension to 200. The LDA-transformed features were used as the DNN input.

The DNN architecture involves 4 hidden layers, and each layer consists of 1,200 units. The output layer is composed of 3,447 units, equal to the total number of Gaussian mixtures in the GMM system. The cross entropy was set as the objective function of the DNN training, and the stochastic gradient descendent (SGD) approach was employed to perform optimization, with the mini batch size set to 256 frames. The learning rate started from a relatively large value (0.008) and was then gradually shrunk by halving the value whenever no improvement on frame accuracy on the development set was obtained. The training stopped when the frame accuracy improvement on the cross-validation data was marginal (less than 0.001). Neither momentum nor regularization was used, and no pre-training was employed since we did not observe a clear advantage by involving these techniques.

In order to inject noises, the averaged energy was computed for each training/test utterance, and a noise segment was randomly selected and scaled according to the expected SNR; the speech and noise signals were then mixed by simple time-domain addition. Note that the noise injection was conducted before the utterance-based CMN. In the noisy training, the training data were corrupted by the selected noises, while the development data used for cross validation remained uncorrupted. The DNNs reported in this section were all initialized from scratch and were trained based on the same alignments provided by the LDA+MLLT GMM system. Note that the process of the model training is reproducible in spite of the randomness on noise injection and model initialization, since the random seed was hard-coded.

In the test phase, the noise type and SNR are all fixed so that we can evaluate the system performance in a specific noise condition. This is different from the training phase where both the noise type and SNR level can be random. We choose the 'big dict' test case suggested in the Kaldi WSJ recipe, which is based on a large dictionary consisting of 150k English words and a corresponding 3-gram language model.

Table 1 presents the baseline results, where the DNN models were trained with clean speech data, and the test data were corrupted with different types of noises at different SNRs. The results are reported in word error rates (WER) on the evaluation data. We observe that without noise, a rather high accuracy (4.31%) can be obtained; with noise interference, the performance is dramatically degraded, and more noise (a smaller SNR) results in more serious degradation. In addition, different types of noises impact the performance in different degrees: the white noise is the most serious corruption which causes a ten times of WER increase when the SNR is 10 dB; in contrast, the car noise is the least impactive: It causes a relatively small WER increase (37% in relative) even if the SNR goes below 5 dB.

Table 1. WER of the baseline system

	Test SNR (dB)					
	5	10	15	20	25	Clean
White	77.23	46.46	21.21	9.30	5.51	4.31
Car	5.94	5.42	4.87	4.77	4.50	4.31
Cafeteria	25.33	14.27	10.07	8.38	6.88	4.31
Restaurant	46.87	22.15	13.27	9.73	7.48	4.31
Train station	34.36	12.72	6.93	5.40	4.43	4.31
Bus	13.88	8.44	6.57	5.51	4.84	4.31
Park	22.10	11.25	7.44	5.87	4.63	4.31

Values are in WER%.

The different behaviors in WER changes can be attributed to the different patterns of corruptions with different noises: white noise is broad-band and so it corrupts speech signals on all frequency components; in contrast, most of the color noises concentrate on a limited frequency band and so lead to limited corruptions. For example, car noise concentrates on low frequencies only, leaving most of the speech patterns uncorrupted.

5.3 Single noise injection

In the first set of experiments, we study the simplest configuration for the noisy training, which is a single noise injection at a particular SNR. This is simply attained by fixing the injected noise type and selecting a small σ_{SNR} so that the sampled SNRs concentrate on the particular level μ_{SNR}. In this section, we choose σ_{SNR}=0.01.

5.3.1 White noise injection

We first investigate the effect of white noise injection. Among all the noises, the white noise is rather special: it is a common noise that we encounter every day, and it is broad-band and often leads to drastic performance degradation compared to other narrow-band noises, as has been shown in the previous section. Additionally, the noise injection theory discussed in Section 6 shows that white noise satisfies Equation 2and hence leads to the regularized cost function of Equation 5. This means that injecting white noise would improve the generalization capability of the resulting DNN model; this is not necessarily the case for most of other noises.

Figure 2 presents the WER results, where the white noise is injected during training at SNR levels varying from 5 to 30 dB, and each curve represents a particular SNR case. The first plot shows the WER results on the evaluation data that are corrupted by white noise at different SNR levels from 5 to 25 dB. For comparison, the results on the original clean evaluation data are also presented. It can be observed that injecting white noise generally improves ASR performance on noisy speech, and a matched noise injection (at the same SNR) leads to the most significant improvement. For example, injecting noise at an SNR of 5 dB is the most effective for the test speech at an SNR of 5 dB, while injecting noise at an SNR of 25 dB leads to the best performance improvement for the test speech at an SNR of 25 dB. A serious problem, however, is that the noise injection always leads to performance degradation on clean speech. For example, the injection at an SNR of 5 dB, although very effective for highly noisy speech (SNR < 10 dB), leads to a WER ten times higher than the original result on the clean evaluation data.

The second and third plots show the WER results on the evaluation data that are corrupted by car noise and cafeteria noise, respectively. In other words, the injected noise in training does not match the noise condition in the test. It can be seen that the white noise injection leads to some performance gains on the evaluation speech corrupted by the cafeteria noise, as far as the injected noise is limited in magnitude. This demonstrated that the white noise injection can improve the generalization capability of the DNN model, as predicted by the noise injection theory in Section 6. For the car noise corruption, however, the white noise injection does not show any benefit. This is perhaps attributed to the fact that the cost function (Equation 1) is not so bumpy with respect to the car noise, and hence, the regularization term introduced in Equation 3 is less effective. This conjecture is supported by the baseline results which show very little performance degradation with the car noise corruption.

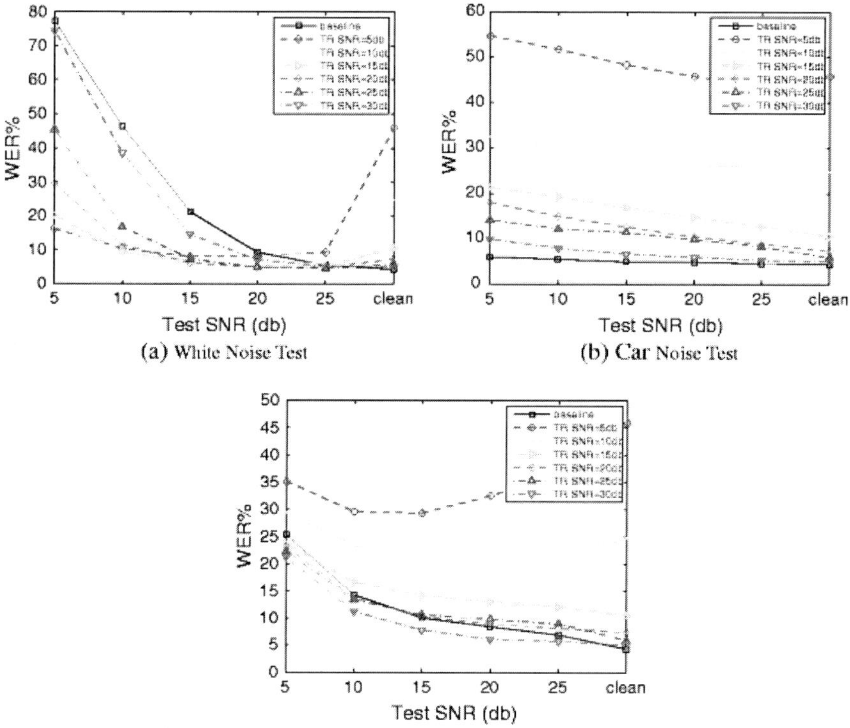

(a) White Noise Test

(b) Car Noise Test

(b) Cafeteria Noise Test

Figure 2. Performance of noisy training with white noise injected **(σ =0 . 01).** 'TR' means the training condition. The 'baseline' curves present the results of the system trained with clean speech data, as have been presented in Table 1. **(a)** White noise test. **(b)** Car noise test. **(c)** Cafeteria noise test.

In both the car and cafeteria noise conditions, if the injected white noise is too strong, then the ASR performance is drastically degraded. This is because a strong white noise injection does not satisfy the small noise assumption of Equation 2, and hence, the regularized cost (Equation3) does not hold anymore. This, on one hand, breaks the theory of noise injection so that the improved generalization capability is not guaranteed, and on the other hand, it results in biased learning towards the white noise-corrupted speech patterns that are largely different from the ones that are observed in speech signals corrupted by noises of cars and cafeterias.

As a summary, white noise injection is effective in two ways: for white noise-corrupted test data, it can learn white noise-corrupted speech patterns and provides dramatic performance improvement particularly at matched SNRs; for test data corrupted by other noises, it can deliver a more robust model if the injection is in a small magnitude, especially for noises that cause a significant change on the DNN cost function. An aggressive white noise injection (with a large magnitude) usually leads to performance reduction on test data corrupted by color noises.

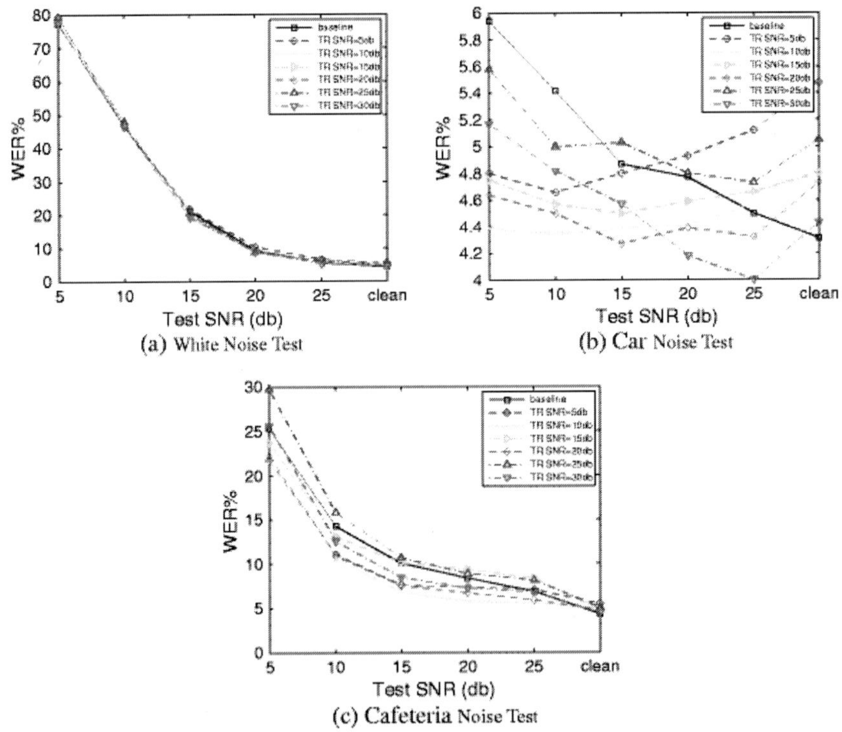

Figure 3. Performance of noisy training with car noise injected (**σ=0.01**). 'TR' means the training condition. The 'baseline' curves present the results of the system trained with clean speech data, as have been presented in Table 1. **(a)** White noise test. **(b)** Car noise test.**(c)** Cafeteria noise test.

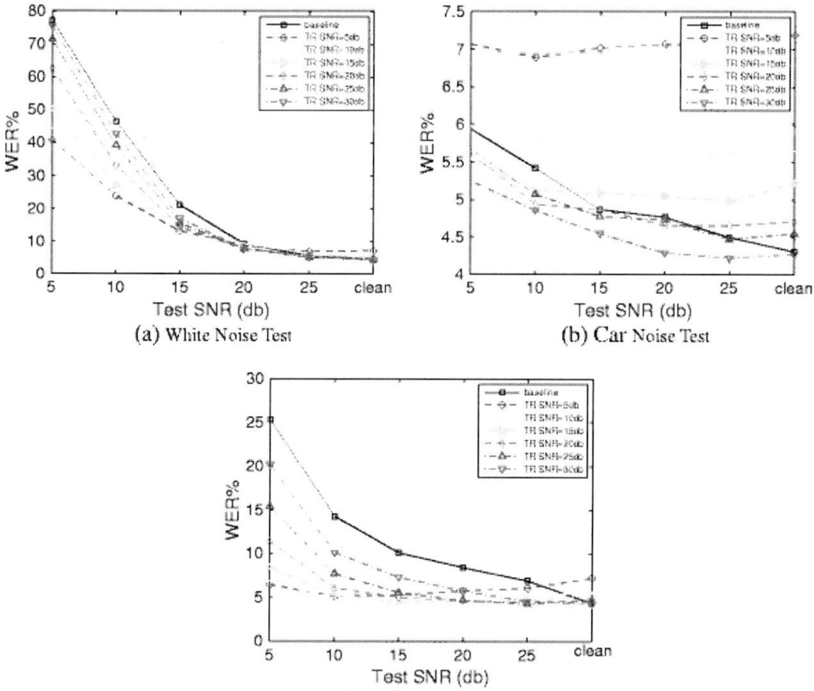

(a) White Noise Test (b) Car Noise Test (b) Cafeteria Noise Test

Figure 4. Performance of noisy training with cafeteria noise injected (**σ =0 . 01**). 'TR' means the training condition. The 'baseline' curves present the results of the system trained with clean speech data, as have been presented in Table 1. **(a)** White noise test. **(b)** Car noise test. **(c)** Cafeteria noise test.

5.3.2 Color noise injection

Besides white noise, in general, any noise can be used to conduct the noisy training. We choose the car noise and the cafeteria noise in this experiment to investigate the color noise injection. The results are shown in Figures 3 and 4, respectively.

For the car noise injection (Figure 3), we observe that it is not effective for the white noise-corrupted speech. However, for the test data corrupted by car noise and cafeteria noise, it indeed delivers performance gains. The results with the car noise-corrupted data show clear advantage with matched SNRs, i.e., with the training and test data corrupted by the same noise at the same SNR, the noise injection tends to deliver better performance gains. For the cafeteria noise-corrupted data, it shows that a mild noise injection (SNR=10 dB) performs the best. This indicates that there are some similarities between car noise and cafeteria noise, and learning patterns of car noise is useful to improve robustness of the DNN model against corruptions caused by cafeteria noise.

For the cafeteria noise injection (Figure 4), some improvement can be attained with data corrupted by both white noise and cafeteria noise. For the car noise-corrupted data, performance gains are found only with mild noise injections. This suggests that cafeteria noise possesses some similarities to both white noise and car noise: It involves some background noise which is generally white, and some low-frequency components that resemble car noise. Without surprise, the best performance improvement is attained with data corrupted by cafeteria noise.

5.4 Multiple noise injection

In the second set of experiments, multiple noises are injected when performing noisy training. For simplicity, we fix the noise level at SNR=15 dB, which is obtained by setting μ_{SNR}=15 and σ_{SNR}=0.01. The hyperparameters $\{\alpha_i\}$ in the noise-type sampling are all set to 10, which generates a distribution on noise types roughly concentrated in the uniform distribution but with a sufficiently large variation.

The first configuration injects white noise and car noise, and test data are corrupted by all the seven noises. The results in terms of absolute WER reduction are presented in Figure 5a. It can be seen that with the noisy training, almost all the WER reductions (except in the clean speech case) are positive, which means that the multiple noise injection improves the system performance in almost all the noise conditions. An interesting observation is that this approach delivers general good performance gains for the unknown noises, i.e., the noises other than the white noise and the car noise.

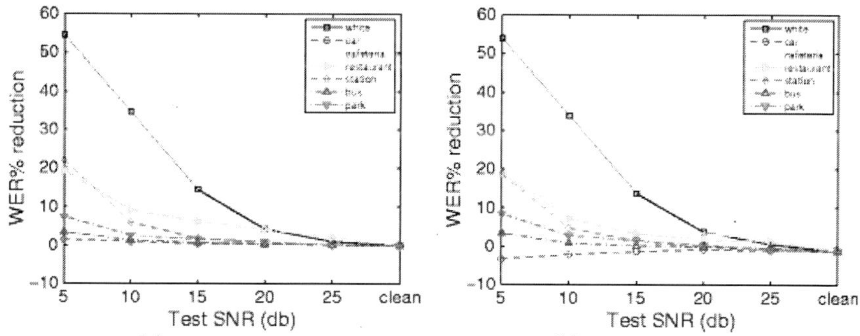

(a) White & Car Noise (b) White & Cafeteria Noise

Figure 5. Performance of multiple noise injection. No clean speech is involved in training. **(a)** White and car noise. **(b)** White and cafeteria noise.

The second configuration injects white noise and cafeteria noise; again, the conditions with all the seven noises are tested. The results are presented in Figure 5b. We observe a similar pattern as in the case of white + car noise (Figure 5a): The performance on speech corrupted by any noise is significantly improved. The difference from Figure 5a is that the performance on the speech corrupted by cafeteria noise is more effectively improved, while the performance on the speech corrupted by car noise is generally decreased. This is not surprising as the cafeteria noise is now 'known' and the car noise becomes 'unknown'. Interestingly, the performance on speech corrupted by the restaurant noise and that by the station noise are both improved in a more effective way than in Figure 5a. This suggests that the cafeteria noise shares some patterns with these two types of noises.

As a summary, the noisy training based on multiple noise injection is effective in learning patterns of multiple noise types, and it usually leads to significant improvement of ASR performance on speech data corrupted by the noises that have been learned. This improvement, interestingly, can be well generalized to unknown noises. In all the seven investigated noises, the behavior of the car noise is abnormal, which suggests that car noise is unique in properties and is better to be involved in noisy training.

5.5 Multiple noise injection with clean speech

An obvious problem of the previous experiments is that the performance on clean speech is generally degraded with noisy training. A simple approach to alleviate the problem is to involve clean speech in the training. This can be achieved by sampling a special 'no-noise' type together with other noise types. The results are reported in Figure 6a which presents the configuration with white + car noise and in Figure 6b which presents the configuration with white + cafeteria noise. We can see that with clean speech involved in the noisy training, the performance degradation on clean speech is largely solved.

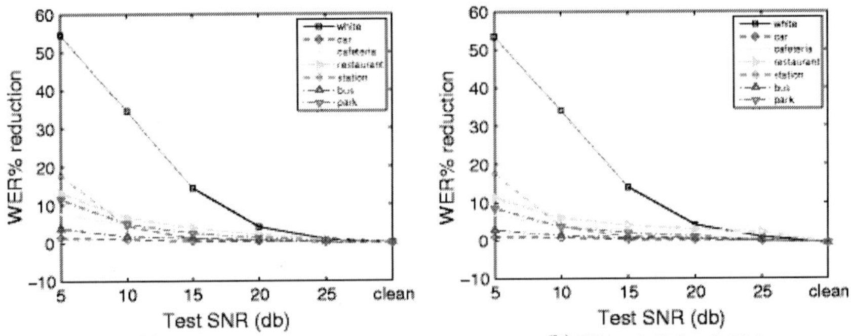

(a) White & Car Noise (b) White & Cafeteria Noise

Figure 6. Performance of multiple noise injection with clean speech involved in training. (a) White and car noise. (b) White and cafeteria noise.

Interestingly, involving clean speech in the noisy training improves performance not only on clean data, but also on noise-corrupted data. For example, Figure 6b shows that involving clean speech leads to general performance improvement on test data corrupted by car noise, which is quite different from the results shown in Figure 5b, where clean speech is not involved in the training and the performance on speech corrupted by car noise is actually decreased. This interesting improvement on noise data is maybe due to the 'no-noise' data that provide information about the 'canonical' patterns of speech signals, with which the noisy training is easier to discover the invariant and discriminative patterns that are important for recognition on both clean and corrupted data.

We note that the noisy training with multiple noise injection resembles the multi-condition training: Both involve training speech data under multiple noise conditions. However, there is an evident difference between the two approaches: In multi-conditional training, the training data are recorded under multiple noise conditions and the noise is unchanged across utterances of the same session; in noisy training, noisy data are synthesized by noise injection, so it is more flexible in noise selection and manipulation, and the training speech data can be utilized more efficiently.

5.6 Noise injection with diverse SNRs

The flexibility of noisy training in noise selection can be further extended by involving multiple SNR levels. By involving noise signals at various SNRs, more abundant noise patterns can be learned. More importantly, we hypothesize that the abundant noise patterns provide more negative learning examples for DNN training, so the 'true speech patterns' can be better learned.

The experimental setup is the same as the previous experiment, i.e., fixing μ_{SNR}=15 dB and then injecting multiple noises including 'non-noise' data. In order to introduce diverse SNRs, σ_{SNR} is set to be a large value. In this study, σ_{SNR} varies from 0.01 to 50. A larger σ_{SNR} leads to more diverse noise levels and higher possibility for loud noises. For simplicity, only the results with white + cafeteria noise injection are reported, while other configurations were experimented and the conclusions are similar.

Firstly, we examine the performance with 'known noises', i.e., data corrupted by white noise and cafeteria noise. The WER results are shown in Figure 7a which presents the results on the data corrupted by white noise and in Figure 7b which presents the results on the data corrupted by cafeteria noise. We can observe that with a more diverse noise injection (a larger σ_{SNR}), the performances under both the two noise conditions are generally improved. However, if σ_{SNR} is too large, the performance might be decreased. This can be attributed to the fact that a very large σ_{SNR} results in a significant proportion of extremely large or small SNRs, which is not consistent with the test condition. The experimental results show that the best performance is obtained with σ_{SNR}=10.

In another group of experiments, we examine performance of the noisy-trained DNN model on data corrupted by 'unknown noises', i.e., noises that are different from the ones injected in training. The results are reported in Figure 8. We observe quite different patterns for different noise corruptions: For most noise conditions, we observe a similar trend as in the known noise condition. When injecting noises at more diverse SNRs, the WER tends to be decreased, but if the noise is over diverse, the performance may be degraded. The maximum σ_{SNR} should not exceed 0.1 in most cases (restaurant noise, park noise, station noise). For the car noise condition, the optimal σ_{SNR} is 0.01, and for the bus noise condition, the optimal σ_{SNR} is 1.0. The smaller optimal σ_{SNR} in the car noise condition indicates again that this noise is significantly different from the injected white and cafeteria noises;

on the contrary, the larger optimal σ_{SNR} in the bus noise condition suggests that the bus noise resembles the injected noises.

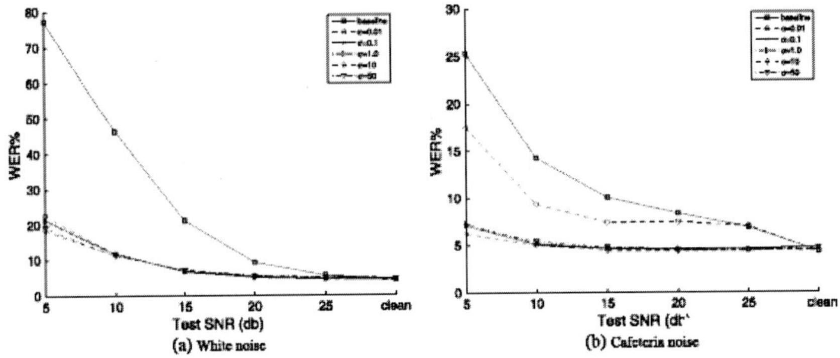

Figure 7. Performance of noise training with different σ_{SNR}. (a) White noise. **(b)** Cafeteria noise. White and cafeteria noises are injected, and μ_{SNR}=15 dB. For each plot, the test data are corrupted by a particular 'known' noise. The 'baseline' curves present the results of the system trained with clean speech data, as have been presented in Table 1.

In general, the optimal values of σ_{SNR} in the condition of unknown noises are much smaller than those in the condition of known noises. This is somewhat expected, since injection of over diverse/loud noises that are different from those observed in the test tends to cause acoustic mismatch between the training and test data, which may offset the improved generalization capability offered by the noisy training. Therefore, to accomplish the most possible gains with the noisy training, the best strategy is to involve noise types as many as possible in training so that (1) most of the noises in test are known or partially known, i.e., similar noises involved in training, and (2) a larger σ_{SNR} can be safely employed to obtain better performance. For a system that operates in unknown noise conditions, the most reasonable strategy is to involve some typical noise types (e.g., white noise, car noise, cafeteria noise) and choose a moderate noise corruption level, i.e., a middle-level μ_{SNR}not larger than 15 dB and a small σ_{SNR} not larger than 0.1.

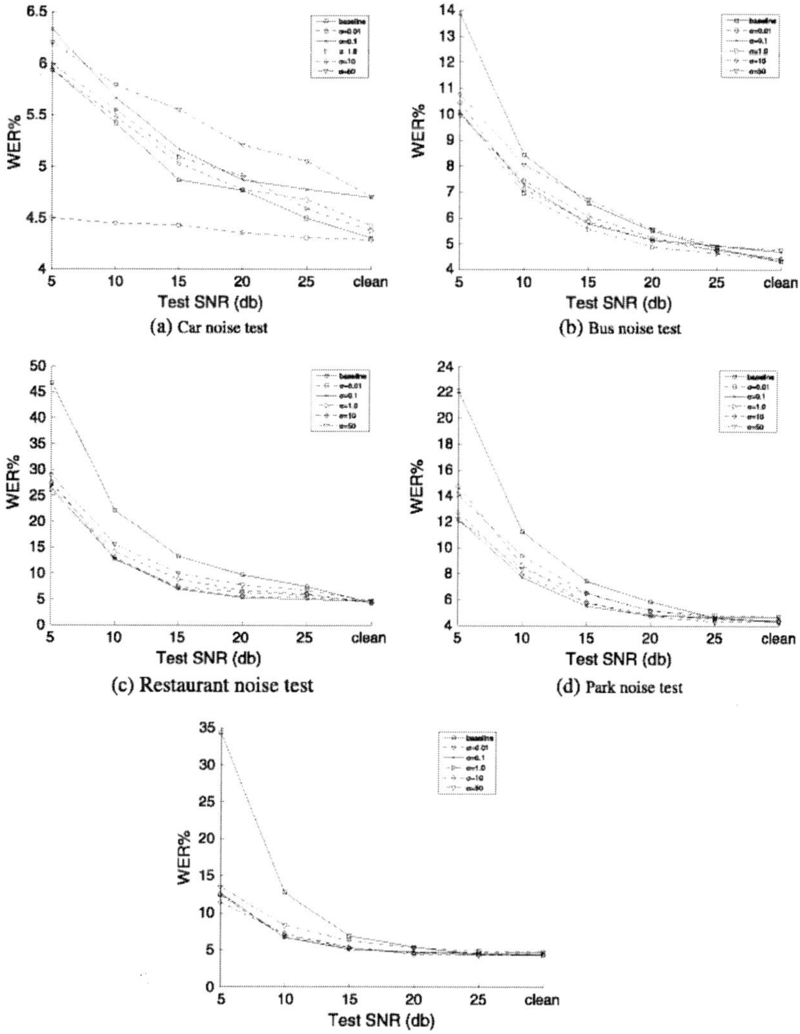

(a) Car noise test (b) Bus noise test (c) Restaurant noise test (d) Park noise test (e) Station noise test

Figure 8. Performance of noise training with different σ_{SNR}. (a) Car noise test. **(b)** Bus noise test. **(c)** Restaurant noise test. **(d)** Park noise test. **(e)** Station noise test. White and cafeteria noises are injected, and μ_{SNR}=15 dB. For each plot, the test data are corrupted by a particular 'unknown' noise. The 'baseline' curves present the results of the system trained with clean speech data, as have been presented in Table 1.

6 CONCLUSIONS

We proposed a noisy training approach for DNN-based speech recognition. The analysis and experiments confirmed that by injecting a moderate level of noise in the training data, the noise patterns can be effectively learned and the generalization capability of the learned DNNs can be improved. Both the two advantages result in substantial performance improvement for DNN-based ASR systems in noise conditions. Particularly, we observe that the noisy training approach can effectively learn multiple types of noises, and the performance is generally improved by involving a proportion of clean speech. Finally, noise injection at a moderate range of SNRs delivers further performance gains. The future work involves investigating various noise injection approaches (e.g., weighted noise injection) and evaluating more noise types.

ACKNOWLEDGEMENTS

This work was supported by the National Science Foundation of China (NSFC) under the Project No. 61371136 and No. 61271389. It was also supported by National Basic Research Program (973 Program) of China under Grant No. 2013CB329302 and the MESTDC PhD Foundation Project No. 20130002120011. Part of the research was supported by Sinovoice and Huilan Ltd..

REFERENCES

1. L Deng, D Yu, Deep learning: methods and applications. Foundations Trends Signal Process. 7, 197–387 (2014).
2. H Bourlard, N Morgan, in *Adaptive Processing of Sequences and Data Structures, ser. Lecture Notes in Artificial Intelligence (1387),*Hybrid HMM/ANN systems for speech recognition: overview and new research directions (USA, 1998), pp. 389–417.
3. H Hermansky, DPW Ellis, S Sharma, in *Proc. of IEEE International Conference on Acoustics, Speech, and Signal Processing (ICASSP),*Tandem connectionist feature extraction for conventional HMM systems (Istanbul, Turkey, 9 June 2000), pp. 1635–1638.

4. GE Dahl, D Yu, L Deng, A Acero, in *Proc. of IEEE International Conference on Acoustics, Speech and Signal Processing (ICASSP),*Large vocabulary continuous speech recognition with context-dependent DBN-HMMs (Prague, Czech Republic, 22 May 2011), pp. 4688–4691.

5. G Hinton, L Deng, D Yu, GE Dahl, A-r Mohamed, N Jaitly, A Senior, V Vanhoucke, P Nguyen, TN Sainath, B Kingsbury, Deep neural networks for acoustic modeling in speech recognition: the shared views of four research groups. IEEE Signal Process. Mag. 29(6), 82–97 (2012).

6. A Mohamed, G Dahl, G Hinton, in *Proc. of Neural Information Processing Systems (NIPS) Workshop Deep Learning for Speech Recognition and Related Applications,*Deep belief networks for phone recognition (Vancouver, BC, Canada, 7 December 2009).

7. GE Dahl, D Yu, L Deng, A Acero, Context-dependent pre-trained deep neural networks for large-vocabulary speech recognition. IEEE Trans. Audio Speech Lang. Process. 20(1), 30–42 (2012).

8. D Yu, L Deng, G Dahl, in *Proc. of NIPS Workshop on Deep Learning and Unsupervised Feature Learning,*Roles of pre-training and fine-tuning in context-dependent DBN-HMMs for real-world speech recognition (Vancouver, BC, Canada, 6 December, 2010).

9. N Jaitly, P Nguyen, AW Senior, V Vanhoucke, in *Proc. of Interspeech,*Application of pretrained deep neural networks to large vocabulary speech recognition (Portland, Oregon, USA, 9–13 September 2012), pp. 2578–2581.

10. TN Sainath, B Kingsbury, B Ramabhadran, P Fousek, P Novak, A-r Mohamed, in *Proc. of IEEE Workshop on Automatic Speech Recognition and Understanding (ASRU),*Making deep belief networks effective for large vocabulary continuous speech recognition (Hawaii, USA, 11 December 2011), pp. 30–35.

11. TN Sainath, B Kingsbury, H Soltau, B Ramabhadran, Optimization techniques to improve training speed of deep belief networks for large speech tasks. IEEE Trans. Audio Speech Lang. Process. 21(1), 2267–2276 (2013).

12. F Seide, G Li, D Yu, in *Proc. of Interspeech,*Conversational speech transcription using context-dependent deep neural networks (Florence, Italy, 15 August 2011), pp. 437–440.

13. F Seide, G Li, X Chen, D Yu, in *Proc. of IEEE Workshop on Automatic Speech Recognition and Understanding (ASRU),*Feature engineering

in context-dependent deep neural networks for conversational speech transcription (Waikoloa, HI, USA, 11 December 2011), pp. 24–29.

14. O Vinyals, SV Ravuri, in *Proc. of IEEE International Conference on Acoustics, Speech and Signal Processing (ICASSP),*Comparing multilayer perceptron to deep belief network tandem features for robust ASR (Prague, Czech Republic, 22 May 2011), pp. 4596–4599.

15. D Yu, ML Seltzer, in *Proc. of Interspeech,*Improved bottleneck features using pretrained deep neural networks (Florence, Italy, 15 August 2011), pp. 237–240.

16. P Bell, P Swietojanski, S Renals, in *Proc. IEEE International Conference on Acoustics, Speech and Signal Processing (ICASSP),*Multi-level adaptive networks in tandem and hybrid ASR systems (Vancouver, BC, Canada, 26 May 2013), pp. 6975–6979.

17. F Grezl, s Fousek P, in *Proc. of IEEE International Conference on Acoustics, Speech and Signal Processing (ICASSP),*Optimizing bottle-neck features for LVCSR (Las Vegas, USA, 4 April 2008), pp. 4729–4732.

18. P Lal, S King, Cross-lingual automatic speech recognition using tandem features. IEEE Trans. Audio Speech Lang. Process. 21(12), 2506–2515 (2011).

19. C Plahl, R Schlüter, H Ney, in *Proc. of Interspeech,*Hierarchical bottle neck features for LVCSR (Makuhari, Japan, 26 September 2010), pp. 1197–1200.

20. TN Sainath, B Kingsbury, B Ramabhadran, in *Proc. of IEEE International Conference on Acoustics, Speech and Signal Processing (ICASSP),*Auto-encoder bottleneck features using deep belief networks (Kyoto, Japan, 25 March 2012), pp. 4153–4156.

21. Z Tüske, R Schlüter, H Ney, M Sundermeyer, in *Proc. of Interspeech,*Context-dependent MLPs for LVCSR: tandem, hybrid or both? (Portland, Oregon, USA, 9 September 2012), pp. 18–21.

22. D Imseng, P Motlicek, PN Garner, H Bourlard, in *Proc. of IEEE Workshop on Automatic Speech Recognition and Understanding (ASRU),*Impact of deep MLP architecture on different acoustic modeling techniques for under-resourced speech recognition (Olomouc, Czech Republic, 8 December 2013), pp. 332–337.

23. J Qi, D Wang, J Xu, J Tejedor, in *Proc. of Interspeech,*Bottleneck features based on gammatone frequency cepstral coefficients (Lyon, France, 25 August 2013), pp. 1751–1755.

24. D Yu, ML Seltzer, J Li, J-T Huang, F Seide, in *Proc. of International Conference on Learning Representations (ICLR),*Feature learning in deep neural networks - a study on speech recognition tasks (Scottsdale, Arizona, USA, 2 May 2013).

25. B Li, KC Sim, in *Proc. of IEEE International Conference on Acoustics, Speech and Signal Processing (ICASSP),*Noise adaptive front-end normalization based on vector Taylor series for deep neural networks in robust speech recognition (Vancouver, BC, Canada, 6 May 2013), pp. 7408–7412.

26. B Li, Y Tsao, KC Sim, in *Proc. of Interspeech,*An investigation of spectral restoration algorithms for deep neural networks based noise robust speech recognition (Lyon, France, 25 August 2013), pp. 3002–3006.

27. ML Seltzer, D Yu, Y Wang, in *Proc. of IEEE International Conference on Acoustics, Speech and Signal Processing (ICASSP),*An investigation of deep neural networks for noise robust speech recognition (Vancouver, BC, Canada, 6 May 2013), pp. 7398–7402.

28. P Vincent, H Larochelle, Y Bengio, P-A Manzagol, in *Proc. of the 25th International Conference on Machine Learning (ICML),*Extracting and composing robust features with denoising autoencoders (Helsinki, Finland, 5 July 2008), pp. 1096–1103.

29. AL Maas, QV Le, O'Neil TM, O Vinyals, P Nguyen, AY Ng, in *Proc. of Interspeech,*Recurrent neural networks for noise reduction in robust ASR (Portland, Oregon, USA, 9 September 2012), pp. 22–25.

30. X Meng, C Liu, Z Zhang, D Wang, in *Proc. of ChinaSIP 2014,*Noisy training for deep neural networks (Xi'an, China, 7 July 2014), pp. 16–20.

31. G An, The effects of adding noise during backpropagation training on a generalization performance. Neural Comput. 8(3), 643–674 (1996).

32. Y Grandvalet, S Canu, Comments on 'noise injection into inputs in back propagation learning'. IEEE Trans. Syst. Man Cybernet. 25(4), 678–681 (1995).

33. CM Bishop, Training with noise is equivalent to Tikhonov regularization. Neural Comput. 7(1), 108–116 (1995).

34. Y Grandvalet, S Canu, S Boucheron, Noise injection: theoretical prospects. Neural Comput. 9(5), 1093–1108 (1997).

35. J Sietsma, RJF Dow, in *Proc. of IEEE International Conference on Neural Networks,*Neural net pruning-why and how (San Diego, California, USA, 24 July 1988), pp. 325–333.

36. K Matsuoka, Noise injection into inputs in back-propagation learning. IEEE Trans. Syst. Man Cybernet. 22(3), 436–440 (1992).

37. R Reed, RJ Marks, Seho Oh, Similarities of error regularization, sigmoid gain scaling, target smoothing, and training with jitter. IEEE Trans. Neural Netw. 6(3), 529–538 (1995).

5

CHAPTER

Speech Dereverberation for Enhancement and Recognition Using Dynamic Features Constrained Deep Neural Networks and Feature Adaptation

Xiong XiaoEmail author, Shengkui Zhao, Duc Hoang Ha Nguyen, Xionghu Zhong, Douglas L. Jones, Eng Siong Chng and Haizhou Li

[1]Temasek Lab@NTU, Nanyang Technological University, 50 Nanyang Drive, 637553 Singapore, Singapore.

[2]Advanced Digital Sciences Center, 1 Fusionopolis Way, 138632 Singapore, Singapore.

[3]School of Computer Engineering, Nanyang Technological University, Nanyang Avenue, 639798 Singapore, Singapore.

[4]Department of Human Language Technology, Institute for Infocomm Research, 1 Fusionopolis Way, 138632 Singapore, Singapore.

ABSTRACT

This paper investigates deep neural networks (DNN) based on nonlinear feature mapping and statistical linear feature adaptation approaches for reducing reverberation in speech signals. In the nonlinear feature mapping approach, DNN is trained from parallel clean/distorted speech corpus to map reverberant and noisy speech coefficients (such as log magnitude spectrum) to the underlying clean speech coefficients. The constraint imposed by dynamic features (i.e., the time derivatives of the speech coefficients) are used to enhance the smoothness of predicted coefficient trajectories in two ways. One is to obtain the enhanced speech coefficients with a least square estimation from the coefficients and dynamic features predicted by DNN. The other is to incorporate the constraint of dynamic features directly into the DNN training process using a sequential cost function.

In the linear feature adaptation approach, a sparse linear transform, called cross transform, is used to transform multiple frames of speech coefficients to a new feature space. The transform is estimated to maximize the likelihood of the transformed coefficients given a model of clean speech coefficients. Unlike the DNN approach, no parallel corpus is used and no assumption on distortion types is made.

The two approaches are evaluated on the REVERB Challenge 2014 tasks. Both speech enhancement and automatic speech recognition (ASR) results show that the DNN-based mappings significantly reduce the reverberation in speech and improve both speech quality and ASR performance. For the speech enhancement task, the proposed dynamic feature constraint help to improve cepstral distance, frequency-weighted segmental signal-to-noise ratio (SNR), and log likelihood ratio metrics while moderately degrades the speech-to-reverberation modulation energy ratio. In addition, the cross transform feature adaptation improves the ASR performance significantly for clean-condition trained acoustic models.

Keywords: Beamforming Deep neural networks Dynamic features Feature adaptation Robust speech recognition Reverberation challenge Speech enhancement

1 INTRODUCTION

Automatic speech recognition (ASR) systems and hands-free speech acquisition systems have achieved satisfactory performance for close-talk microphones. However, the performance of these systems is still poor for far-talk microphones where the distance between the speaker and the microphone is large. This is because the speech signals recorded by the far-talk microphones are significantly corrupted by background noise and room reverberation. Hence, improving the robustness of the ASR and other speech-processing systems for far-talk speech is an important task for the deployment of such systems in more realistic environments.

It is well known that reverberation is produced by multi-path propagation of an acoustic signal from its source to the microphone in enclosed spaces. The distortion of reverberation to an acoustic signal can be modeled by the acoustic impulse response (AIR), which may last for hundreds of milliseconds. Reverberation cancelation has been tried by many researchers using deconvolution techniques that estimate and apply the inverse of the AIR to the reverberant microphone outputs. Several significant contributions have been made in these areas [1–7]. However, the available techniques are sensitive to estimation error of the AIR, which is difficult to estimate in realistic environments. In addition, as the talker may change location in a room, the geometry between the talker and the microphone receiver will change accordingly, and consequently, the acoustic impulse response is time-varying. The additive background noise further increases the difficulty for accurately estimating the AIR.

Besides the studies on reverberation cancellation, other studies focus on reverberation suppression. Both spatial processing using multiple microphones and spectral enhancement belong to the reverberation suppression methods. Microphone array processing techniques such as beamforming provide spatial filtering to suppress specular reflections so that the speech signal from the desired direction of arrival (DOA) can be enhanced. The most direct and straightforward technique is the delay and sum (DS) beamfomer [8]. Several variants of the DS beamformer with adaptations also exist [8–12]. Generally, adaptive beamformers have been found to be efficient in applications to suppress localized additive noise sources. The DS beamformer can partially reduce reverberation coming from directions other than the look-direction. As the reverberant speech signal consists of highly dependent distortions that are delayed versions of the signal itself, the adaptive beamformers may attenuate the direct-path speech signal while reducing reverberation. Very recently, a conjunction of DS beamformer and minimum variance distortionless response (MVDR) beamformer has shown favorable performance for speech enhancement in the room environment [13].

To further reduce the reverberation from the look-direction, spectral-subtraction techniques may be applied. Lebart et al. has shown the effectiveness of spectral subtraction for dereverberation [14, 15]. The authors assume a statistical model of the room impulse response comprising Gaussian noise modulated by a decaying exponential function. The power spectral density of the later impulse response is identified and removed by spectral subtraction.

Although the above-mentioned approaches to dereverberation can be effective for both speech enhancement and ASR [16], blind identification of other features is often required. The reverberation conditions have high impact on the identification performance, thus affecting the dereverberation performance.

In this work, we investigated a different approach for speech dereverberation that is based on learning from data. If a parallel corpus of clean speech and the corresponding reverberant speech is available, it is possible to learn a mapping that maps reverberant speech coefficients to clean speech coefficients. Supposing that the parallel corpus is representative of the real test environment, and the mapping function is accurate, the learning-based approach is a viable way to deal with reverberation. In fact, the concept of the learning-based approach is not new. For example, in noise-robust ASR, a popular feature compensation method is called SPLICE [17, 18], which learns a set of linear transforms to map noisy feature vectors to clean feature vectors. In voice conversion [19], it is a common practice to learn a set of linear transforms to map a source speaker's speech coefficients, such as the log-magnitude spectrum, to a target speaker's speech coefficients. A major limitation of these methods is that linear transforms are too limited to accurately predict clean speech coefficients, especially when the relationship between the clean and distorted speech coefficients are highly nonlinear.

Recently, there are studies on using neural networks (NN) to learn the nonlinear mapping between clean and distorted speech coefficients. Neural networks are universal mapping functions that could be used for both classification and regression problems. NN has been used for speech enhancement for a long time [20]. A NN with more than one hidden layer is usually called a deep NN, or DNN. Recently, DNN has become popular after a pretraining step, called restrictive Boltzmann machine (RBM) pretraining [21, 22], was introduced to initialize the network parameters to some reasonable values such that backpropagation can then be used to train the network efficiently on task-dependent objective functions. The advantage of a DNN over one-hidden-layer NN is that the deep structure of the DNN allows much more efficient representation of many nonlinear transformations/functions [22]. In the past several years, DNN and other neural networks have been applied to many speech processing tasks. In [23], DNN was used for acoustic modelling in ASR systems and now it has become the de-facto standard acoustic model. In [24], another DNN architecture, called the deep recurrent neural network (DRNN), is used to estimate clean speech features (MFCC) from noisy features. In [25], a special case of recurrent neural networks, called long short-term memory (LSTM), is used to map reverberant features to clean features. In [26], a DNN is used to predict the speech mask, which is then used for enhancing speech for robust ASR. It is also found that adapting the mask-estimating DNN using a linear input transform further improves the ASR performance. While the previous two studies focus on predicting low-dimensional feature vector for ASR, in [27], deep neural networks (DNN) are used to directly estimate the high-dimension log-magnitude spectrum for speech denoising.

This method was later applied as a preprocessor for a robust ASR task [28]. In this study, we use DNN to estimate both the low-dimensional speech feature vectors for the ASR task and a high-dimensional log-magnitude spectrum vector for the speech enhancement task. Although in [25], the authors show that LSTM outperforms DNN significantly for the ASR task, the DNN used in that study is very limited in terms of network size.

In this study, we extend our previous work on DNN-based speech dereverberation [29]. DNN is trained from parallel data of clean and distorted speech coefficients to map distorted speech to clean speech. To improve the performance of DNN mapping for speech enhancement which requires a smooth and natural coefficient trajectory, we proposed two methods that make use of the information of dynamic features. The motivation is that the predicted speech coefficient trajectory should have dynamics (represented by dynamic features) that are similar to real clean speech coefficient trajectories. Specifically, we propose least-square (LS) estimation of log-magnitude spectrum from the static, delta, and acceleration log-magnitude spectrum predicted by DNN. We also propose a new sequential cost function for DNN training that takes into account the mean-squared error of the dynamic spectrum.

Although DNN and other neural-network-based speech coefficients mapping approach have the potential to produce an accurate clean speech estimate, they rely on a *representative parallel* speech corpus for training the neural networks. To address this limitation, we also propose a feature adaptation method that only requires clean speech data during training. At the test phase, a linear transform is estimated to map the reverberant features such that the mapped features fit the clean speech model better. This is in spirit similar to the popular feature space maximum likelihood linear regression (fMLLR) [30] that uses the maximum likelihood criterion to estimate the linear transform. Our proposed method, called cross transform [31], can be seen as an extension of fMLLR in that the cross transform exploits both temporal information (between frames) and spectral information (within frame) in feature mapping, while fMLLR only uses spectral information and short-term temporal information (up to 0.1 s) through delta and acceleration features.

The rest of the paper is organized as follows. Section 2 describes the system designs of the speech enhancement system and the ASR system. Section 3 reviews briefly the beamforming methods used in our system to process multi-channel speech and the conventional spectral subtraction-based dereverberation method. Sections 4 and 5 introduce the DNN-based speech coefficients mapping approach and the cross transform feature adaptation methods in detail, respectively. In Section 6, experimental results and analysis are presented. Conclusions and future research directions are discussed in Section 7.

2 SYSTEM MODULES

Our study is focused on reducing reverberation and noise in speech signals for speech enhancement and speech features for ASR. There are three stages of processing, i.e., (1) the beamforming, (2) log-magnitude spectrum enhancement for the speech enhancement task, and (3) speech features (such as MFCC) enhancement for the ASR task. The three processing stages and their combinations are illustrated in Fig. 1.

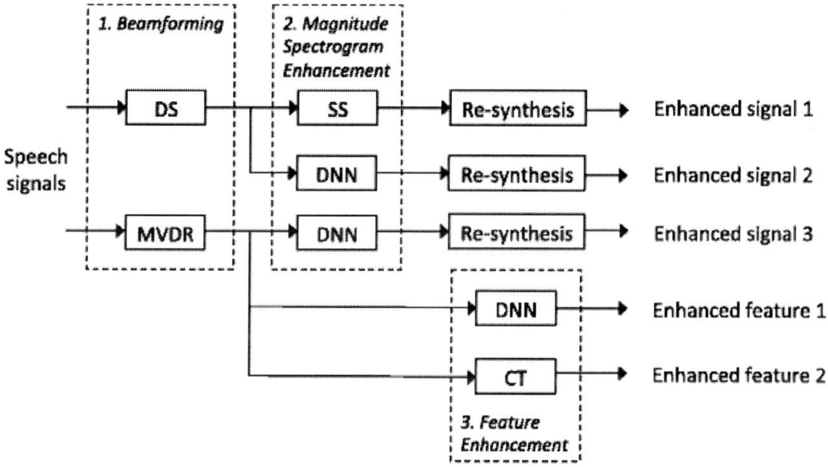

Figure. 1. Illustration of three processing stages: beamforming log-magnitude spectrum enhancement, feature enhancement. DS and MVDR are the delay and sum and minimum variance distortionless response beamforming, respectively. SS refers to spectral subtraction, while DNN stands for deep neural network-based speech coefficient mapping. CT is the cross transform feature adaptation. Three enhanced signals are produced for the speech enhancement task, and two enhanced features are produced for the ASR task

For beamforming, we investigate two popular methods, i.e., DS beamforming and MVDR beamforming. For spectrogram enhancement, we use the DNN-based speech coefficient mapping method with dynamic feature constraint. We also study the spectral subtraction method for late reverberation reduction. For speech feature enhancement, we also use the proposed cross transform feature adaptation. When multiple channels are available, a speech enhancement system is the cascade of Stages 1 and 2, while a feature enhancement system is the cascade of Stages 1 and 3. For single-channel processing, Stage 1 will be skipped. In the next three sections, we will describe the three stages in more detail.

3 CLASSIC APPROACHES

3.1 Problem formulation

Considering a multichannel speech acquisition system in an enclosed environment, the mth microphone receives the reverberant speech signal $x_m(n)$ with the room impulse response $h_m(n)$ as follows

$$x_m(n) = h_m(n) \otimes s(n) + v_m(n), m = 1, 2, \ldots, M \tag{1}$$

where $s(n)$ is the source signal and $v_m(n)$ is the additive observation noise; the symbol ⊗ denotes the linear convolution; M is the number of microphones in the system. The observed signal, $x_m(n)$, at microphone m can be described as the superposition of the direct-path signal and a finite set of reflections of the direct-path signal. The early part of $h_m(n)$ is referred to as early reverberation which causes spectral changes and leads to a perceptual effect referred to as coloration [32], while the late part (which is referred to as later reverberation) changes the waveform's temporal envelope as exponentially decaying tails are added at sound offsets.

The aim of speech dereverberation is to find a system, with input $x_m(n)$ and output s^(n)s^(n), which is an estimate of $s(n)$. The criteria in the estimation, $s(n)$, is application-dependent. It may be related to perceptual quality or ASR performance. The room impulse response $h_m(n)$ could be either time-varying or short-term fixed, which is also application-dependent.

3.2 The DS beamforming

The DS beamformer has a very simple form, and it was developed based on the fact that times of arrival (TOA) of the incoming signal $s(n)$ at different microphones are different. Adding all of the microphone signals $x_m(n)$ together with appropriate amounts of time delay reinforces the incoming signal at the steered direction with respect to noise and reverberant signals arriving from different directions. To obtain more reliable estimation of the time difference of arrivals (TDOAs), cross-correlation methods such as the GCC-PHAT are usually applied [33]. The DS beamformer has a signal-independent formulation, and the output of the DS beamformer improves the signal-to-noise ratio (SNR) [8]. The advantage of the DS beamformer is that it is simple and computationally efficient. There is usually very low distortion in the output of the DS beamformer.

3.3 The MVDR beamforming

The MVDR beamformer has a slightly more complicated form than the DS beamformer. It involves the estimation of the noise covariance matrix in the estimation of the optimal weight vector. The optimal weight vector minimizes the total output signal power at each frequency bin while constraining the filtering response of the signal from the look direction to unity [34]. The effect of the MVDR beamformer is to attenuate the signals that are uncorrelated with the target signal and which are coming from directions different from the target. The MVDR beamformer is usually more effective than the DS beamformer when the interference signals are uncorrelated with the target signal, but it introduces more distortion to the target signal in the dereverberation as shown in our experimental results.

3.4 Spectral subtraction

The DS and MVDR beamformers function as spatial filters and effectively improve the reverberant speech in general. However, there is very low attenuation for the reflected signals and noise coming from a similar direction as the desired signal. A post-processing stage is usually adopted to further attenuate the residual reverberation and noise after the beamforming. There are many single-channel enhancement techniques that can be applied, and the spectral subtraction technique [14] has been popular for reliable performance. It uses the exponential model of the room impulse response and the quasi-stationary characteristics of speech signals. In the formulation of amplitude spectral subtraction, both the a priori SNR and the a posteriori SNR are estimated based on a smoothing exponentially decaying form. In addition, the reverberation time is required in the formulation, and we applied the improved maximum-likelihood (ML) estimator [35] in our experiments.

4 DNN-BASED SPEECH COEFFICIENTS MAPPING WITH A DYNAMIC FEATURE CONSTRAINT

Neural networks are universal function approximators that can model complicated nonlinear relationships between system inputs and outputs. The use of deep architecture neural networks, such as the DNN used in this paper, is efficient in representing complex relationships [22]. Generally speaking, given a set of input/output vector pairs, we can train a DNN to learn a mapping that accurately predicts the output given the input. In this section, we describe how to use a DNN to learn the mapping from reverberant and noisy speech coefficients to clean speech coefficients and the details of dynamic feature constraint.

4.1 DNN-based mapping

The task of DNN-based speech mapping is illustrated in Fig. 2. At the bottom of the figure, there is a sequence of input vectors, which in our study are speech coefficient vectors computed from reverberant and noisy speech. The type of speech coefficients is task-dependent and will be discussed in the next section. At the top of the figure, there is a sequence of desired output vectors that the DNN is trying to predict. In our study, the desired output vectors are the speech coefficient vectors computed from clean speech. The input vector sequence and the desired output vector sequence should be aligned at the frame level, and we call this data parallel data (also called stereo data in SPLICE [17]). The frame-level alignment requirement can be easily satisfied in speech dereverberation tasks. For example, if the reverberant and noisy speech is generated from clean speech by convolving with a known RIR and adding recorded noise samples, the generated distorted speech will be aligned perfectly with the clean speech. Another way to generate the parallel data is to record speech signals using close-talk and far-talk microphones simultaneously; then, the close-talk recording can serve as the DNN's desired output and, the far-talk recording(s) will be used as input to the DNN. Hence, it is relatively simple to generate a large amount of parallel training data.

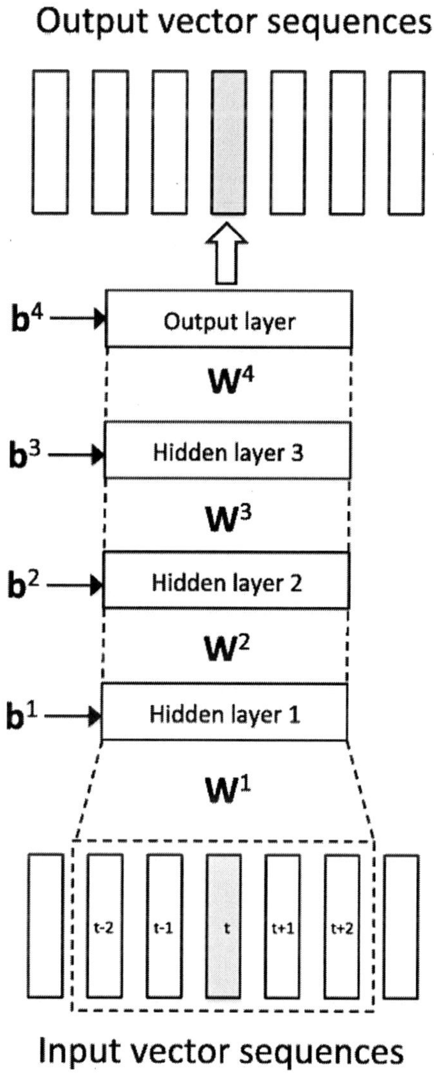

Figure. 2. The architecture of the DNN for speech coefficient mapping

A DNN consists of several hidden layers, each including a linear transform and a nonlinearity function, also called an activation function. The output of a hidden layer can be computed as

$$\mathbf{a}^L = f(\mathbf{z}^L) \tag{2}$$

$$\mathbf{z}^L = \mathbf{W}^L\mathbf{a}^{L-1} + \mathbf{b}^L \tag{3}$$

where $\mathbf{z}^L$ and $\mathbf{a}^L$ are the input and output of the Lth hidden layer, and $f()$ is the activation function that operates on the input matrix element by element. $\mathbf{W}^L$ is the vector weight connecting the nodes in layer L–1 to the nodes in layer L, and $\mathbf{b}^L$ is the bias of the nodes at layer L. In summary, the output of a hidden layer is obtained by first computing an affine transform of the previous layer's output and then applying the activation function. One popular choice for the activation function is the sigmoid function $f_{sig}(x)=1/(1+e^{-x})$ which is used in this study.

In Fig. 2, there are three hidden layers in the illustrative DNN. The input vectors is the first affine transformed by $\mathbf{W}^1$ and $\mathbf{b}^1$, and then passed through the activation function to obtain the output of the hidden layer 1. The hidden layer 1 output is again affine transformed by $\mathbf{W}^2$ and $\mathbf{b}^2$ and passed through the activation function to get the output of hidden layer 2. This process continues with hidden layer 3. Finally, the output of hidden layer 3 is affine transformed by $\mathbf{W}^4$ and $\mathbf{b}^4$ of the output layer to generate the final output of the DNN. As the speech coefficient mapping task is a regression task and the output is real-valued rather than class labels as in classification problems, the output layer has a linear activation function $f_{lin}(x)=x$.

As a speech coefficient vector is computed from a single frame which is typically quite short (e.g., 25 ms), it is important to use a sequence of speech coefficient vectors as the input of the DNN. There are two reasons why the speech vectors from neighbouring frames are important to predict the clean speech vector of the current frame. First, without context information, it is difficult to determine the underlying phone identity of the current frame using only a short frame of 25 ms. One frame is not enough even for accurate phone classification, so it would not be sufficient for predicting the underlying clean vector. Second, due to the effect of reverberation, the current frame is affected by previous frames which may be dozens of frames away. The T60 time considered in normal meeting room can be as high as 1s, which is equivalent to 100 speech frames if the frame shift is 10 ms. This may suggest that there is a relationship between two frames that are as far away as 100 frames. Therefore, it is important to feed a local patch of speech vectors to DNN. Figure 2 shows the example of using five consecutive frames as DNN input. The optimal number of input vectors will be determined experimentally.

4.2 DNN training

Although DNN has a long pipeline of processing, it is obvious that the DNN's output is a highly nonlinear but continuously differentiable function of the input. Hence, the parameters of DNN, such as the weights and bias, can be trained from parallel data by using a gradient descent method. As the speech coefficient mapping is a regression task, it is natural to choose the cost function as the mean-squared error (MSE) between the DNN's output and the desired output, i.e., the speech coefficients of the underlying clean speech for current frame. The back-propagation (BP) algorithm is used to implement the gradient descent to train the DNN parameters. Specifically, we used the stochastic gradient descent (SGD) method to update the DNN after the model sees a few hundred of training frames. The SGD algorithm is known to work well for large-scale DNN training problems.

One of the major difficulties in training a DNN is the initialisation of the parameters. Usually, random initialisation will result in slow training, and often, the training will become trapped in a local minimum of the parameter space. To address this issue, RBM pretraining [21] is used to initialise the DNN's parameters before the MSE training. The RBM pretraining is an unsupervised learning and does not require any labeling of the training data. It tries to learn the intrinsic structure in the input, which is the reverberant and noisy speech in our study. The RBM pretraining initialises the DNN parameters to reasonable values and makes the MSE training (also called fine tuning) much easier. In our study, we have observed that the RBM training is critical to the successful training of a DNN with more than one hidden layer.

Another issue with DNN training is to choose the proper parallel training data. To achieve good test performance, it is required that the training environments should be sufficiently similar to the potential test environment. In many cases, it is not clear what the test environment is, so it may be a good approach to make the training data as diverse as possible. For example, the training of parallel data should cover different room RIRs, different noise types, different signal-to-noise ratios (SNR), and different speakers. The mapping problem is basically a many-to-one mapping, i.e., we want to map many versions of distorted speech coefficients that are different due to reverberation and noise characteristics to the same underlaying clean speech coefficients. In other words, if a clean speech signal is corrupted in 100 different ways, we want the DNN to map the 100 different speech coefficients to the same coefficients of the original clean speech signal. Such many-to-one mapping is difficult to achieve by conventional linear mapping methods such as fMLLR or piecewise linear mapping methods such as SPLICE due to their limited flexibility. A DNN has much more modelling power than linear transforms due to its nonlinear activation function and deep layered structure, allowing efficient representation of complex mapping [22]. In this study, we use the multi-condition training scheme defined for the ASR task to train the DNN for both speech enhancement and ASR feature compensation. As the multi-condition training data is generated from the clean-condition training data by adding reverberation and noise effects, we can obtain the perfect frame level alignment between the two corpus. There are about 30 h of parallel training data (15 h clean and 15 h distorted speech) for DNN training. The multi-condition data are distorted by multiple types of RIRs and noises; hence, it is expected to cover the test environments in the REVERB challenge evaluation data reasonably well.

4.3 Speech coefficients generation and preprocessing

The type of coefficients used as input and desired output of DNN mapping is task-dependent. For example, in speech enhancement, we use log-magnitude spectrum as the speech representation; it has a dimension of 257 when using a frame-length of 25 ms and a FFT length of 512. The log-magnitude spectrum is required to recover high-quality speech waveform for human listening. On the other hand, to enhance speech features for ASR, we only need to use the 39-dimensional MFCC as speech coefficient vectors, as finer spectral detail is not useful for differentiating speech classes.

It is usually beneficial to preprocess the DNN's input to achieve easier model training and better performance. We apply two stages of feature normalisation to the DNN inputs. In the first stage, for the speech enhancement task, we conducted experiments to understand whether utterance-wise mean normalisation should be applied to log-magnitude spectrogram to reduce channel effects on the data. For the ASR feature compensation task, utterance-wise cepstral mean and variance normalisation (CMVN) is applied to the MFCC features to reduce channel and reverberation effects. The use of CMVN is motivated by the observation that on the baseline ASR system, CMVN processed features produced better results than raw MFCC or CMN processed features. In the second stage, global mean and variance normalisation (MVN) is applied to normalise the distribution of the DNN inputs to zero mean and unit variance on a corpus level. The bias and scale used for the global MVN is also used to normalise any test data so that the training data and test data are processed in the same way.

4.4 Incorporation of dynamic feature constraint

A limitation of the DNN-based speech coefficient mapping scheme in Fig. 2 is that each frame is predicted independently, and we cannot guarantee that the predicted frame sequence is smooth and sounds natural [1]. Hence, we investigated two DNN speech-enhancement schemes that improve the smoothness of the enhanced spectrogram. As the proposed methods can also be used to features other than the log-magnitude spectrum, we will use the term "feature" to represent log-magnitude spectrum.

4.4.1 Least-squares estimation of static features

We train the DNN to predict both the clean features and their time derivatives from distorted features. Similar to time-derivative features in speech recognition, we used both delta features (first-order time derivative) and acceleration features (second-order time derivative). The delta and acceleration feature vectors are concatenated to the original feature vector (called the static feature) to form the new target vector for DNN learning. Hence, the target vector's dimension becomes three times of the original one. During the enhancement phase, the static, delta, and acceleration features are all predicted. The final enhanced features can be found by solving a least-squares (LS) problem described as follows.

Given a sequence of static feature vectors, we can approximate their time derivatives as follows [36]

$$\mathbf{y}_D(t) = \frac{\sum_{l=1}^{L} l \times (\mathbf{y}_S(t+l) - \mathbf{y}_S(t-l))}{\sum_{l=1}^{L} 2l^2} \quad (4)$$

where $\mathbf{y}_S(t)$ is the static feature vector at frame t, $\mathbf{y}_D(t)$ is the delta feature vector at frame t, L is the order of computing the derivatives and set to two in this study. The acceleration features can be obtained by applying Eq. (4) to the delta features. The delta and acceleration features are called dynamic features. They are the band-pass filtered versions of the static features that carry the temporal information of the static features. The DNN is trained to predict the static, delta, and acceleration features at the same time.

Let $\mathbf{Y}=[\mathbf{Y}_S,\mathbf{Y}_D,\mathbf{Y}_A]$ denote the output of the DNN which is a T×3MT×3M matrix, where TT is the number of frames in the current utterance and MM is the dimension of the feature vectors. The subscripts S, D, and A represent the static, delta, and acceleration features, respectively. Since the DNN is not aware of the physical relationship between the three components of the target vector, the static, delta, and acceleration components of **Y** do not obey the physical relationship defined in (4). For speech enhancement purposes, we do not need the delta and acceleration features, but we can use them to improve the estimation of the static features.

Let $\mathbf{X}_S$ be the static-feature matrix we want to estimate from **Y**. Let $\mathbf{X}_D$ and $\mathbf{X}_A$ be the delta and acceleration feature matrices of $\mathbf{X}_S$ computed according to (4). Hence, $\mathbf{X}_D$ and $\mathbf{X}_A$ are completely determined by $\mathbf{X}_S$ linearly as follows

$$\mathbf{X}_D = \mathbf{D}\mathbf{X}_S \tag{5}$$

$$\mathbf{X}_A = \mathbf{A}\mathbf{X}_S \tag{6}$$

where **D** is the T×TT×T matrix that performs the linear filtering on $\mathbf{X}_S$ to generate the delta features. Similarly, **A** is the linear transform for generating the acceleration features from the static features. The parameters of **D** and **A** are determined by TT and Eq. (4). The formulation of the delta and acceleration features as the linear transform of the static features is motivated by the work in [19].

We estimate $\mathbf{X}_S$ by solving the following least-squares problem

$$\hat{\mathbf{X}}_S = \arg\min_{\mathbf{X}_S} \mathcal{L}(\mathbf{X}_S) \tag{7}$$

$$\mathcal{L}(\mathbf{X}_S) = ||\mathbf{X}_S - \mathbf{Y}_S||_F^2 + w_D||\mathbf{X}_D - \mathbf{Y}_D||_F^2 + w_A||\mathbf{X}_A - \mathbf{Y}_A||_F^2 \tag{8}$$

where ||X||2F||X||F2 is the Frobinus norm of **X**, and w_D and w_A are the weights of cost contributed by the delta and acceleration features. Usually, we want to use a value larger than 1 for these two weights as the dynamic ranges of the delta and acceleration features are much smaller than those of static features. By investigating the variances of the log magnitude spectrum features, we found that the average variance of static features is about 20 and 114 times as large as that of the delta and acceleration features, respectively. Therefore, w_D and w_A are empirically set to 20 and 114, respectively, to make the static, delta, and acceleration features contribute similiarly to the cost function. From Eq. (7), we are searching for static features that obey the physical relationship between static, delta, and acceleration log spectrograms, and at the same time fit the DNN's output. Compared to the DNN's output $\mathbf{Y}_S$ which is estimated independently for each frame, the $\mathbf{X}_S$ will have better temporal continuity as it is estimated from the whole utterance.

The closed-form solution of the least-squares problem in Eq. (7) is

$$\hat{\mathrm{X}}_S = \mathrm{R}^{-1}\mathrm{P} \tag{9}$$

$$= \mathrm{R}^{-1}\mathrm{Y}_S + w_D\mathrm{R}^{-1}\mathrm{Y}_D + w_A\mathrm{R}^{-1}\mathrm{Y}_A \tag{10}$$

$$\mathrm{R} = \mathrm{I} + w_D\mathrm{D}^T\mathrm{D} + w_A\mathrm{A}^T\mathrm{A} \tag{11}$$

$$\mathrm{P} = \mathrm{Y}_S + w_D\mathrm{Y}_D + w_A\mathrm{Y}_A \tag{12}$$

where **I** is a T×TT×T identity matrix. The LS solution can be interpreted as a weighted sum of transformed static, delta, and acceleration features as shown in Eq. (10). Hence, it is clear that enhanced delta and acceleration features will help improve the static features.

The LS solution requires the inversion of the T×TT×T matrix **R**, and the computational cost of the matrix inversion can be high when TT is large. In practice, we can reduce the computational cost by breaking a long sentence into several segments during silence frames, and find the LS solution for each segment independently. Another way to reduce the computational cost is to store the inversion $\mathbf{R}^{-1}$ for every possible length TT.

4.4.2 Sequential training of DNN

The LS solution presented in the previous section requires expensive matrix inversion. In this section, we present another method that directly optimizes the DNN using a sequential cost function similar to Eq. (8) in which no LS post-processing is necessary.

The sequential cost function is illustrated in Fig. 3. Note that to save space, only the last two layers of the DNN is drawn. After the static features are predicted by the DNN, the delta and acceleration features are obtained from the static feature vector sequence by applying the **D**and **A** matrices. Due to the need to compute the dynamic spectra, we cannot randomize the training frames and need to train the DNN sequentially. One simple way is to use each utterance as a minibatch. The predicted static, delta, and acceleration spectra are then used to compute the cost function

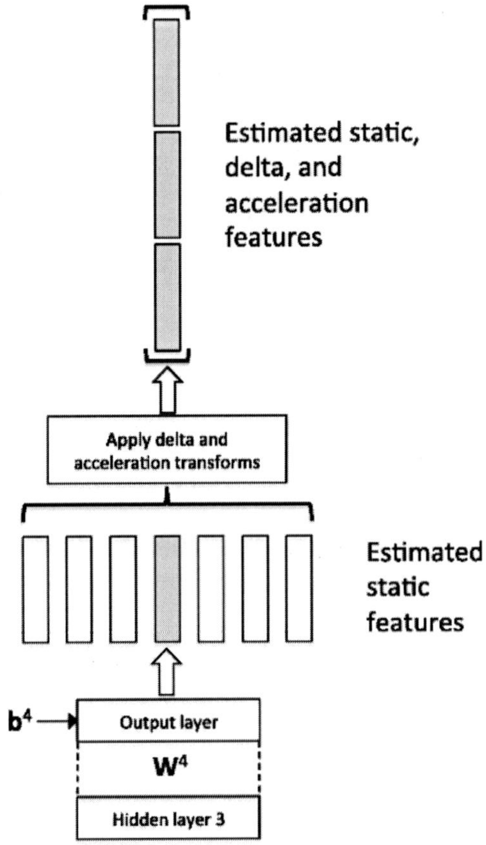

Figure. 3. The architecture of the DNN coefficient mapping using a sequential training cost function

$$\mathcal{L}_{\mathrm{DNN}}(\mathbf{X}_S) = ||\mathbf{X}_S - \mathbf{Z}_S||_F^2 + w_D||\mathbf{D}\mathbf{X}_S - \mathbf{Z}_D||_F^2 \\ +w_A||\mathbf{A}\mathbf{X}_S - \mathbf{Z}_A||_F^2 \tag{13}$$

where $\mathbf{Z}_S$, $\mathbf{Z}_D$, and $\mathbf{Z}_A$ are the static, delta, and acceleration spectra of the clean target speech signal. By optimizing the DNN using the sequential cost function (13), the predicted static spectra will tend to have delta and acceleration features that are close to the clean (natural) one. The use of a sequential cost function can be seen as a special case of multi-task learning where the error gradient of the delta and acceleration spectra prediction are used to help train the static feature prediction. One advantage of this approach over the LS solution discussed in the previous section is that there is no need to perform matrix inversion. In practice, we use the sequential training to fine-tune the DNN trained to predict static and/or dynamic features.

5 CROSS TRANSFORM FEATURE ADAPTATION

In the DNN-based speech coefficient mapping, parallel data of clean and distorted speech is required to train the mapping network. In this section, we study the scenario where only the clean speech signal is available at the system-building phase for ASR. This is also known as clean-condition training of an acoustic model. As a result, there is a significant mismatch between the clean-trained model and the distorted test speech features, and the speech recognition performance will be significantly affected.

There are two major approaches to reduce the mismatch between the clean model and distorted test features. One is through the model adaptation approaches, which adapt the clean model towards the distorted speech features. Some examples of the model adaptation method include the (constrained) maximum likelihood linear regression (CMLLR/MLLR) [30], maximum a posteriori (MAP) [37], and vector Taylor series (VTS) [38–40] based adaptation methods. Another approach to reduce train/test mismatch is to adapt the distorted features towards the clean model. Examples include the feature space maximum-likelihood linear regression (fMLLR, equivalent to global CMLLR), SPLICE feature compensation [17], etc. In this paper, for the clean-condition training scheme of the ASR task, we apply a new feature adaptation method called cross transform that we proposed in [31]. For each test utterance, speaker, or condition, a linear transform is estimated to adapt the test features towards the clean acoustic model. For completeness, we briefly describe the cross transform in the following section.

5.1 Cross transform feature adaptation

To compensate speech features for robust ASR, there are two popular feature-processing schemes, i.e., the linear transformation of feature vectors and the temporal filtering of feature trajectories, as illustrated in Fig. 4. Linear transformation uses all dimensions of the current frame to predict new features that fit the acoustic model under the maximum-likelihood (ML) criterion [30, 41]. On the other hand, temporal filtering uses the context information in neighboring frames to estimate features that fit the acoustic model [42–45]. While linear transformation uses inter-dimensional correlation information (or spectral information) to process features, temporal filtering uses inter-frame correlation information (or temporal information). In the past, these two types of information are usually not used together for feature adaptation.

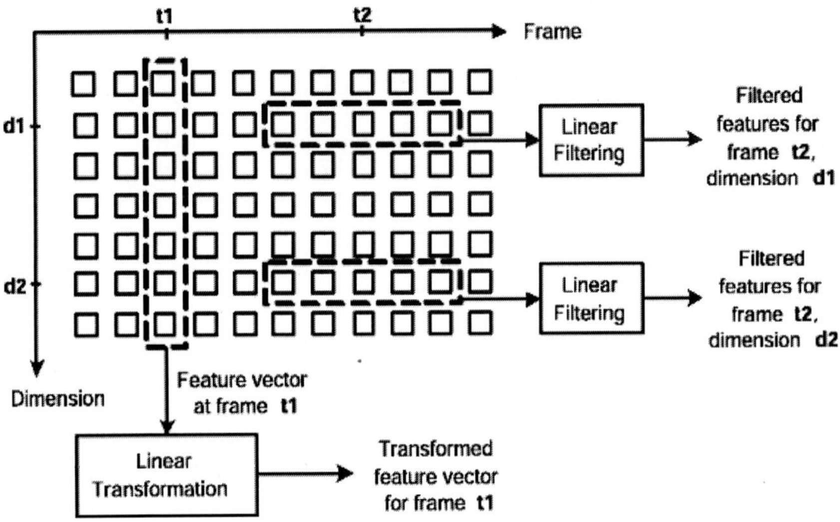

Figure. 4. Temporal filtering of feature trajectories versus linear transformation of feature vectors

To use both spectral and temporal information for feature processing, the simplest way is to predict the clean feature vectors from a sequence of input feature vectors as follows

$$\mathbf{y}_t = \sum_{\tau=-L}^{L} \mathbf{B}_\tau \mathbf{x}_{t+\tau} + \mathbf{c} = \mathbf{W}\tilde{\mathbf{x}}_t, \tag{14}$$

where $\mathbf{x}_t$ and $\mathbf{y}_t$ are D-dimensional input and output feature vectors, respectively. $\mathbf{B}_\tau$, $\tau=-L,\ldots,L$ are the transformation matrices, and $\mathbf{W}=[\mathbf{B}_{-L},\ldots,\mathbf{B}_L,\mathbf{c}]$ and x~t=[xTt−L,...,xTt+L,1]Tx~t=[xt−LT,...,xt+LT,1]T are the concatenated transformation matrices and inputs, respectively. Although the transform in (14) is possible in theory, it is hard to apply in practice as there are too many parameters in **W** and hence a lot of data are required for its reliable estimation. For example, if we set L=16 (i.e., use a context of 33 frames, then there are $33D^2+D$ parameters), which is not feasible to reliably estimate from a small amount of test data (e.g., one test utterance). Therefore, in this study, we make **W** sparse by setting most of its elements to zero. Specifically, to predict the feature at frame t and dimension d, y(d)tyt(d), we only use the local feature trajectory and feature vector that contains x(d)txt(d) as shown in Fig. 5. The simplified transform is simply the combination of the linear transform and temporal filter illustrated in Fig. 4. As the shape of the transform often looks like a cross, we call it the cross transform.

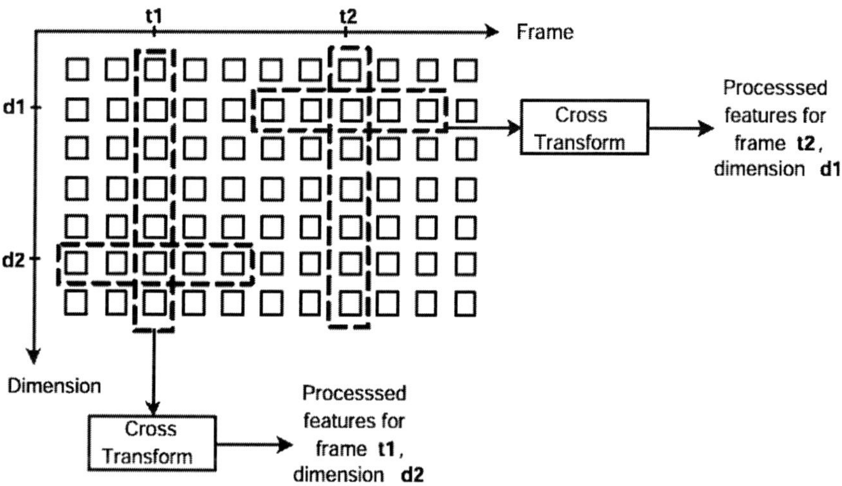

Figure. 5. Illustration of cross transform

Similar to maximum normalized likelihood linear filtering in [45], the parameters of the cross transform can be estimated by minimizing an approximated KL divergence between the distribution of the processed features, p_y, and the distribution of clean training features, p_Λ. In this work, p_y is modelled by a single Gaussian and p_Λ by a GMM with parameter set $\Lambda=\{c_j,\boldsymbol{\mu}_j,\boldsymbol{\Sigma}_j|j=1,...,J\}$ and $\boldsymbol{\Sigma}_j$ being diagonal. The optimal **W** is found by minimizing the following approximated KL divergence

$$f(\mathbf{W}) = -\frac{\lambda}{2}\log\det\left(\mathbf{W}\boldsymbol{\Sigma}_{\tilde{\mathbf{x}}}\mathbf{W}^T\right) + \frac{\beta}{2T}||\mathbf{W}-\mathbf{W}_0||_2 - \frac{1}{T}\sum_{t=1}^{T}\log\sum_{j=1}^{J}c_j\mathcal{N}(\mathbf{W}\tilde{\mathbf{x}}_t;\mu_j,\boldsymbol{\Sigma}_j), \quad (15)$$

Where $\Sigma x\sim$ is the covariance matrix of $x\sim$. Tunable parameters β and λ are used to control the contributions of the L2 norm term and log determinant term in the cost function, respectively. $\mathbf{W}_0$ is the initial value of the weight matrix $\mathbf{W}$. When constructing $\mathbf{W}_0$, the sub-matrix $\mathbf{B}_\tau$contains all 0's except that $\mathbf{B}_0$ is an identity matrix. In this way, the application of $\mathbf{W}_0$ will result in the same output features as the input features. An intuitive explanation of the cost function is that we want the likelihood of the transformed features on the clean reference model $\Lambda$to be high. At the same time, the covariance matrix of the transformed features is encouraged to have a large log-determinant to prevent the variance of the transformation features from shrinking. The cost function can be iteratively minimized via an EM algorithm. For the detailed solution of the cross transform, readers are referred to [31].

5.2 Comparison between cross transform and DNN-based feature compensation

A major difference between the feature adaptation methods (like fMLLR and cross transform) and the DNN feature compensation is how the free parameters are estimated. The parameters of the feature adaptation are learned from the test data itself and hence dynamically updated during test, while the DNN parameters are trained from parallel training data and fixed once trained. When the test environment is known during system building and it is possible to collect data with similar characteristics for training, using DNN-based feature compensation is a suitable approach. On the other hand, feature-adaptation methods such as the cross transform does not require the knowledge of the test environment and availability of parallel training data, making them universally applicable in all test environments. However, the linear transforms used in fMLLR and the cross transform are less powerful than DNN.

6 EXPERIMENTS

The techniques are evaluated on the REVERB Challenge 2014 tasks [46]. In this section, we first describe the task and evaluation metrics, followed by the implementation parameter settings for the techniques. Then, we present the evaluation results on both speech enhancement and ASR tasks.

6.1 Task, data, and evaluation metrics

The REVERB Challenge 2014 [46] is a benchmark task to evaluate dereverberation techniques for both human listening and ASR. The distortion considered is mainly reverberation, with a moderate amount of additive background noise. There are two types of evaluation data. One type is simulated reverberant and noisy speech, generated by adding noise and reverberation to clean utterances from the WSJCAM0 [47] corpus, which is the British version of the WSJ0 corpus [48]. The other type is a real meeting recording from the MC-WSJ-AV [49] corpus, which is the re-recorded version of WSJCAM0 in a meeting-room environment. Both types of data are provided for system development (dev set) and evaluation (eval set). In this experiment, we report results on the eval set only.

In the speech recognition task, there are two training schemes, i.e., (1) the clean-condition scheme in which only clean data is available for training the acoustic model; (2) multi-condition training scheme in which reverberant and noisy speech with similar characteristics as the simulated test data are available for training. The clean-condition training data are taken from the WSJCAM0 [47] corpus, while the multi-condition training data is artificially generated by corrupting the clean-condition training data in a similar way as the generation of simulated test data.

Speech enhancement methods are evaluated by several metrics, such as cepstral distance (CD) [50], log-likelihood ratio (LLR) [50], frequency-weighted segmental SNR [50], speech-to-reverberation modulation energy ratio (SRMR) [51], and optional PESQ [52]. For real room data, only the non-intrusive SRMR metric is used. In addition, subjective listening is planned by the organizer of the challenge. The ASR system is evaluated by word error rate (WER). As we do not have a PESQ license, we will not report PESQ results in this paper. For more details of the corpus and tasks, please visit the REVERB Challenge website (http://reverb2014.dereverberation.com).

6.2 Settings of methods

6.2.1 DS beamformer

In the implementation of the DS beamformer, we segmented the speech utterances into segments of 64 ms long with 75 % overlap. We then applied pre-emphasis and a Hanning window of 64 ms long to the segments. A 1024-point short-time Fourier transform (STFT) was used to obtain the frequency-domain signals. The frequency components of the array channels were aligned according to the TODAs computed by the GCC-PHAT method [33] where the first channel in each record was selected as the reference channel. Since the maximum delay between any microphone pairs in the array is 0.59 ms, the TDOAs in samples were calculated from the cross-correlation peaks that appeared within 0.59 ms. The speed of sound was set to 340 m/s in our implementation. The aligned channels were summed with a normalization to obtain the frequency components of the DS output. Then, we applied the inverse STFT and the overlap-save method to obtain the time-domain signal of 16 ms long. The final output of the DS beamformer was obtained after the de-emphasis. The output of the DS beamformer served as the input signals for the spectral subtraction module and the DNN module.

6.2.2 MVDR beamformer

In the implementation of the MVDR beamformer, we used the same window size and overlap as in the DS beamformer. The frequency-domain components of all the array channels and the TDOAs were obtained similarly as in the DS beamformer. To estimate the noise covariance matrix, we applied an energy-based voice activity detector to detect the absence of speech signals. When the speech signals are absent, the noise covariance matrix can be updated.

6.2.3 Spectral subtraction

The spectral subtraction algorithm [14] was implemented separately from the beamformers. Only the outputs of the beamformers were passed to the spectral subtraction algorithm. In the spectral subtraction algorithm, we obtained the frequency-domain signals using the STFT of 256 points with pre-emphasis and a Hanning window of 16 ms long and 75 % overlap. The reverberation time used in the algorithm was estimated from the beamformer output by the ML method [35]. Noting that this estimator takes the advantage of a long input signal, we repeatedly refined the reverberation time estimation by using the up-to-date output signals of the beamformers for each utterance.

6.2.4 DNN-based speech coefficient mapping

The DNN-based speech coefficients mapping is applied to both log-magnitude spectrogram enhancement for speech enhancement task, and also MFCC enhancement for ASR task. For speech enhancement, the speech signal is transformed into frequency domain using a 25-ms Hamming window and 10-ms frame shifts. The logarithm of the magnitude spectrum has a dimensionality of 257 and is used as the input features of the DNN, and each input is a concatenation of multiple frames. The enhanced log-magnitude spectrum produced by the DNN is combined with the original distorted phase spectrum to re-synthesize the enhanced speech signal.

For ASR, a concatenation of the MFCC feature vectors is used as the DNN input. Each MFCC feature vector has 39 dimensions, including the first 13 cepstral coefficents (c0–c12) and their first and second derivatives. The MFCC features are normalized by utterance-based CMVN and then enhanced by DNN-based speech coefficient mapping. The DNN takes 15 frames of MFCC as input, hence the input layer dimension is 15×39=585. We empirically choose to use three hidden layers with 2048 hidden nodes in each layer. The output layer is 39-dimensional, including both the static and dynamic features. The feature compensation DNN is pretrained using RBM training and refined using the MSE criterion. The enhanced MFCC features are used for both ASR training and testing.

When there are multiple input channels, DS or MVDR beamformers are applied to produce the enhanced single-channel speech signal first, and then DNN-based speech coefficient mappings are applied on the single-channel signal.

6.2.5 Cross transform feature adaptation

The cross transform uses a context size of frames (i.e., L=16) to capture long-term temporal information to effectively suppress reverberation. The clean reference GMM model is trained from the clean-condition training data with about 4400 Gaussian components. The hyper-parameters β and λ are set to 1 and 0.9, respectively.

6.3 Speech enhancement

We evaluate the DNN approach for speech enhancement and compare it to the approach of DS beamformer plus spectral subtraction (SS). We report the objective measures in this section.

6.3.1 Effect of input context size and hidden layer size

Table 1 shows the performance of speech enhancement obtained by three DNNs of different input context sizes and hidden layer sizes. A single microphone input is used and the performance of SS is also shown for comparison. By comparing DNN1 and DNN2, it is observed that using longer input context and larger hidden layer size improves the performance metrics in most cases except for SRMR of real test data. The poorer results on real rooms may be because that the DNNs are trained from simulated room data and hence do not generalise well on real room due to mismatch in distortion characteristics. From DNN2 to DNN3, the network input is further increased from 15 to 19 frames. However, the results of DNN3 is similar to or even slightly worse than that of DNN2. This may suggest that 15 frames are enough for speech dereverberation, or the DNN3 model is overfitted to the training data as it contains more parameters. Therefore, we decided to use 15 frames as the input context size and three hidden layers, each with 3072 sigmoid nodes, for the following experiments.

Table 1. Performance of speech enhancement methods using single-channel input on simulated and real room recordings. The results are averaged over near and far test cases

Processing			Simulated rooms							Real
			CD		SRMR	LLR		SNR		SRMR
Name	Architecture	CMN	mean	med.	mean	mean	med.	mean	med.	mean
None	-	No	3.97	3.69	3.68	0.58	0.51	3.62	5.39	3.18
SS	-	No	3.82	3.51	4.0	0.56	0.51	4.75	6.89	3.94
Effect of input context size and hidden layer size										
DNN1	11x257-2048-2048-2048-257	Yes	2.64	2.41	5.78	0.52	0.48	7.19	8.09	4.54
DNN2	15x257-3072-3072-3072-257	Yes	2.53	2.31	5.80	0.51	0.47	7.54	8.31	4.36
DNN3	19x257-3072-3072-3072-257	Yes	2.50	2.28	5.77	0.50	0.47	7.55	8.35	4.36

"mean" represents the mean value of the scores of utterances, while "med." represents the median of the scores. "CMN" indicates whether utterance-wise mean normalization is applied during both DNN training and testing. A DNN architecture of "11x257-2048-2048-2048-257" means that 11 frames of 257D log-magnitude spectrum are used as input, followed by three hidden layers each with 2048 nodes, and the output layer predicts the 257D log-magnitude spectrum of clean speech

6.3.2 *Effect of beamforming*

The performance comparisons between MVDR and DS beamforming are shown in the first two rows of Table 2. It is observed that DS produces better results than MVDR except for SRMR. This could be because DS produces less distortions than MVDR in reverberant environments. It is also observed that when SS is applied after DS, significantly better results are obtained than DS alone except for LLR.

Both MVDR and DS beamforing are used as the preprocessing unit of the DNN-based speech enhancement (DNN4). It is observed that DS+DNN4 generally produces better results than MVDR+DNN4. This shows that the DNN-based speech enhancement should work with a beamformer with low distortions. Therefore, we will use DS as the preprocessor for DNN-based speech enhancement in the following experiments.

Table 2. Performance of speech enhancement methods using eight channel inputs on simulated and real room recordings. The results are averaged over near and far test cases

Processing				Simulated rooms							Real
				CD (dB)		SRMR	LLR		SNR (dB)		SRMR
Name	Target /train	Estimation	CMN	mean	med.	mean	mean	med.	mean	med.	mean
MVDR	-	-	No	3.64	3.28	4.85	0.48	0.43	5.31	7.76	4.12
DS	-	-	No	3.11	2.76	4.34	0.410	0.360	6.60	9.24	3.84
DS+SS	-	-	No	3.00	2.67	4.56	0.410	0.360	7.16	9.68	4.62
Effect of beamforming											
MVDR+DNN4	257/random	-	Vis/Tgt	2.28	2.07	5.88	0.470	0.440	8.44	8.88	4.51
DS+DNN4	257/random	-	Vis/Tgt	*2.01*	*1.85*	*5.92*	0.467	0.440	8.56	8.88	4.40
Effect of CMN											
DS+DNN5	257/random	-	No	2.15	1.96	4.80	0.205	0.155	12.07	12.55	*4.95*
DS+DNN6	257/random	-	Vis	2.18	2.00	5.27	0.235	0.198	11.11	11.49	4.24
DS+DNN4a	257/random	-	Vis/Tgt2	2.02	1.86	5.16	0.278	0.237	10.93	11.55	3.76
Effect of dynamic features											
DS+DNN7	3x257/random	Use static	No	2.15	1.96	4.88	0.205	0.158	12.04	12.59	*4.95*
DS+DNN7LS	3x257/random	LS (9)	No	2.07	1.90	4.83	0.195	0.150	12.42	12.99	4.78
DS+DNN8	257-3x257/seq	Use static	No	2.04	1.86	4.61	*0.193*	*0.147*	*12.64*	*13.22*	4.62
Effect of clean phase											
DS+DNN8c	257-3x257/seq.	Use static	No	1.84	1.66	4.90	0.165	0.123	13.37	13.88	-

"mean" represents the mean value of the scores of utterances, while "med." represents the median of the scores. "random" means that the frames of each minibatch of DNN training are randomly selected from the whole training corpus, while "seq." refers to the case in which each utterance is used as a minibatch. An output size of "3x257" means that the static, delta, and acceleration spectra are all predicted. The target size of "257-3x257" refers to the sequential training in Section 4.4.2. All DNNs use 15 frames of input and 3072 nodes per hidden layer. DNN8c is the same as DNN8 except that clean phase is used. Best results of each metric (not including DNN8c) are shown in italics

6.3.3 Effect of CMN preprocessing on different evaluation metrics

One important question for DNN-based speech dereverberation is whether the CMN should be applied for each training and testing utterance. The motivation of using CMN is that it may reduce some variations in the training data and make the mapping from the distorted speech spectrum to the clean speech spectrum easier. We show the performance of speech enhancement with and without CMN preprocessing in Table 2. By comparing DS+DNN4 and DS+DNN5, the CMN has a significant but mixed effect on the evaluation metrics. Specifically, the SNR and LLR are much better without CMN, while CD is better with CMN applied. In addition, applying CMN causes SRMR degradation for simulated data but the reverse is true for real data.

To understand the different trends, it is necessary to look into the detailed implementation of the evaluation metrics. For CD computation, as CMN is also applied to the reference (clean) and enhanced cepstral coefficients before the calculation of distance, applying CMN to both input and target of DNN training leads to lower CD than without CMN. On the other hand, CMN is not applied when computing LLR and SNR, so applying CMN on the target log-magnitude spectrum during DNN training effectively causes a mismatch between the enhanced spectrum and the reference spectrum. This mismatch is similar to filtering the speech with a channel. Therefore, DS+DNN4 performs even worse than the DS baseline for LLR and the median value of SNR. To reduce the mismatch, we add back the average clean log-magnitude spectrum (a single vector of 257 dimensions) to all enhanced log-magnitude spectra (see DS+DNN4a). The results show that this leads to significant improvement of LLR and SNR, but degardation for SRMR. We also tried another setting, i.e., only apply CMN to the input to reduce channel mismatch (DS+DNN6). The results are even worse than not applying CMN at all except for SRMR.

In summary, we found that not applying CMN leads to significantly better LLR and SNR, moderate degradation to CD, significant degradation to SRMR on simulated data but improvement to SRMR on real data. Hence, we will not apply CMN in the following experiments.

6.3.4 Effect of dynamic feature estimation

We now investigate the effect of predicting dynamic log-magnitude spectra and using them to improve the static spectra. The results are shown in the rows DNN7, DNN7LS, and DNN8 of Table 2. The DNN7 is trained to predict both the static and the dynamic log-magnitude spectra. During testing, only the predicted static spectra are used for resynthesizing waveform. By comparing DNN7 and DNN5, we observe no significant difference in performance due to the additional task of predicting the dynamic spectrum in DNN7. This shows that the DNN is able to predict the static and dynamic spectrum simultaneously without degrading the performance of static spectrum prediction. The DNN7LS uses the same trained DNN as DNN7, except that the static spectra are obtained by using the LS estimation of Eq. (9). The results show that DNN7LS outperforms DNN7 in terms of CD, LLR, and SNR, but degrades SRMR a bit, especially for real data. DNN8 is trained by using the sequential training cost function in Section 4.4.2. Compared to DNN7LS, DNN8 further improves CD, LLR, and SNR, but also further degardes the SRMR. An important advantage of DNN8 is that it does not need to perform the computationally expensive LS estimation during test time. The detailed results of DS+DNN8 are listed in Table 3.

Table 3. Detailed results obtained by DS+DNN8 on the six test conditions

Cases	Simulated rooms				Real
	CD (dB)	SRMR	LLR	SNR (dB)	SRMR
far1	1.64/1.52	4.85	0.12/0.09	14.33/14.52	4.81
far1	2.76/2.49	4.83	0.31/0.24	10.18/11.36	-
far1	2.44/2.21	4.16	0.28/0.22	10.30/11.13	-
near1	1.44/1.33	4.72	0.09/0.07	15.15/15.34	4.43
near1	2.00/1.82	4.60	0.17/0.12	13.04/13.64	-
near1	1.97/1.80	4.49	0.19/0.14	12.82/13.30	-
avg.	2.04/1.86	4.61	0.193/0.147	12.64/13.22	4.62

For CD, LLR, and SNR, the numbers before and after "/" represents the mean and median of the scores, respectively

We also show the mean-squared errors (MSE) between the clean log-magnitude spectra and its DNN-predicted versions to get a better understanding of how the dynamic spectra help to improve the prediction of the static spectrum. The MSE averaged over the six simulated test conditions of eval set are shown in Table 4. Here, the log-magnitude spectra of the enhanced speech is taken from the DNN's output layer directly to avoid the effect of imperfect phase. For DS+DNN7LS, the static log-magnitude spectrum are first obtained by finding the LS solution of (9), then the static and acceleration spectra are obtained by applying Eq. (4). By comparing DS+DNN7 and DS+DNN7LS, we can conclude that the LS solution not only reduces the MSE of the static spectra but also the delta and acceleration spectra. This shows that the LS solution is an effective way to exploit the physical relationship between the static and dynamic spectra to produce a better prediction of the clean speech's spectrum. The sequential training produces similar results as the LS solution. This is achieved with just passing the input through the DNN without the LS post-processing which may be computationally expensive.

Table 4. Mean-squared error (MSE) between the log-magnitude spectra of reference (clean) and DNN enhancement

Processing	Static	Delta	Acceleration
DS	226.21	10.76	2.06
DS+DNN5	91.81	6.53	1.31
DS+DNN7	91.34	6.28	1.22
DS+DNN7LS	*87.70*	*5.99*	*1.18*
DS+DNN8	88.77	*5.99*	1.20

The enhanced spectra are taken from the DNN's output layer without going through the resynthesis to avoid the effect of imperfect phase. The MSE is averaged over all the six simulated test conditions of eval set

6.3.5 Subjective listening

We performed informal listening of the enhanced speech. Perceptually, it is found that the SS and DS+SS methods produces moderate reduction of reverberation and also improve speech qualities. The DNN-based system significantly removes the reverberation from the speech. However, it also degrades the speech quality, especially when the distortion is strong. To find out which part of the DNN system causes the quality degradation, we use the DNN8 predicted magnitude spectrum together with the phase spectrum of the clean speech to re-synthesize the enhanced waveform. The results are presented as DNN8c in Table 2. It can be seen that the use of clean phase produces a significant improvement to all objective measures. An informal listening test also confirmed that the waveform reconstructed from DNN enhanced magnitude and clean phase is much better than that from DNN-enhanced magnitude and original reverberant and noisy phase, especially when the reverberation is strong, such as in far rooms. The analysis shows that it is necessary to improve the phase in addition to the magnitude.

6.4 Speech recognition

6.4.1 Clean-condition training

We used the HTK-based ASR system from the REVERB Challenge 2014 organizer for evaluation on clean-condition training. Detailed results are shown in Table 5. From the table, we have several observations. First, cross transform (CT) reduces the WER significantly for both the single-channel scenario and multiple-channel scenario where it is used after MVDR beamforming. In addition, the improvement is obtained for both simulated and real data. This verified the effectiveness of the cross transform for real reverberant recordings. Second, the cross transform performs similarly to the 256-class CMLLR model adaptation (MA), despite that many more free parameters are being used in CMLLR than in cross transform. Third, if cross transform feature adaptation and the CMLLR model adaptation are applied in sequence, the WER is further reduced. This shows that although both cross transform and CMLLR are linear transforms of the features, they are complementary to each other because they use different information. Specifically, cross transform uses both the spectral and temporal information (up to 0.33 s) while CMLLR mainly uses spectral information and limited temporal information (up to 0.1 s). Another reason that cross transform and CMLLR are complementary may be due to that one is applied in utterance mode and the other is in batch mode. In utterance mode, the transform is able to adapt to each speaker and utterance-specific distortion characteristics, while in batch mode the transform is adapted to the average speaker and distortion. In summary, the results on cross transform show that long-term temporal information is important in improving the speech recognition performance of reverberant speech.

Table 5. ASR performance (WER) using clean condition training data on the evaluation data

CT	MA	Simulated rooms						Real		Avg.
		Room1A		Room2A		Room3A		Room1		
		Near	Far	Near	Far	Near	Far	Near	Far	
					Single microphone					
N	N	19.0	25.6	34.5	69.8	47.1	78.3	80.2	76.6	53.9
Y	N	15.6	20.7	24.2	45.3	30.9	57.5	63.1	62.4	40.0
N	Y	14.1	17.9	21.3	45.1	28.3	59.5	66.4	65.9	39.8
Y	Y	14.5	18.2	21.2	38.8	26.8	50.3	57.3	58.0	35.6
					Two microphones, with MVDR					
N	N	18.0	23.3	27.7	59.8	40.1	71.2	75.1	73.7	48.6
Y	N	14.5	19.0	20.6	38.8	26.6	51.0	56.5	58.6	35.7
N	Y	13.5	17.0	18.9	36.8	24.5	51.4	58.8	59.3	35.0
Y	Y	13.7	17.4	18.3	33.4	23.3	45.2	51.2	53.1	31.9
					Eight microphones, with MVDR					
N	N	17.0	21.3	23.6	40.3	30.5	53.2	59.3	58.1	37.9
Y	N	14.3	17.2	18.0	27.9	21.7	36.2	43.1	46.4	28.1
N	Y	13.6	16.4	17.3	26.6	20.1	35.6	44.4	46.1	27.5
Y	Y	13.7	16.2	15.8	24.1	19.5	32.3	38.1	42.6	25.3

CT stands for cross transform, while MA refers to the 256-class based CMLLR model adaptation

6.4.2 **Multi-condition training**

For the multi condition training scheme, we developed an ASR system based on the Kaldi toolkit [53] and DNN acoustic model. This is because when multi-condition training is used, a DNN acoustic model provides much better results than the GMM acoustic model. The DNN-based acoustic model uses 9 frames of 39D MFCC features as input, and we found that using longer context did not lead into better results. There are seven hidden layers in the model, each layer with 2048 sigmoid hidden nodes. The output layer of the DNN contains about 3500 classes, i.e., the number of tied triphone states. We use seven hidden layers and 2048 nodes. The DNN acoustic model is first pretrained using RBM unsupervised training, then trained using cross entropy training, and finally refined by sequential MMI training, all using Kaldi's DNN recipe [53]. Note that the DNN acoustic model is different from the DNN-based speech coefficient mapping described in Section 4. In the following experiments, the MFCC features are first enhanced by the DNN-based speech coefficient mapping, and then fed to the DNN acoustic model for speech recognition.

The performance of the ASR system using multi-condition training is shown in Table 6. For comparison, we also show two results obtained from the clean-condition trained DNN acoustic model. From the results, we have several observations. First, by comparing Rows 1 and 3, the DNN acoustic model itself is not robust against reverberation distortion. The robustness is coming from the multi-condition training. Second, when the multi-condition training data is used to train the DNN-based feature mapping, and the acoustic model is still clean-trained (Row 2, MAP = Yes), the performance is close to when the multi-condition training data are directly used to train the DNN acoustic model (Row 3). In addition, if both DNNs are trained from multi-condition training data, we obtained the best results for the single-channel scenario (Row 4). This shows that it is useful to use two DNNs for reverberant speech recognition, one for feature compensation, and one for acoustic modelling. This observation is true for the 2-channel and 8-channel scenarios also. There may be two reasons for the usefulness of DNN feature compensation. One is that DNN feature compensation uses more information than the DNN acoustic model, as both clean- and multi-condition data are used in its training. Another reason is that it may be useful to explicitly recover the clean features rather than let the DNN acoustic model automatically discover useful features for speech recognition.

Table 6. WER on the evaluation data using DNN based acoustic models. "MAP" refers to the DNN based MFCC feature mapping

MAP	Simulated rooms						Real		Avg.
	Room1A		Room2A		Room3A		Room1		
	near	far	near	far	near	far	near	far	
	Single channel + Clean condition training								
No	10.6	19.3	23.2	69.3	30.2	74.6	68.0	66.2	45.2
Yes	9.3	10.6	12.7	21.4	16.5	25.1	40.2	39.0	*21.9*
	Single channel + Multi condition training								
No	8.7	9.4	10.5	16.5	13.4	20.0	35.4	34.3	18.5
Yes	8.9	8.8	8.8	13.9	11.4	15.5	32.2	32.7	*16.5*
	MVDR(2ch) + Multi condition training								
No	8.6	9.6	9.1	14.9	11.6	18.3	33.3	30.7	17.0
Yes	8.5	8.6	7.9	12.4	10.1	14.8	29.1	29.1	*15.1*
	MVDR(8ch) + Multi condition training								
No	7.8	8.3	8.3	10.8	9.8	13.3	24.8	25.1	13.5
Yes	7.5	8.2	7.4	9.7	8.9	11.3	22.7	24.4	*12.5*

7 CONCLUSIONS

In this paper, we studied two methods for speech dereverberation for both speech enhancement and ASR tasks. In the DNN-based speech coefficient mapping, parallel training data of reverberant speech (observation) and clean speech (desired output) are used to train the DNN to predict clean speech. This mapping approach is applied to both speech enhancement and ASR feature enhancement tasks. For speech enhancement, we also proposed a LS postprocessing and a sequential cost function to incorporate the constraint of dynamic features to improve the smoothness of the enhanced magnitude spectrum. Results in both tasks show the effectiveness of the DNN-based mapping. The proposed LS postprocessing and sequential cost function improves the CD, SNR, and LLR evaluation metrics but cause slight degradation for SRMR. We also noticed that the DNN mapping causes distortion to enhanced speech waveforms especially when the reverberation is strong. This is partially due to the reverberant phase spectrogram being used with the DNN-enhanced magnitude spectrogram to re-synthesise the speech waveforms. It will be interesting to study the possibility of predicting the clean phase spectrogram together with the clean magnitude spectrogram.

We also studied the cross transform feature adaptation method that does not rely on parallel training data and can be applied to any unknown test environment for ASR. The cross transform only relies on the information of the clean reference model (a GMM in our study) and the current test utterance or speaker, and hence is not restricted by the training/testing environment mismatch. To effectively remove reverberation effects from the speech features, the cross transform uses long-term temporal information as input (up to 0.33 s), which is much longer than traditional feature/model adaptation methods such as fMLLR/CMLLR. Experimental results confirmed the effectiveness of cross transform in improving the ASR performance in real reverberation test scenarios. In addition, the cross transform is complementary to CMLLR model adaptation as they use different information sources.

In the future, we will continue to pursue the two research directions we studied in this paper. For DNN-based speech coefficient mapping, one important question is how quickly the prediction accuracy degrades as the test condition deviates from the training conditions. Another question is how much diverse training data can the DNN-based mapping learn well. Both questions are related to whether such a pretrained mapping machine is a practical solution to real-world speech enhancement and ASR tasks where the test environment is usually unpredictable. For the cross transform, we may extend it in several ways. One way is to use a nonlinear transform such as an MLP to replace the linear transform to increase the flexibility of the method. This is motivated by the fact that the distortion in the cepstral domain is usually highly nonlinear. Another way is to use a more powerful clean reference model to learn the intrinsic structure of the speech features. It is the clean reference model that provides guidance to the transform estimation; hence, a better reference model could lead to a more accurate translation estimation.

8 ENDNOTE

[1] Even if recurrent neural network is used to predict clean speech coefficients, there is no explicit constraint on the temporal structure of the predicted coefficient trajectories.

AUTHORS' CONTRIBUTIONS

XX designed the DNN based speech enhancement systems and performed experiments. He also contributed in the design of the cross transform and coordinated the works done in this paper. SZ implemented the beamforming modules and performed related experiments with the help of XZ. DHHN designed and performed experiments on cross transform. DLJ,

ESC and HL helped to revise the manuscript and approved it for publication. All authors read and approved the final manuscript.

REFERENCES

1. TH Li, Estimation and blind deconvolution of autoregressive systems with nonstationary binary inputs. J. Time Ser. Anal.**14**(6), 575–588 (1993).

2. R Chen, TH Li, Blind restoration of linearly degraded discrete signals by gibbs sampling. IEEE Trans. Signal Process.**43:**, 2410–2413 (1995).

3. O Cappe, A Doucet, M Lavielle, E Moulines, Simulation-based methods for blind maximum-likelihood filter deconvolution. IEEE Trans. Signal Process.**73**(1), 3–25 (1999).

4. S Gannot, M Moonen, Subspace methods for multimicrophone speech dereverberation. EURASIP J. Appl. Signal Process.**2003**(11), 1074–1090 (2003).

5. M Triki, DTM Slock, in *Proc. IEEE International Conference on Acoustics, Speech, and Signal Processing*, 5. Delay and predict equalization for blind speech dereverberation (Toulouse, France, 2006), pp. 97–100.

6. M Delcroix, T Hikichi, M Miyoshi, Precise dereverberation using multichannel linear prediction. IEEE Trans. Audio, Speech, Lang. Process.**15**(2), 430–440 (2006).

7. S Subramaniam, A Petropulu, C Wendt, Cepstrum-based deconvolution for speech dereverberation. IEEE Trans. Speech Audio Process.**4**(5), 392–396 (1996).

8. BDV Veen, KM Buckley, Beamforming: A versatile approach to spatial filtering. IEEE ASSP Mag. **5**(2), 4–24 (1988).

9. J Allen, D Berkley, Multimicrophone signal processing technique to remove room reverberation from speech signals. J. Acoust. Soc. Am.**62:**, 912–915 (1977).

10. R Zelinski, in *Int. Conf. on Acoust. Speech and Sig. Proc.* A microphone array with adaptive post-filtering for noise reduction in reverberant rooms (New York, USA, 1988), pp. 2578–2581.

11. S Fischer, Beamforming microphone arrays for speech acquisition in noisy environments. Speech Commun.**20:**, 215–227 (1996).

12. E Habets, J Benesty, I Cohen, S Gannot, J Dmochowski, New insights into MVDR beamformer in room acoustics. IEEE Trans. Audio, Speech Lang. Process.**18**(1), 158–170 (2010).

13. E Habets, J Benesty, A two stage beamforming approach for noise reduction and dereverberation. IEEE Trans. Audio, Speech Lang. Process.**21**(5), 945–958 (2013).

14. K Lebart, JM Boucher, PN Denbigh, A new method based on spectral subtraction for speech dereverberation. ACUSTICA. **87**(3), 359–366 (2001).

15. FS Pacheco, R Seara, in *Proc. of the Fifth International Telecommunications Symposium (ITS2006)*, 4. Spectral subtraction for reverberation reduction applied to automatic speech recognition (Fortaleza-CE, Brazil, 2006), pp. 581–584.

16. T Yoshioka, MJ Gales, Environmentally robust asr front-end for deep neural network acoustic models. Comput. Speech Lang.**31**(1), 65–86 (2015).

17. L Deng, A Acero, M Plumpe, XD Huang, in *Proc. ICSLP '00*. Large-vocabulary speech recognition under adverse acoustic environment (Beijing, China, 2000), pp. 806–809.

18. X Xiao, J Li, ES Chng, H Li, in *IEEE International Conference on Acoustics, Speech and Signal Processing (ICASSP)*. Feature compensation using linear combination of speaker and environment dependent correction vectors (Florence, Italy, 2014), pp. 1720–1724.

19. T Toda, AW Black, K Tokuda, Voice conversion based on maximum-likelihood estimation of spectral parameters trajectory. IEEE Trans. Audio, Speech, Lang. Process.**15**(8), 2222–2235 (2007).

20. EA Wan, AT Nelson, in *Handbook of neural networks for speech processing*, ed. by S Katagiri. Networks for speech enhancement (Artech House, Boston, 1998).

21. GE Hinton, S Osindero, Y Teh, A fast learning algorithm for deep belief nets. Neural Comput. **8**(7), 1527–1554 (2006).

22. Y Bengio, 2. Foundations and Trends®; in Machine Learning. Learning deep architectures for AI, (2009), pp. 1–127.

23. GE Hinton, L Deng, D Yu, GE Dahl, A Mohamed, N Jaitly, A Senior, V Vanhoucke, P Nguyen, T Sainath, B Kingsbury, Deep neural networks for acoustic modeling in speech recognition: the shared views of four research groups. Signal Process. Mag. IEEE. **29**(6), 82–97 (2012).

24. AL Maas, QV Le, TM O'Neil, O Vinyals, P Nguyen, AY Ng, in *Interspeech 2012*. Recurrent neural networks for noise reduction in robust asr (CiteseerPortland, Oregon, 2012).

25. F Weninger, J Geiger, M Wöllmer, B Schuller, G Rigoll, Feature enhancement by deep lstm networks for asr in reverberant multisource environments. Comput. Speech Lang.**28**(4), 888–902 (2014).

26. B Li, KC Sim, A spectral masking approach to noise-robust speech recognition using deep neural networks. IEEE/ACM Trans. Audio, Speech Lang. Process. (TASLP). **22**(8), 1296–1305 (2014).

27. Y Xu, J Du, L-R Dai, C-H Lee, A regression approach to speech enhancement based on deep neural networks. IEEE/ACM Trans. Audio, Speech, Lang. Process. **23**(1), 7–19 (2015).

28. J Du, Q Wang, T Gao, Y Xu, L Dai, C-H Lee, in *Interspeech 2014*. Robust speech recognition with speech enhanced deep neural networks (Singapore, 2014).

29. X Xiao, S Zhao, DHH Nguyen, X Zhong, DL Jones, ES Chng, H Li, in *Proceeding of REVERB challenge workshop*. The NTU-ADSC systems for reverberation challenge (Florence, Italy, 2014).

30. MJF Gales, Maximum likelihood linear transformations for HMM-based speech recognition. Comput. Speech Lang.**12:**, 75–98 (1998).

31. DHH Nguyen, X Xiao, ES Chng, H Li, in *ICASSP 2014*. Generalization of temporal filter and linear transformation for robust speech recognition (Florence, Italy, 2014).

32. H Kuttruff, *Room acoustics*, 4th edn. (Taylor & Francis, 270 Madison Avenue, New York, NY, 2000).

33. CH Knapp, GC Carter, The generalized correlation method for estimation of time delay. IEEE Trans. Acoust., Speech Signal Process.**24**(4), 320–327 (1976).

34. OLF III, An algorithm for linearly constrained adaptive array process. IEEE Proc.**60**(8), 926–935 (1972).

35. HW Löllmann, E Yilmaz, M Jeub, P Vary, in *International Workshop on Acoustic Echo and Noise Control (IWAENC)*. An improved algorithm for blind reverberation time estimation (Tel Aviv, Israel, 2010).

36. S Furui, Speaker independent isolated word recognizer using dynamic features of speech spectrum. IEEE Trans. Acoustics, Speech Signal Process.**34**(1), 52–59 (1986).

37. JL Gauvain, CH Lee, Maximum *a posteriori* estimation for multivariate Gaussian mixture observations of Markov chains. IEEE Trans. Speech Audio Process.**2**(2), 291–298 (1994).

38. PJ Moreno, *Speech recognition in noisy environments. PhD thesis* (ECE, Carnegie Mellon University, 1996).

39. A Acero, L Deng, T Kristjansson, J Zhang, in *Proc. ICSLP '00*. HMM adaptation using vector Taylor series for noisy speech recognition (Beijing, China, 2000), pp. 869–872.

40. J Li, L Deng, D Yu, Y Gong, A Acero, A unified framework of HMM adaptation with joint compensation of additive and convolutive distortions. Comput. Speech Lang.**23**(3), 389–405 (2009).

41. Y Li, H Erdogan, Y Gao, E Marcheret, in *Proc. ICSLP '02*. Incremental on-line feature space MLLR adaptation for telephony speech recognition (Denver, USA, 2002), pp. 1417–1420.

42. H Hermansky, N Morgan, RASTA processing of speech. IEEE Trans. Speech Audio Process.**2**(4), 578–589 (1994)

43. C-P Chen, JA Bilmes, MVA processing of speech features. IEEE Trans. Audio, Speech, Lang. Process.**15**(1), 257–270 (2007).

44. X Xiao, ES Chng, H Li, Normalization of the speech modulation spectra for robust speech recognition. IEEE Trans. Audio, Speech, Lang. Process.**16**(8), 1662–1674 (2008).

45. X Xiao, ES Chng, H Li, in *Proc. ICASSP '13*. Temporal filter design by minimum KL divergence criterion for robust speech recognition (VancouverCanada, 2013).

46. K Kinoshita, M Delcroix, T Yoshioka, T Nakatani, E Habets, R Haeb-Umbach, V Leutnant, A Sehr, W Kellermann, R Maas, S Gannot, B Raj, in *Proceedings of the IEEE Workshop on Applications of Signal Processing to Audio and Acoustics (WASPAA-13)*. The REVERB challenge: a common evaluation framework for dereverberation and recognition of reverberant speech (New Paltz, NY, 2013).

47. T Robinson, J Fransen, D Pye, J Foote, S Renals, in *Proc. ICASSP '95*. WSJCAM0: a British English speech corpus for large vocabulary continuous speech recognition (Detroit, MI, 1995), pp. 81–84.

48. DB Paul, JM Baker, in *Proceedings of the Workshop on Speech and Natural Language (HLT-91)*. The design for the wall street journal-based csr corpus (Stroudsburg, PA, 1992), pp. 357–362.

49. M Lincoln, I McCowan, J Vepa, HK Maganti, in *Proc. ASRU '05*. The multi-channel wall street journal audio visual corpus (MC-WSJ-AV): specification and initial experiments (Cancun, Mexico, 2005), pp. 357–362.

50. Y Hu, P Loizou, Evaluation of objective quality measures for speech enhancement. IEEE Trans. Audio, Speech, Lang. Process.**16**(1), 229–238 (2008).

51. TH Falk, C Zheng, W-Y Chan, A non-intrusive quality and intelligibility measure of reverberant and dereverberated speech. IEEE Trans. Audio, Speech, Lang. Process.**18**(7), 1766–1774 (2010).

52. A Rix, M Hollier, A Hekstra, JG Beerends, Perceptual evaluation of speech quality (PESQ), the new ITU standard for end-to-end speech quality assessment, Part I-time-delay compensation. J. Audio Eng. Soc.**50**(10), 755–764 (2002).

53. D Povey, A Ghoshal, G Boulianne, L Burget, O Glembek, N Goel, M Hannemann, P Motlicek, Y Qian, P Schwarz, J Silovsky, G Stemmer, K Vesely, in *Proc. ASRU '11*. The kaldi speech recognition toolkit (Waikoloa, HI, 2011).

6

CHAPTER

Robust Dialogue Act Detection Based On Partial Sentence Tree, Derivation Rule, and Spectral Clustering Algorithm

Chia-Ping Chen, Chung-Hsien WuEmail author and Wei-Bin Liang

[1] *Department of Computer Science and Engineering, National Sun Yat-sen University, 70 Lien-Hai Road, Kaohsiung, Taiwan*

[2] *Department of Computer Science and Information Engineering, National Cheng Kung University, Tainan, Taiwan*

ABSTRACT

A novel approach for robust dialogue act detection in a spoken dialogue system is proposed. Shallow representation named partial sentence trees are employed to represent automatic speech recognition outputs. Parsing results of partial sentences can be decomposed into derivation rules, which turn out to be salient features for dialogue act detection. Data-driven dialogue acts are learned via an unsupervised learning algorithm called spectral clustering, in a vector space whose axes correspond to derivation rules. The proposed method is evaluated in a Mandarin spoken dialogue system for tourist-information services. Combined with information obtained from the automatic speech recognition module and from a Markov model on dialogue act sequence, the proposed method achieves a detection accuracy of 85.1%, which is significantly better than the baseline performance of 62.3% using a naïve Bayes classifier. Furthermore, the average number of turns per dialogue session also decreases significantly with the improved detection accuracy.

1 INTRODUCTION

Spoken dialogue systems (SDS) are computer systems with which a user interacts through natural speech [1]. Services based on SDS have been deployed in a wide range of domains, from simple goal-oriented applications, such as DARPA Airline Travel Information System project for flight information [2], AT&T "How May I Help You?" for call routing [3], and systems for trip planning [4–6], to complex conversational applications, such as chatbot A.L.I.C.E. [7] and a variety of conversational agents using avatars [8].

The designer of an SDS often faces the following critical issues. First, with noisy speech or spontaneous speech with disfluency [9, 10], abundant errors made by automatic speech recognition (ASR) can lead to misunderstanding or even pre-mature termination of a dialogue session (i.e., task failure). Second, the spoken language understanding (SLU) unit is often very expensive to develop, due to the manual annotation of certain features for semantic content. Examples of semantic features are part-of-speech tags [11], semantic roles [12, 13], prosodic features [14], and keywords [15]. Third, the dialogue manager (DM) requires a sound dialogue strategy for management based on the state of a dialogue. Such a strategy could be quite complex in order to deal with all sorts of uncertainty, such as errors in ASR.

A dialogue act (DA) describes the purposes or effects of an utterance in a dialogue [16, 17]. In principle, an utterance can convey multiple DAs. It is a succinct representation of the current intention of the speaker. DAs are closely related to speech acts (SA) [18], but they are specialized to dialogue systems [19]. While SAs are generic, DAs often vary from SDS to SDS. Since we are building an SDS, the notion of DA is more appropriate than SA to our study.

In this article, we describe an SDS with robust DA detection. Knowledge sources exploited include ASR confidence, semantic representation of ASR output, and the history of DA. First, the detrimental effects caused by ASR errors are abated by using partial sentence trees. Second, an unsupervised learning approach can determine data-driven DAs automatically, reducing annotation costs. Third, when DA can be reliably detected, the complexity of DM strategy can be significantly reduced. The motivation for focusing on robust DA detection is that the issues with ASR error, SLU cost, and DM complexity can be greatly alleviated.

A wealth of methods for DA detection have been introduced in the literature. The simplest and strongest "memorylessness" property basically assumes that the current (DA) is independent of the past. Thus, DA detection is based on a set of features derived from the current utterance. In this case, classification-based methods have been studied, including support vector machines (SVM) [12, 20], naïve Bayes classifiers (NBC) [21–23], and multi-layer perceptrons (MLP) [14, 21]. When the memorylessness assumption is relaxed, the dependence between past and current DAs has been modeled by *n*-grams [24, 25], hidden Markov models [26, 27], and Bayesian networks [28]. Recently, methods based on weighted finite state transducers (WFST) [4, 29–31] or partially observable Markov decision processes (POMDP) [32–34] have been studied for DM.

Our method for DA detection is completely different. First, DAs are data-driven by clustering via the spectral clustering algorithm, with each cluster identified as a DA. The clustering happens in a space defined by derivation rules (DR). Classification of DA for unseen utterances is based on a novel derivation rule-dialogue act (DRDA) matrix, which is created by counting the occurrences of each DR in each utterance cluster. As a result, a column in the DRDA matrix represents a DA in the vector space spanned by DRs. As an example, in our system, the utterance How can I go to Anping-Fort by car? is mapped to DA-33 (Car_Destination, as listed in Table 1), and takes an action which leads to the generation of system response "The suggested line is that... ".

The rest of this article is organized as follows. The basic framework of SDS is introduced in Section 2. The proposed robust DA detection method is stated in Section 3. Details of the implementation are described in Section 4. Experiments and discussion on the results are presented in Section 5. Lastly, concluding remarks are given in Section 6.

2 SPOKEN DIALOGUE SYSTEM

A dialogue session between a user and a statistical SDS consists of a chain of interleaving user turns and system turns, as illustrated in Figure 1. ASR outputs a string of words (or *N*-best list) **W** based on utterance *U*. SLU parses **W** and output a semantic representation. DM updates the belief on dialogue states, and accordingly decides the system's action based on a policy. Natural language generation (NLG) converts system's action to a surface representation in the textual form, which is passed to the text-to-speech (TTS) module for speech waveform generation. The cycle repeats when the user responds with the next utterance.

Table 1. List of dialogue acts

Numbers	DA	Numbers	DA
1	Greeting	2	Ending
3	Query_Service	4	Query_Spot
5	Query_Opening	6	Query_Introduction
7	Query_Contact	8	Query_Telephone
9	Query_Address	10	Query_Ticket
11	Query_Route	12	Query_Opening_Spot
13	Query_Introduction_Spot	14	Query_Contact_Spot
15	Query_Telephone_Spot	16	Query_Address_Spot
17	Query_Ticket_Spot	18	Query_Route_Spot
19	Query_Station	20	Query_Bus
21	Bus_From	22	Bus_Destination
23	Bus_From_Destination	24	Query_THSR
25	THSR_From	26	THSR_Destination
27	THSR_From_Destination	28	Query_TRA
29	TRA_From	30	TRA_Destination
31	TRA_From_Destination	32	Car_From
33	Car_Destination	34	Car_From_Destination
35	Route_From	36	Route_Destination
37	Route_From_Destination	38	Particle

The ASR module turns user's utterance into word hypotheses. A telephone-based SDS inevitably needs to deal with noisy speech and spontaneous speech, rendering the job of ASR module difficult. Furthermore, errors made by ASR may propagate along the system, making the jobs of other modules difficult. As a result, ASR accuracy is critical to the performance of SDS.

The SLU module, as depicted in Figure 2, converts ASR output into semantic representation. In the proposed system, the ASR output is first converted to a partial sentence tree (PST) [35] in the PST Construction block. The basic idea of PST is to replace unreliable word hypotheses by fillers. As a result,

PST is less vulnerable to recognition errors. From PST, partial sentences are formed and parsed. The parse results contain derivation rules (DR), which are extracted in the DR Generation block. The NEC (name entity class) inventory is referenced and certain words are replaced by word classes.

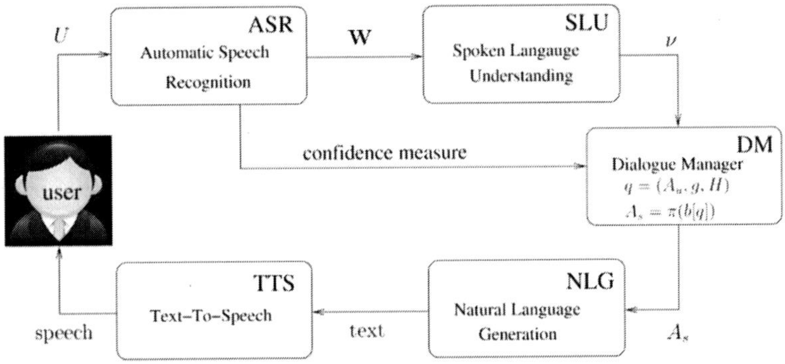

Figure 1. Block diagram of a spoken dialogue system. At turn *t*, the user utters *U*, which is recognized by ASR to be **W**. *v* is a semantic representation of user's intended dialogue act. *q* is the dialogue state, where A_u is the hypothesized user's dialogue act. *g* is user's goal, and *H* is dialogue history. *b* is a distribution over dialogue states. A_s is the system's action. The function π is called policy and it encodes the strategy of the dialogue manager.

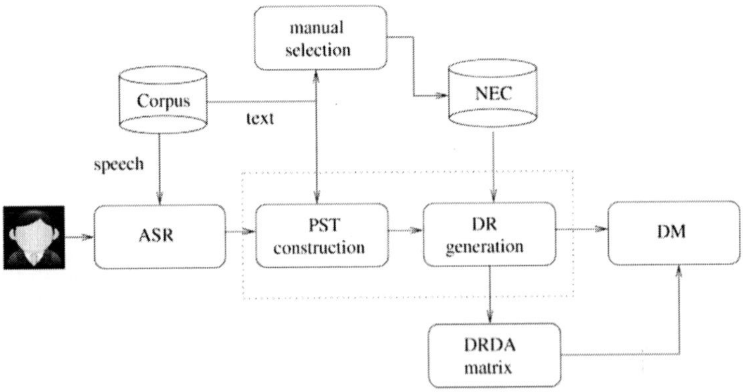

Figure 2. The spoken language understanding (SLU) module. During training, derivation rules are extracted based on partial sentence tree construction, and a derivation rule-dialogue act (DRDA) matrix is constructed. During testing, the trained DRDA matrix is used in DM for DA detection. Name entity class (NEC) inventory is referenced to convert certain words to word classes.

The core of an SDS is the dialogue manager. DM adopts sound strategy to keep dialogue sessions alive until they are successfully finished. An optimal action is taken at each turn based on the dialogue state, including user's goal, user's DA, and dialogue history. To cope with uncertainty, a belief on the states can be maintained, and the policy for taking action can be based on the belief.

3 DIALOGUE ACT DETECTION

To infer dialogue act, a statistical model involving DA is required. The model assumption of the generation process for user's utterance is described as follows. Based on user's goal and the dialogue history, a user decides a DA, convert it into words, and produces an utterance. This is depicted in Figure 3. Note that each variable in the figure is indexed by turn *t*. However, to keep the notation and graph from being cluttered, we drop the subscript *t*. It is not difficult to see that the critical evidence to infer the current dialogue act should depend on ASR output, lexical items, and dialogue history. Thus, we can write

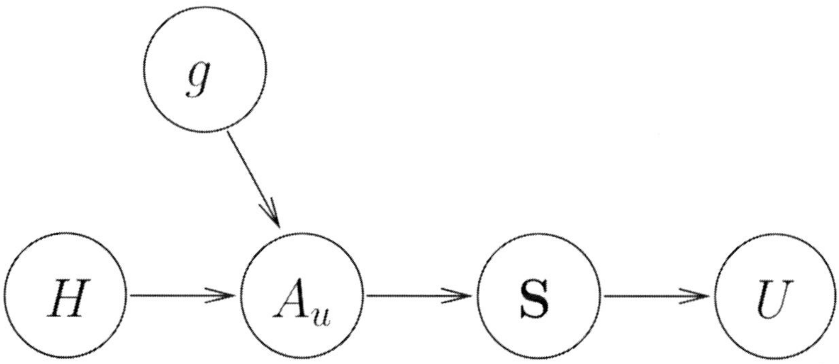

Figure 3. The generation process of user's utterance. In this graph, g is user's goal, H is dialogue history, A_u is user's intended dialogue act,**S** is the uttered sentence, and U is the acoustical observation. Note that the uttered sentence **S** and the recognition hypothesis of ASR**W** are different.

$$A_u^* = \arg\max_{A_u \in \Omega} \max_{\mathbf{W}} f(\mathbf{W}, U) g(A_u, \mathbf{W})\, h(A_u, H), \tag{1}$$

where $\Omega = \{A^1, \ldots, A^q\}$ is the set of DAs. In (1), $f(\mathbf{W}, U)$ is called ASR score, $g(A_u, \mathbf{W})$ is called lexical scorem and $h(A_u, H)$ is called history score.

These scores are related to conditional probability functions. For the ASR score, we use the acoustic model and the language model in the ASR system. Specifically,

$$f(\mathrm{W},\ U) \approx p_{\mathrm{AM}}(U|\mathrm{W})P^{\alpha}_{\mathrm{LM}}(\mathrm{W}), \tag{2}$$

where $p_{\mathrm{AM}}(\cdot)$ is the acoustic model probability, $P_{\mathrm{LM}}(\cdot)$ is the language model probability, and α is the language model scale factor. For the history score, a back-off bi-gram model for DA sequence is used [4, 30, 31]. That is,

$$h(A_u,\ H) \approx Pr(A_t = A_u|A_{t-1}). \tag{3}$$

Essentially, equation (3) models DA sequence as a Markov chain. We assume that the current user's DA depends on the history only through the previous user's DA. For the lexical score, a novel measure is proposed and the details are described in the following section.

4 METHOD FOR LEXICAL SCORE

One main contribution of this research is to demonstrate that a novel method for estimating lexical score $g(A_u, \mathbf{W})$ works quite well. The proposed method incorporates several steps, including partial sentence tree construction, derivation rule extraction, utterance representation in a vector space, the dialogue act set generation via spectral clustering, dialogue act representation using relative frequency weighted by normalized entropy, and finally a cosine distance measure between dialogue act and utterance. Taking the risk of being tedious, we describe the details of these steps in the following sections in order to make the overall procedure clear.

4.1 Construction of partial sentence tree

In an SDS, it is often beneficial to partition the vocabulary into a set of keywords K$\mathcal{K}$ and a set of non-keywords Q$\mathcal{Q}$. Each word w∈K$w \in \mathcal{K}$ should be quite indicative of DA. Using K$\mathcal{K}$ and Q$\mathcal{Q}$, the set of sentences with at least one keyword can be represented as

$$\mathcal{S} = \mathcal{Q}^{*}(\mathcal{K}\ \mathcal{Q}^{*})^{+} \tag{4}$$

where $\mathcal{A}^*$ is the Kleene star (a.k.a. Kleene closure) of $\mathcal{A}$, and $\mathcal{A}^+$ is the Kleene plus of $\mathcal{A}$.

Given a sentence $s \in \mathcal{S}$, a partial sentence (PS) of s contains all keywords in s, while replacing some non-keywords in s by tokens called Filler. For a sentence with n non-keywords, there are 2^n PS's. These PS's can be compiled in a tree called partial sentence tree (PST). A path in PST from the root to a leave corresponds to a PS. The PST of sentence s is henceforth denoted by Ts $\mathcal{T}_s$. For example, Figure 4 gives the PST for the sentence

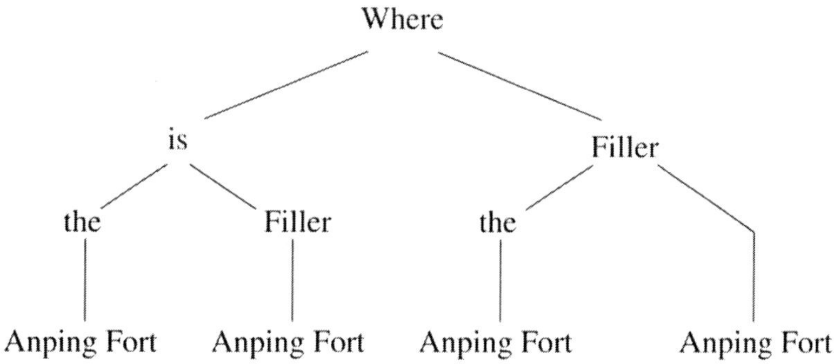

Figure 4. Construction of the partial sentence tree for the sentence where is the Anping-Fort. With 2 non-keywords, there are 4 partial sentences.

$$s: \text{Where is the Anping - Fort} \qquad (5)$$

In this example, Where and Anping-Fort are keywords, while is and the are non-keywords. The $2^2 = 4$ PS's embedded in the PST.

PST is a robust representation of ASR output. That is, even if some words are not recognized correctly, the semantics of an utterance can still be conveyed with the recognized keywords.

In the actual implementation, the ASR output is post-processed before PST construction. First, a word hypothesis, say w, is replaced by a Filler if the z-score [36] is below a threshold

$$z(w) = \frac{f(w) - \mu}{\sigma}, \qquad (6)$$

where $f(w)$ is the recognition probability for word w, μ is the mean and σ^2 is the variance computed from all samples. In addition, recognized keywords are replaced by the named entity classes (NEC) or the greeting/ending classes, to have a compact representation.

4.2 Extraction of derivation rules

After PST construction, each PS in the PST is parsed by the Stanford parser (S-parser) [11]. Let the grammar of the S-parser be denoted as a 5-tuple [37]

$$G = (\mathcal{V},\ \Sigma,\ \mathcal{P},\ S,\ D), \tag{7}$$

where V$\mathcal{V}$ is the set of variables, Σ is the set of terminals, P$\mathcal{P}$ is the set of production rules, S is the sentence symbol, and D is a function defined on P$\mathcal{P}$ for rule probability. In our implementation, a derivation rule (DR) is defined to be a derivation of the form

$$A \rightarrow B \rightarrow w, \tag{8}$$

where A,B∈V$A, B \in \mathcal{V}$ and $w \in \Sigma$. Note that equation (8) is a lexicalized rule. For illustration, parse results of the partial sentences are shown in Table 2. One can see that a lexical word in a PS produces a DR. Given a text corpus, a set of DRs R={R1,R2,...,Rl}$\mathcal{R} = \{R^1, R^2, \ldots, R^l\}$ can be extracted and compacted.

The motivation for using DR is to exploit the part-of-speech (POS) information. In particular, POS tags help to disambiguate noun-verb homonyms that occur quite often in Chinese.

4.3 Vector representation of sentences

Using each DR as a feature, we can represent a sentence s as a binary vector v_s, where

$$v_s(i) = \begin{cases} 1, \text{ if } R^i \in \mathcal{T}_s, \\ 0, \text{ otherwise,} \end{cases} \tag{9}$$

Table 2. Examples of the parse result (left) and the extracted derivation rules (right) corresponding to the four partial sentences in Figure 4

PS: where is the spot	
(Root	DR1: WHADVP WRB Where
(SINV	DR2: VP VBZ is
(FRAG	DR3: NP DT the
(WHADVP (WRB Where)))	DR4: NP NNP Spot
(VP (VBZ is))	
(NP (DT the) (NNP Spot)))	
PS: where is filler spot	
(ROOT	DR1: WHADVP WRB Where
(SBARQ	DR2: SQ VBZ is
(WHADVP (WRB Where))	DR3: NP NNP Filler
(SQ (VBZ is)	DR4: NP NNP Spot
(NP (NNP Filler) (NNP Spot)))))	
PS: where filler the spot	
(ROOT	DR1: WHADVP WRB Where
(SBARQ	DR2: SQ VBZ is
(WHADVP (WRB Where))	DR3: NP NNP Filler
(SQ (VBZ is)	DR4: NP NNP Spot
(NP (NNP Filler) (NNP Spot)))))	
PS: where filler the spot	
(ROOT	DR1: WHADVP WRB Where
(FRAG	DR2: VP VB Filler
(WHADVP (WRB Where))	DR3: NP DT the
(VP (VB Filler)	DR4: NP NNP Spot
(NP (DT the) (NNP Spot)))))	
PS: where filler spot	
(ROOT	DR1: NP NNP Where
(NP (NNP Where) (NNP Filler) (NNP Spot)))	DR2: NP NNP Filler
	DR3: NP NNP Spot

where Ts$\mathcal{T}_s$ is the PST for s. For example, the representative vector

$$v_s = [1\ 0\ 1\ 0]^T \tag{10}$$

means that R^1 and R^3 are used in Ts$\mathcal{T}_s$, and that there are $l = 4$ derivation rules.

4.4 Generation of dialogue acts

We use a set of data-driven DAs to save the prohibitive cost of manual annotation. We apply the recently-proposed *spectral clustering algorithm*[38] to cluster utterances in the training set. The spectral clustering algorithm is chosen because a conventional clustering algorithm (e.g., *k*-means) is often sensitive to centroid selection (for initialization). After clustering, each cluster found is identified as a DA.

Our implementation of spectral clustering is outlined as follows. Suppose there are n utterances in the training set

$$\mathcal{D} = \{s_1, s_2, \ldots, s_n\}. \tag{11}$$

Each utterance is represented by a vector according to equation (9). From D$\mathcal{D}$, we construct an $n \times n$ similarity matrix M, where the similarity $M_{kk'}$ between two utterances s_k and $s_{k'}$ is defined as the cosine measure between vskv_{s_k} and vsk$v_{s_{k'}}$. The normalized Laplacian matrix of M is defined as

$$L \triangleq I - D^{-\frac{1}{2}} M D^{-\frac{1}{2}}, \tag{12}$$

where D is a diagonal matrix with entries

$$D_{kk'} = \delta_{kk'} \sum_{j=1}^{n} M_{kj}. \tag{13}$$

We find the eigenvectors of the q smallest eigenvalues of L. Note that the eigenvectors can be made orthonormal since L is real-symmetric. We put these eigenvectors in an $n \times q$ orthogonal matrix Q, and cluster the row vectors to q clusters. Each cluster is identified as a data-driven DA.

On a theoretical side, consider the conversion of M into a binary-valued matrix M^$\hat{M}$ via a threshold τ, i.e.,

$$\hat{M}_{kk'} = \begin{cases} 1, & M_{kk'} < \tau, \\ 0, & \text{otherwise}. \end{cases} \tag{14}$$

M^$\hat{M}$ can be regarded as the adjacency matrix of a graph $G = (\mathcal{N}, \mathcal{E})$, where node set N$\mathcal{N}$ corresponds to $\mathcal{D}$, and edge set E corresponds to the non-zero entries in M'. It can be shown [38] that the multiplicity of the eigenvalue 0 for L^$\hat{L}$, the normalized Laplacian matrix of $\hat{M}$, equals the number of disjoint connected components in G, which can be identified as clusters in D$\mathcal{D}$.

4.5 Derivation rule-dialogue act matrix

A cluster of utterances found via spectral clustering algorithm is identified as a DA. In our implementation, we use an entropy-based representation for DA. The representation of DA is described as follows. Let n_{ij} be the accumulated count that DR R^i occurs in the utterance cluster of A^j. From n_{ij}, a probability function of DA conditional on DR is defined as follows

$$\gamma_{ij} = \hat{P}(\mathrm{DA} = A^j | \mathrm{DR} = R^i) \triangleq \frac{n_{ij}}{\sum_{j'=1}^{q} n_{ij'}}, \quad i = 1, \ldots, l, \quad j = 1, \ldots, q. \tag{15}$$

The normalized entropy for the probability conditional on DR R^i is

$$\varepsilon_i = -\frac{1}{\log q} \sum_{j=1}^{q} \gamma_{ij} \log \gamma_{ij}, \quad i = 1, \ldots, l. \tag{16}$$

Note that $0 \leq \epsilon_i \leq 1$, and a DR R^i with a lower ϵ_i is more discriminative for DA. From equations (15) and (16), a matrix Γ of size $l \times q$ can be constructed with entries

$$\Gamma_{ij} = (1 - \varepsilon_i)\gamma_{ij}. \tag{17}$$

We call Γ the derivation rule-dialogue act (DRDA) matrix. The jth column in Γ is a vector representation for a DA A^j in the vector space spanned by DRs.

4.6 Similarity between utterance and dialogue act

In our implementation, the lexical score $g(A_u, \mathbf{W})$ in equation (1) is decomposed into two terms

$$g(A_u, W) \approx g_R(A_u, s) g_N(A_u, W), \tag{18}$$

where $g_R(Au, s)$ is called DR score and $g_N(A_u, \mathbf{W})$ is called named entity score. For DR score, the following similarity measure is used

$$g_R(A_u = A^j, s) = \max_{\sigma \in T_s} \frac{\mathbf{b}_\sigma^T \mathbf{a}_j}{|\mathbf{b}_\sigma| \, |\mathbf{a}_j|}, \tag{19}$$

where $\mathbf{b}_\sigma$ is the vector representation for PS σ in TsT_s, and $\mathbf{a}_j$ is the vector representation for DA A^j (i.e., column j in DRDA matrix Γ). For named entity score, we use the naïve Bayes approximation

$$g_N(A_u = A^j, W) = \prod_{\alpha \in W} \nu(A^j, \alpha) \tag{20}$$

where α is a named entity. Note that $\nu(A^j, \alpha)$ is estimated from a training corpus by the relative frequency of α occurring in A^j.

5 EXPERIMENTS AND DISCUSSION

We evaluate the proposed method for dialogue act detection on an SDS for Tainan city tourist-information services.

5.1 Data collection

We adopt the setup utilized in [4, 6] to collect the dialogue speech data. The data collection setup is shown in Figure 5, and an exemplar in the collected dialogue data is shown in Table 3. An operator play the role of SDS, which helps users to plan trips in Tainan. Twenty six male and eleven female subjects play the role of users. For our prototype system, users are asked to use utterances with single DA. Dialogue speech data is recorded in a lab environment, using 16,000-Hz sampling rate and 16-bit PCM format. There are 294 dialogues.

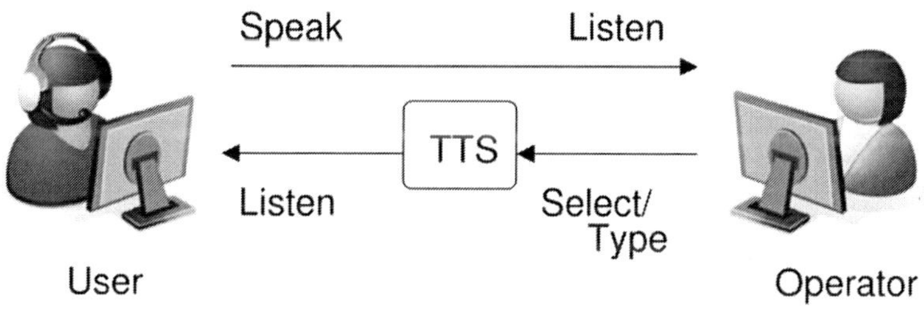

Figure 5. The environmental setting of data collection. The operator acts like an SDS, and the user acts like s/he is interacting with an SDS.

Table 3. The beginning part of a collected dialogue

Role	Dialogue act	Utterance
System	Greeting	Welcome
User	Query_Service	What service can you provide?
System	Ans_Service	I can provide the information of historic spot and timetable of railway
User	Query_Intro	Can you give an introduction to Anping-Fort?
System	Ans_Intro	Anping-Fort is also known as Fort Zeelandia It was first built by the Dutch in 1624 as ...

This is collected in the way illustrated in Figure 5

Two types of speech data are collected. The first type, called S-data, is from the operator playing the role of SDS. S-data contains travel information collected from on-line resources, such as Wikipedia and Google map. S-data set consists of 2, 653 utterances, with 317 different words. The second type, called U-data, is from subjects playing the role of users. U-data consists of 2, 636 utterances, with 297 different words. The vocabulary size is small as we have a domain-specific task. From U-data, 87 keywords corresponding to 28 named entity classes/semantic classes and 796 derivation rules are obtained from the S-parser. Examples of the selected NECs and semantic classes are given in Table 4. The collected data contains sightseeing information, queries for the time schedules of two railway systems (Taiwan Railways Administration (TRA) and Taiwan High-Speech Rail (THSR)), and greeting/ending words in dialogues.

Table 4. Examples of named entity classes (NEC) and semantic classes

NEC/semantic class	Named entities/words
City	Tainan, Taipei, Kaohsiung
Spot	Anping-Fort, Fort-Provintia, Sun-Moon Lake
Date	Today, Tomorrow, Yesterday
Time1	Morning, Noon, Afternoon
Time2	o'clock, hour, minute
Greeting	Welcome, Hello
Ending	Thanks, Bye

We use fivefold cross-validation method for system development. That is, the data is divided into five parts. In a round-robin fashion, four parts are used as training data, and one part is used as test data. We develop our system such that the average accuracy of DA detection over five test sets is optimal.

5.2 ASR module

The ASR module is an HTK-based Mandarin speech recognizer [39]. A syllable in Mandarin is modeled as the concatenation of an initial model and a final model. The acoustic model set includes 115 right-context-dependent initial models, 38 context-independent final models, 37 particle models, (e.g., EN, MA, OU), 47 syllable-level models for hyper-articulated speech, and 14 filler models (e.g., short pause, breathing, and footfall). Each initial model is a three state HMM, while each final model is a five state HMMs. The observation probability density of a state is a Gaussian mixture model (GMM) with no more than 32 components. The speech feature vector is composed of 39 components, including 12 mel-frequency cepstral coefficients (MFCCs), log energy, and the velocity and acceleration features. For real-world data with a variety of speakers, a reliable acoustic model is needed. Thus, an acoustic model set trained by the TCC-300 Mandarin corpus is adapted by the collected dialogue speech data via maximum-likelihood linear regression (MLLR). The lexicon contains 297 words. The bi-gram language model is estimated by SRILM toolkit [40].

Table 5 shows the performance of ASR module with clean and simulated noisy speech. Note that the real-world scenario of noise corruption is applied in the collection of the noisy speech (footfall noise, human speech, or both). That is, a speaker stands in front of a microphone and the noise is played behind the speaker. From the results, we can see that the recognition accuracy does not severely degrade in the presence of noises behind a user.

Table 5. Word accuracy rates of automatic speech recognition in clean and three noisy conditions

Conditions	Clean	Football	Human	Both noises
accuracy rate (%)	84.8	82.7	81.4	80.9

5.3 The *z*-score threshold

Ideally, an effective threshold for *z*-score strikes a good balance between reliable recognition and keeping sufficient keywords for subsequent semantic representation in SLU. We analyze the rejected word hypotheses with *z*-scores below the threshold of 2 (which corresponds to the confidence level of 0.95), and find that only 3.4% of the keywords are incorrectly rejected. The threshold of 2 is therefore used. Such performance can be attributed to the fact that users often pause naturally before or after a keyword.

5.4 The number of dialogue acts

While generic speech acts are relatively well-defined, DAs are often specialized to particular domains and they need to be specified. In this research, since we adopt data-driven DAs by clustering, the number of DAs (clusters) become a critical parameter in system design. In order to decide this number, we investigate the system performance when it is varied. The detection accuracies are shown in Table 6. We can see that 38 DAs (q = 38) achieves the best performance[a]. Therefore, we use 38 DAs. To make more sense, each cluster is given an artificial but meaningful label (tag, name), as shown in Table 1. For example, Query_Introduction_Spot is assigned to the cluster formed by "queries of introduction to sightseeing spot".

Table 6. Accuracy rates of dialogue act detection with various numbers of Das

Number of DAs	36	37	38	39	40
accuracy rate (%)	79.6	81.7	82.9	79.2	78.8

5.5 Evaluation of feature sets

Just like the set of DRs, an alternative set of semantic features can be used as the coordinate axes to construct the corresponding vector set for DD. Applying spectral clustering, a matrix analogs to the DRDA matrix can be constructed according to the steps described in Section 4.

Including the proposed DR, 5 sets of features are investigated. In baseline, keywords are used as features. In NEC, named entity classes are used. In PS, partial sentences are used. In uwDR, derivation rules without normalized entropy weighting are used.

DA detection accuracies are summarized in Table 7. In this table, the column 40%-SIM means 40% of the words in the reference transcripts are retained, and similarly for 60%-SIM and 100%-REF. The recognition accuracy of ASR is 84.8% (15.2% word error rate), so we have a column of 84.8%-ASR. The middle columns are the results with simulated noisy speech, corrupted by footfall (football), human speech (human), and both noises (both).

Table 7. Accuracy rates of dialogue act detection with various feature sets in various noisy conditions

	40%-SIM	60%-SIM	Football	Human	Both	84.8%-ASR	100%-REF
baseline	17.2	32.6	44.3	43.1	42.6	49.6	60.9
NEC	22.4	36.8	52.1	51.0	49.8	56.8	76.9
PS	29.8	49.2	75.2	74.6	73.5	76.2	91.1
uwDR	26.3	48.0	81.1	80.8	80.2	81.6	92.1
DR	26.3	47.4	82.3	81.9	81.6	82.9	93.3

In the case of 84.8%-ASR, we can see that NEC (56.8%) is better than baseline (49.6%), and that PS (76.2%) is better than NEC. The incorporation of uwDR (81.6%) and DR (82.9%) lead to further improvements. Thus, the difference between baseline and the proposed DR is very significant. We notice that an ambiguous Chinese word may correspond to different DAs with its different meanings. For instance, in open door and drive car, the words open and drive are the same word in Chinese. Using DRs helps disambiguation. For the cases of 40%-SIM and 60%-SIM, the results show clear improvement of NEC and PS over the baseline. Using DRs, however, does not further improve in these scenarios as the keywords are randomly discarded. We can see that recognizing the keywords is particularly important in highly adverse acoustic conditions. We also evaluate using the simulated noisy speech data in SDS. One can observe an interesting result that the performance of DR with the simulated noisy data and the clean data are very close. In PS, non-keywords are removed or replaced by Fillers. Thus, most of the partial sentences of simulated noisy speech are almost the same as those obtained from the clean speech.

5.6 Evaluation of the history score

The above results on DA detection are obtained without considering the dependency between DAs. Next, we evaluate the effectiveness of the history score. In order to balance the contribution of the lexical score and the history score, we generalize equation (1) to the following form,

$$A_u^* = \arg\max_{A_u \in \Omega} \, [g(A_u, \mathbf{W})]^{\beta_g} \, [h(A_u, H)]^{\beta_h}, \tag{21}$$

where $0 \leq \beta_g \leq 1$ is the weight of the lexical score, and $\beta_h = 1 - \beta_g$ is the weight of the history score.

A few comments on using equation (21) are in order. First, we note that when the ASR module outputs only one-best hypothesis, the maximization over **W** in equation (1) becomes trivial. It follows that the term $f(\mathbf{W}, U)$ can be dropped since it does not depend on A_u. In addition, as the values of $g(A_u, \mathbf{W})$ and $h(A_u, H)$ are in different ranges, simple linear combination may not work as one score can easily be dominated by the other. Therefore, we use the linear combination in the log domain, which is equivalent to the product in equation (21). In fact, a similar case based on the same consideration is the language model scale factor commonly used in ASR.

Table 8 shows the results of different β_h, and the best performance is achieved when β_h = 0.7. The evaluation results demonstrate that the dialogue history is informative.

Table 8. Accuracy rates of dialogue act detection with various history score weights

Value of β_h	0.3	0.4	0.5	0.6	0.7	0.8	0.9
accuracy rate (%)	83.9	84.1	84.3	84.6	85.1	84.9	84.9

5.7 Comparison with other methods

The performance of the proposed approach for DA detection is compared with other methods. In the NBC method, the keywords are used as the semantic features, and they are used in calculating DA probabilities. In the co-occurrence (co-oc) method, a priori algorithm [41] is used to calculate the co-occurrence of keywords in each DA. In the SVM and maximum entropy (ME) methods, a DA classifier is trained using keywords. In latent semantic analysis (LSA), the keyword-DA matrix is treated as a conventional word-document matrix, and then the LSA is applied. The results are listed in Table 9. We can see that the proposed approach achieves the best accuracy.

Table 9. Accuracy rates of dialogue act detection with five feature sets

Approaches	NBC	co-oc	SVM	ME	LSA	Proposed
accuracy rate (%)	62.3	62.6	75.8	76.3	78.6	85.1

5.8 Evaluation on end-to-end measure

In addition to DA detection accuracy, we also conduct evaluation on end-to-end measures, i.e., from the start of a session to the end of the session. End-to-end measures are arguably better for performance evaluation as the ultimate goal of an SDS is to enable a user to complete a session correctly and quickly.

Three systems are evaluated, including the NBC, the proposed system (proposed), and the proposed system without using the history information (no history). Five subjects are recruited. Subjects perform exactly same task without knowing the order of the systems. This order is random for a test subject. A task is considered completed as soon as a subject acquires the appointed information. Table 10 shows the average dialogue turns per task of the evaluated systems. The proposed approach achieves the minimum of the average number of turns.

Table 10. End-to-end measure of system performance evaluation.

	NBC	No history	Proposed
average number of turns	11	9.2	8.2

The average numbers of turns per dialogue session of three systems

6 CONCLUSION

In this article, a robust dialogue act detection method using named entity classes, partial sentence trees, derivation rules, and entropy-based dialogue act-derivation rule matrix is investigated. Data-driven dialogue acts are created by the spectral clustering algorithm. Our implementation of a spoken dialogue system for tourist-information services incorporating the proposed method achieves 85.1% detection accuracy, outperforming a naïve Bayes classification based method (62.3%). It also reduces the number of dialogue turns per dialogue session on average. The results show that partial sentence tree and derivation rules are indeed succinct and informative features for dialogue act detection. Furthermore, spectral clustering is a successful method for automatic and unsupervised learning of dialogue acts from in-domain training data.

ENDNOTE

[a]Queries to 3 kinds of vehicles - bus, TRA, and THSR, are in different clusters when $q = 38$, but in the same cluster when $q = 36$. This partially explains the difference in performance between using 36 DAs and 38 DAs.

REFERENCES

1. Fraser N: *Handbook of Standards and Resources for Spoken Language Systems. Volume chap. 6*. Edited by: Gibbon D, Moore R, Winski R. Mouton de Gruyter, Berlin; 1997:564-564.

2. Price PJ: Evaluation of spoken language systems: the ATIS domain. In *Proc the workshop on Speech and Natural Language*. Hidden Valley, Pennsylvania; 1990:91-95.

3. Gorin A, Riccardi G, Wright JH: How may i help you? *Speech Commun* 1997, 23: 113-127. 10.1016/S0167-6393(97)00040-X

4. Hori C, Ohtake K, Misu T, Kashioka H, Nakamura S: Dialog management using weighted finite-state transducers. In *Proc INTERSPEECH-2008*. Brisbane, Australia; 2008:211-214.

5. Liu J, Xu Y, Seneff S, Zue V: CITYBROWSER II: a multimodal restaurant guide in Mandarin. In *Proc International Symposium on Chinese Spoken Language Processing*. Kunming, China; 2008:1-4.

6. Misu T, Kawahara T: Bayes risk-based dialogue management for document retrieval system with speech interface. *Speech Commun* 2010, 52: 61-71. 10.1016/j.specom.2009.08.007

7. Wallace R: *The Artificial Linguistic Internet Computer Entity (A. L. I. C. E.)*. 2001. [http://www.alicebot.org]

8. Cassell J, Bickmore T, Billinghurst M, Campbell L, Chang K, Vilhjálmsson H, Yan H: Embodiment in conversational interfaces: rea. In *Proc the SIGCHI Conference on Human Factors in Computing Systems: the CHI is the limit*. Pittsburgh, Pennsylvania; 1999:520-527

9. Yeh JF, Wu CH: Edit Disfluency detection and correction using a cleanup language model and an alignment model. *IEEE Trans Speech Audio Process* 2006, 14(5):1574-1583.

10. Wu CH, Liang WB, Yeh JF: Interruption point detection of spontaneous speech using inter-syllable boundary-based prosodic features.*ACM Trans Asian Lang Inf Process* 2010. 10, 6:16:21

11. Levy R, Manning C: Is it harder to parse Chinese, or the Chinese Treebank? In *Proc 41st Annual Meeting on Association for Computational Linguistics (ACL)*. Sapporo, Japan; 2003:439-446.

12. Liu CH, Wu CH: Semantic role labeling with discriminative feature selection for spoken language understanding. In *Proc INTERSPEECH*. Brighton, United Kingdom; 2009:1043-1046.

13. Coppola B, Moschitti A, Riccardi G: Shallow semantic parsing for spoken language understanding. In *Proc Annual Conference of the North American Chapter of the Association for Computational Linguistics-Human Language Technologies*. Boulder, Colorado; 2009:85-88.

14. Wright H: Automatic utterance type detection using suprasegmental features. In *Proc International Conference on Spoken Language Processing*. *Volume 4*. Sydney, Australia; 1998:1403-1406.

15. Kawahara T, Lee CH, Juang BH: Flexible speech understanding based on combined key-phrase detection and verification. *IEEE Trans Speech Audio Process* 1998, 6(6):558-568. 10.1109/89.725322

16. Bunt H: Context and dialogue control. *THINK Quarterly* 1994, 3: 19-31.

17. Prasad R, Walker M: Training a dialogue act tagger for human-human and human-computer travel dialogues. In *Proc Annual Meeting of the Association for Computational Linguistics*. *Volume 2*. Philadelphia, Pennsylvania; 2002:162-173.

18. Austin JL: *How to Do Things with Words*. Edited by: Urmson JO, Sbisá M. Harvard University Press, Cambridge, MA; 1962.

19. Stolcke A, Ries K, Coccaro N, Shriberg E, Bates R, Jurafsky D, Taylor P, Martin R: Dialogue act modeling for automatic tagging and recognition of conversational speech. *Comput Linguist* 2000, 26(3):339-373. 10.1162/089120100561737

20. Tur G, Hakkani-Tür D, Heck L: What is left to be understood in ATIS. In *Proc IEEE Workshop on Spoken Language Technologies*. Berkeley, California; 2010:19-24.

21. Levin L, Langley C, Donna Gates AL, Wallace D, Peterson K: Domain specific speech acts for spoken language translation. In *Proc the 4th SIGdial Workshop on Discourse and Dialogue*. Sapparo, Japan; 2003.

22. Grau S, Sanchis E, Castro MJ, Vilar D: Dialogue act classification using a Bayesian approach. In *Proc Conference on Speech and Computer*. St Petersberg; 2004:495-499.

23. Ivanovic E: Dialogue Act Tagging for Instant Messaging Chat Sessions. In *Pro the ACL Student Research Workshop, Association for Computational Linguistics*. Ann Arbor, Michigan; 2005:79-84.

24. Seneff S, Wang C, Hazen TJ: Automatic induction of *N*-gram language models from a natural language grammar. In *Proc EUROSPEECH-2003*. Geneva, Swiss; 2003:641-644.

25. Hara S, Kitaoka N, Takeda K: Automatic detection of task-incompleted dialog for spoken dialog system based on dialog act N-gram. In*Proc INTERSPEECH-2010*. Makuhari, Japan; 2010:3034-3037.

26. Ries K: Hmm and Neural network based speech act detection. In *Proc IEEE International Conference on Acoustics, Speech, and Signal Processing*. *Volume 1*. Phoenix, Arizona; 1999:497-500.

27. Wu CH, Yan GL: Speech act modeling and verification of spontaneous speech with disfluency in a spoken dialogue system. *IEEE Trans Speech Audio Process* 2005, 13(3),330-344.

28. Keizer S, Nijholt A: Dialogue act recognition with Bayesian networks for Dutch dialogues. In *Proc the 3rd SIGdial workshop on Discourse and dialogue*. *Volume 2*. Philadelphia, Pennsylvania; 2002:88-94.

29. Hori C, Ohtake K, Misu T, Kashioka H, Nakamura S: Recent advances in WFST-based dialog system. In *Proc INTERSPEECH*. Brighton, United Kingdom; 2009:268-271.

30. Hori C, Ohtake K, Misu T, Kashioka H, Nakamura S: Statistical dialog management applied to WFST-based dialog systems. In *Proc IEEE International Conference on Acoustics Speech and Signal Processing*. Taipei, Taiwan; 2009:4793-4796.

31. Ohtake K, Misu T, Hori C, Kashioka H, Nakamura S: Dialogue acts annotation for NICT Kyoto tour dialogue corpus to construct statistical dialogue systems. In *Proc LREC2010*. Valletta, Malta; 2010:2123-2130.

32. Williams JD, Young S: Partially observable Markov decision processes for spoken dialog systems. *Comput Speech Lang* 2007, 21: 393-422. 10.1016/j.csl.2006.06.008

33. Young S: Still talking to machines (cognitively speaking). In *Proc INTERSPEECH2010*. Makuhari, Japan; 2010:1-10.

34. Williams JD, Young S: Scaling POMDPs for spoken dialog management. *IEEE Trans Acoustic Speech Lang Process* 15(7):2116-2129.

35. Wu CH, Chen YJ: Recovery from false rejection using statistical partial pattern trees for sentence verification. *Speech Commun* 2004, 43(1-2):71-88. 10.1016/j.specom.2004.02.003

36. Larsen RJ, Marx ML: *An Introduction to Mathematical Statistics and Its Applications*. 3rd edition. Prentice Hall, Lebanon, Indiana, USA; 2000. ISBN: 0139223037

37. Jurafsky D, Martin JH: *Speech and Language Processing*. 2nd edition. Pearson Prentice Hall, New Jersey; 2009.

38. von Luxburg U: A tutorial on spectral clustering. *Stat Comput* 2007, 17(4):395-416. 10.1007/s11222-007-9033-z

39. Young SJ, Kershaw D, Odell J, Ollason D, Valtchev V, Woodland P: *The HTK Book Version 3.4*. Cambridge University Press, Cambridge; 2006.

40. Stolcke A: SRILM - an extensible language modeling toolkit. In *Proc International Conference on Spoken Language Processing*. Denver, Colorado; 2002:901-904.

41. Agrawal R, Imielinski T, Swami AN: Mining association rules between sets of items in large databases. In *ACM SIGMOD*. Washington, D.C; 1993:207-216.

7
CHAPTER

A Recognition-Based Approach to Segmenting Arabic Handwritten Text

Ashraf Elnagar, Rahima Bentrcia

Department of Computer Science, College of Sciences, University of Sharjah, Sharjah, UAE

ABSTRACT

Segmenting Arabic handwritings had been one of the subjects of research in the field of Arabic character recognition for more than 25 years. The majority of reported segmentation techniques share a critical shortcoming, which is over-segmentation. The aim of segmentation is to produce the letters (segments) of a handwritten word. When a resulting letter (segment) is made of more than one piece (stroke) instead of one, this is called over-segmentation. Our objective is to overcome this problem by using an Artificial Neural Networks (ANN) to verify the resulting segment. We propose a set of heuristic-based rules to assemble strokes in order to report the precise segmented letters. Preprocessing phases that include normalization and feature extraction are required as a prerequisite step for the ANN system for recognition and verification. In our previous work [1] , we did achieve a segmentation success rate of 86% but without recognition. In this work, our experimental results confirmed a segmentation success rate of no less than 95%.

Keywords: Character Segmentation, Handwritten Recognition Systems, Arabic Handwriting, Neural Networks, Multi-Agents

1. INTRODUCTION

Automatic recognition of handwritings is developing well as a result of research contributions in this field. There are two main types of character recognition systems, namely, on-line and off-line systems. On-line systems recognize handwritings input on a tablet or any a similar device by a digital pen or stylus. Off-line systems deal with images of handwritings stored. The temporal information in the first type would positively contribute to the recognition process. Such information is absent in the second type, which makes this problem in particular more challenging.

In this paper, we study the problem of Arabic handwritten characters recognition, [2] . Several factors contribute to the difficulty of recognizing Arabic handwritings, which is, mainly, attributed to the quality of the writing (the poorer the writing, the harder it is to be recognized). This subject is still under research because of its potential array of applications. So many services need to automate human processes for time and accuracy purposes. One application appears in automating the process of reading and recognizing handwritten accounts names and checks amounts in banks. Sorting incoming mails by recognizing the handwritten addresses is another main application required in post-mail offices. One more application can be seen in retrieving the ancient Arabic handwritten manuscripts.

Our recognition system is embedded in the segmentation system that was proposed in [3] as illustrated in Figure 1. After word segmentation, the resulting segments are normalized and a set of twenty features is extracted and fed into an artificial neural network. The recognition outputs range from class 1 to class 46, as clarified in Table 1, where each class represents the location of a single letter in the word or the location of a group of letters that share similar shape characteristics. Some segments may not be recognized because of the poor writing, so they are combined with the following segment and a new set of twenty features is extracted again and passed to the neural network. This process is repeated until the segment is recognized. A set of grouping rules is also applied to specific recognized characters.

The rest of the paper is organized as follows. Section 2 presents related work. Segmentation phase is described in Section 3 while the recognition phase is discussed in Section 4. Section 5 presents the experimental results, followed by the Conclusion and future direction.

2. RELATED WORK

Most of the work on handwriting recognition was done on Latin text. This lack in Arabic handwriting recognition systems is highly related to the difficulty of segmenting words into characters because of the cursive nature of Arabic handwriting. Therefore, Arabic recognition methods can be divided into those which first segment the word to be recognized, and those that recognize the whole word. In this work we are focusing on the segmentation of Arabic text rather than digits' strings such as in [3] [4] .

Earlier surveys discussed both Arabic printed and handwritten texts, [1] [4] - [6] . One of the segmentation based methods for automatic recognition of printed Farsi, Arabic, and Urdu texts was proposed by Parhami and Taraghi in 1981, [7] . In this approach, sub-words were segmented and recognized according to geometrical features such as concavities, loops, and connectivity. No performance results were reported for this algorithm but smaller type fonts may not recognized perfectly.

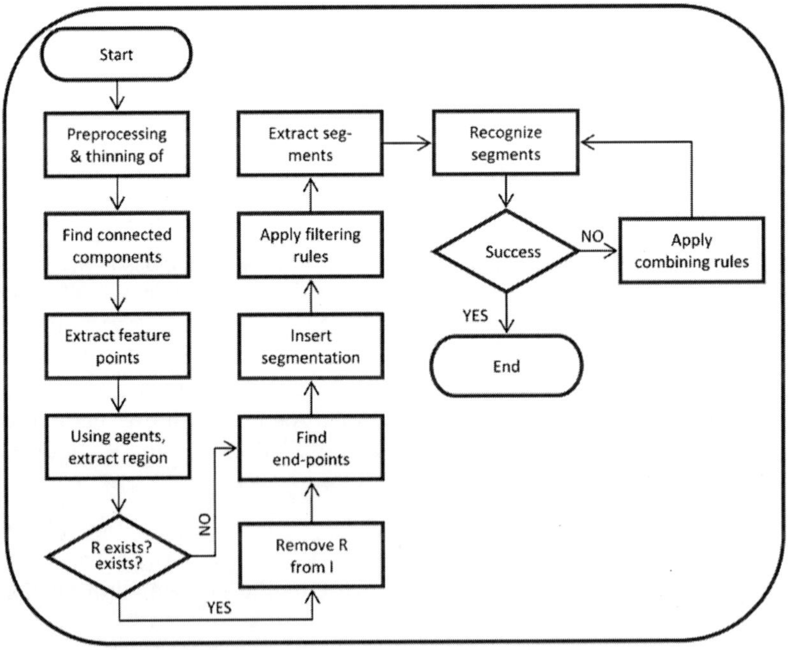

Figure 1. Flow-chart of the major steps of the main system.

Table 1. The output classes of the proposed recognition system.

Letter	Class #	Letter	Class #	Letter	Class #
فـ قـ	31	سـ شـ	17	ـا	1
ف ق	32	س ش	18	أ	2
ـك	33	ـص ـض	19	ـب ـت ـث	3
ك	34	ـصـ ـضـ	20	ـبـ ـتـ ـثـ	4
ـكـ	35	صـ ضـ	21	بـ تـ ثـ	5
ـل	36	ص ض	22	ب ت ث	6
لـ	37	ـط ـظ	23	ج ح خ	7
ـمـ	38	ط ظ	24	ـجـ ـحـ ـخـ	8
ـم	39	عـ غـ	25	جـ حـ خـ	9
مـ	40	ـفـ ـقـ ـعـ ـغـ	26	ج ح خ	10
ـه	41	ـعـ ـغـ	27	ـد ـر ـل	11
م	42	ع غ	28	ل د ر	12
ـن	43	ـف ـق	29	ي	13
ن	44	هـ	30	ـي	14
ـو	45	ـس ـش			15
و	46	ـسـ ـشـ			16

In 1986, Amin and Masini proposed a system for segmentation and recognition that used horizontal and vertical projections and shape-based primitives [8] . On 100 multi-font words, it achieved a character recognition rate of 85% and a word recognition rate of 95%.

Gillies et al. constructed a recognition system for Arabic text, [9] , where words were over-segmented using two different splitting methods, then the resulting segments are ordered and combined in groups and sent to a trained neural network which recognized whole characters from the grouping options. These were passed to a Viterbi search to predict the word. Using a testing set of 138 page images, digitized to 200 × 200, the system achieved a recognition rate of 93%. However, this rate degraded to 89% when the same set was used with a size of 100 × 200.

In 2002, Hamami and Berkani developed a structural approach to handle many fonts and it included rules to prevent over-segmentation [10] .

Hidden Markov Model (HMM) is used also to recognize words by using words features. In 2001, Dehghanet. Al split words into overlapping vertical segments [11] , then, they extracted column features and passed them to HMM.

Al-Qahtani and Khorsheed presented a system based on Hidden Markov Model Toolkit in 2004, [12] [13] . One system did not require the segmentation stage and recognized Arabic scripts using HTK. The second system decomposed the text into line images and divided each line image into smaller overlapped frames. Then it extracted statistical features from each frame and passed them to HTK.

Two segmentation free recognition methods appeared in 1995 by Al-Badr and Haralick. In the first system, [14] , the whole word was recognized by detecting a set of shape primitives which matched to a constrained set of symbol models. The recognition rate was 99.7% for synthetically degraded symbols and 94.1% for scanned symbols. For isolated words, the system achieved 99.4% for noise-free words, 95.6% for synthetically degraded words, and 73% for scanned words. The second system was developed to recognize machine printed Arabic words without prior segmentation. The idea was based on shape primitives that were detected with mathematical morphology operations, [15] . The recognition rate was 99.4% for noise-free texts and 73% for scanned texts.

Khorsheed and Clocksin proposed in 1999 another holistic system where features were extracted from a word's skeleton for recognition without prior segmentation [16] .

In 2000, Amin introduced another holistic approach where global features such as loops and peaks were extracted from the input word [17] , and passed to the C4.5 machine learning system to generate a decision tree for classifying the word. The success rate of the system was 92% using 1000 Arabic words with different fonts.

Another method was presented by Pechwitz and Maergner [18] , where the recognition system was based on a semi-continuous 1-dimensional HMM. From each input word, features were collected using sliding window approach. The recognition results achieved 89%, using the IFN/ENIT database of Arabic handwritten words for testing.

In this work, a recognition-based segmentation method for Arabic handwriting is developed. The method used a multi-agent approach to segment words, [1] , and relied on recognition to verify the validity of the candidate segmentation points. Comparing the previous methods of segmentation approaches and our approach, this segmentation method is not only resolved the shortcomings of the previous related methods but also achieved better results by avoiding under segmentation. This depended on the high performance of the agents and the right decision to select artificial neural network with grouping rules which improved detecting the candidate segmentation points.

3. SEGMENTATION PHASE

Our segmentation system, which we proposed in [3] , was basically based on a multi-agent approach to identify the segmentation points.

Initially, the image of Arabic handwritten text was binarized and cleaned from noise. Then, the text was segmented into lines and each line was segmented into words. The resulting words were thinned and the main connected components in each word were determined and passed to agents that extracted three types of feature points before starting their work.

The identification of initial cutting points strongly depends on seven agents. Six agents are major, which are: loop agent, letter Seen agent, under-baseline-cavities agent, above-baseline-right-cavity agent, above-baseline-left-cavity agent, and above-baseline-narrow-left-cavity agent. The other agent which is the baseline agent is a minor one since it was used by major agents to facilitate their task. First, the agents detected regions that look like some of Arabic characters, these regions were subtracted from the whole word and the remaining parts were left for further processing. Next, all end points features were extracted from the remaining regions and an initial cutting point was inserted between every two successive end points'. Finally, a set of filtering rules was applied to remove the extra segmentation points. The experiments reported very good results where the success rate was 86%.

4. RECOGNITION PHASE

This phase is very important in our segmentation system, [3] . Since segmenting words into characters is a challenging task, especially for Arabic handwritings, a verification tool is needed to measure the segmentation performance. Artificial neural network was selected to decide if the resulting segment is a letter or a stroke and then needs further processing.

Generally, artificial neural networks are very common in pattern recognition field. Our decision to use ANN as a recognition model was based on the excellent features that it possesses compared to other recognition tools. A well-trained neural network can perform complex functions and solve challenging problems that are difficult for conventional computers or human beings since it is based on learning what it sees. In addition, neural networks can be modified easily and retrained when the requirements of the problem are changed. Finally, its integration property allows several recognition tools to work properly and cooperate with neural networks.

This feature may increase the efficiency of the problem solution. The following sections describe the main steps in our approach.

4.1. Features Extraction

In this step, each segment image is converted into numerical features which describe the segment. The feature extraction methods used in character segmentation systems are probably the most important factor in achieving a good segmentation/recognition rate. After segmenting the word, its output segments are normalized into 250 × 250 images. Then, twenty structural features are extracted from them. Fifteen Fourier descriptors are extracted from the segments contour and normalized to remove character variations in shift, size, and rotation, [19] [20] . The other five features include number of loop, number of black points to total number of points" ratio, the existence of connection to the right and left of the segment [21] , and height to width ratio.

A different number of Fourier descriptors are tested and the final set includes 15 descriptors. The selection of these features was based on their ability of describing the general shape of any closed curve such as characters by a set of Fourier coefficients. Suppose that a character consists of a sequence of points (x_i, y_i), where $i = 1, 2, \ldots, N$ and N is the number of points in character's boundary. Each of these points can be represented as a complex number $a(n) = x(n) + iy(n)$. The discrete Fourier transformation u(n) represents the coordinate sequence a(n) as follows:

$$u(n) = \sum_{k=0}^{N-1} a(k) e^{\frac{i2\pi kn}{N}}$$

The first 15 coefficients (descriptors) are selected as our features. This is referred to that the general properties of the character shape are kept in the first (low) coefficients. Because characters varied in size, location and maybe rotation angle, Fourier descriptors can be manipulated to be character rotation, scale, and shift invariant. To make Fourier descriptors rotation and shift invariant, only their absolute values are used, and to make them scale invariant, the coefficient are normalized by dividing them by the first coefficient a(1), [19] .

4.2. Reconstruction and Recognition

Artificial neural networks are computational models which take their inspiration from the models and theories of the human brain. The most popular neural network is the multilayer feed-forward network where neurons are grouped as layers and connections between neurons in consecutive layers are permitted. The inputs are fed from the input layer and outputs are at the output layer.

In this work, after images normalization, a vector of 20 features is extracted from each segment image and classified using a feed forward neural network trained by back-propagation learning algorithm [2] . The structure of this ANN, shown in Figure 2, consists of four layers: one input layer of 20 neurons, two hidden layers of 100 neurons and one output layer of 46 neurons. The neurons in the hidden layers and the output layer are working using tan-sigmoid and linear algorithms, respectively, and the network is trained using traincgf function. The final selection of the ANN's structure and the used algorithms was determined after trying so many other structures and testing several algorithms. The ANNs which are trained using "traincgf" give better results compared to those that use other training algorithms. Moreover, traincgf has smaller storage requirements and faster convergence in some recognition problems.

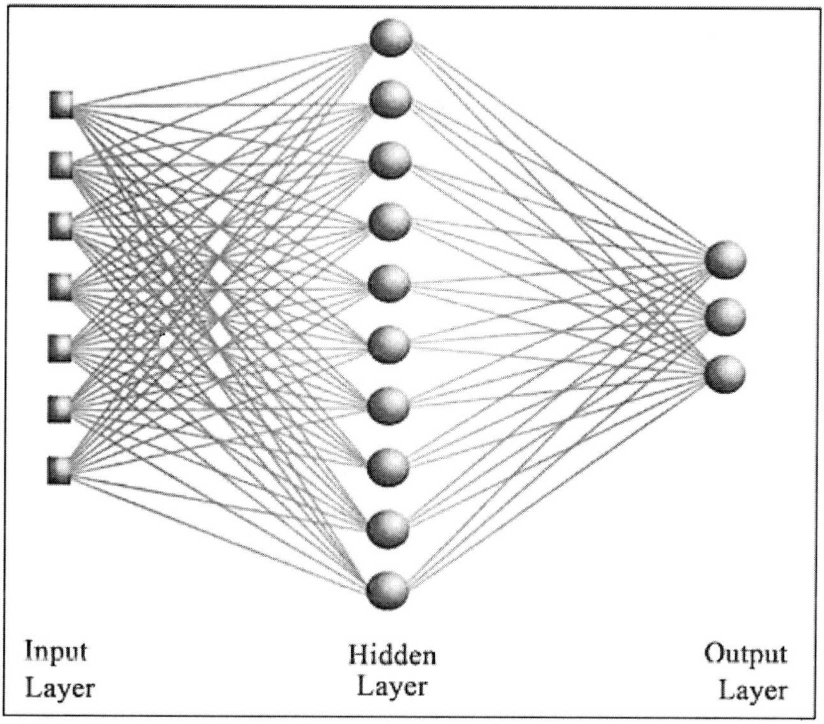

Figure 2. General structure of the ANN in which the hidden layer consists of 2 layers.

The 46 outputs represent the classes that each segment may belong to, and each class includes letters that have similar shape (body) in a specific location in the word; in the beginning of the word, in the middle, in the end, or isolated. The list of output classes appears in Table 1.

The proposed ANN is trained using 2000 characters; more than 40 characters from each class, written by different people. Then, testing was accomplished by selecting examples from each class and passing them to the ANN. A total of 250 characters were used as testing examples. The obtained recognition rate exceeds 87%.

4.3. Restoration and Grouping

This step is required when the word is over-segmented and additional segmentation points were determined. As a result, pseudo characters that passed to the neural network are not correctly recognized. To remedy this situation, the extra segmentation points are removed and the adjacent segments are combined and passed again to the neural network, [22] . This process is repeated until the candidate character is recognized.

A preprocessing step was applied first to remove segmentation points that yield to segments with width less than a threshold. This process eliminates most of the strokes which wrongly found in letters such as "ainـع" and "haaـحـ". The following examples depict this case in Figure 3. As clarified in the figure, the small segment of letter "ع" in the word "الـ شرايـ ع", and of the letter "و" in the word "صحراوي", and of the letter "ء" in the word "الـ رجاء" are eliminated and combined to their related segments to form complete letters.

Because word segmentation is a precise process, a set of rules is used to cooperate with the embedded recognition system in order to keep the correct segments (characters) and combine the wrong ones in a correct way.

The grouping rules are based on the recognition results of segments. As observed in the segmentation stage, a letter is segmented in the worst case into three segments and this happened in letters that belong to the classes: 15, 16, 17, 18, and in some types of the handwritten letters of classes 7, 10, 19, 20, 21, and 22. In addition, characters of classes 2, 3, 6, 11, 12, 13, 23, 24, 29, 32, 43, and 44, shown in Table 1, are segmented into two segments in the most types of handwritings. Figure 4 clarifies these cases of triple (three segments) and double (two segments) segmentation.

The main objective of the cooperation between the recognition model and the grouping rules is to handle the over segmented letters introduced in Figure 4. The following diagram, shown in Figure 5, demonstrates this cooperation strategy.

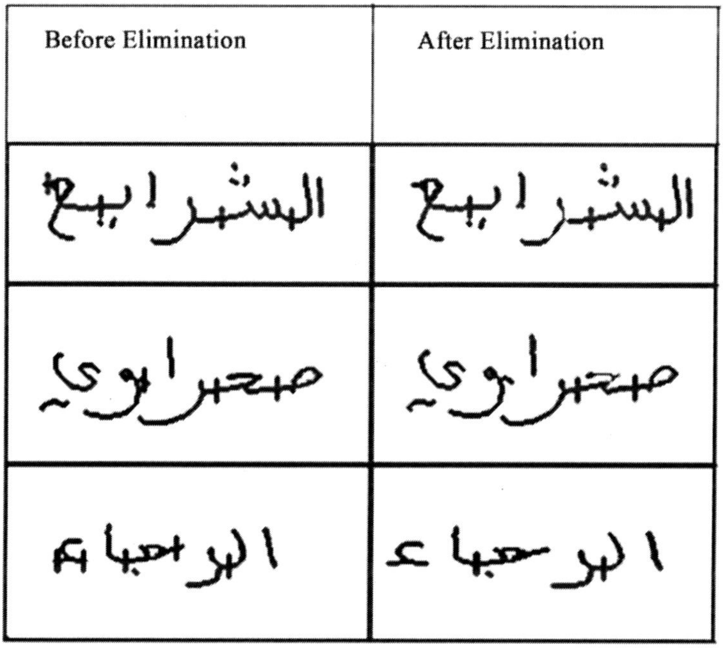

Figure 3. The word before and after extra segmentation points.

Class no.	Double Segmentation	Triple Segmentation
3		
6		
13		
24		
29		
10		
18		
21		
22		

Figure 4. The double and triple segmentation of some characters.

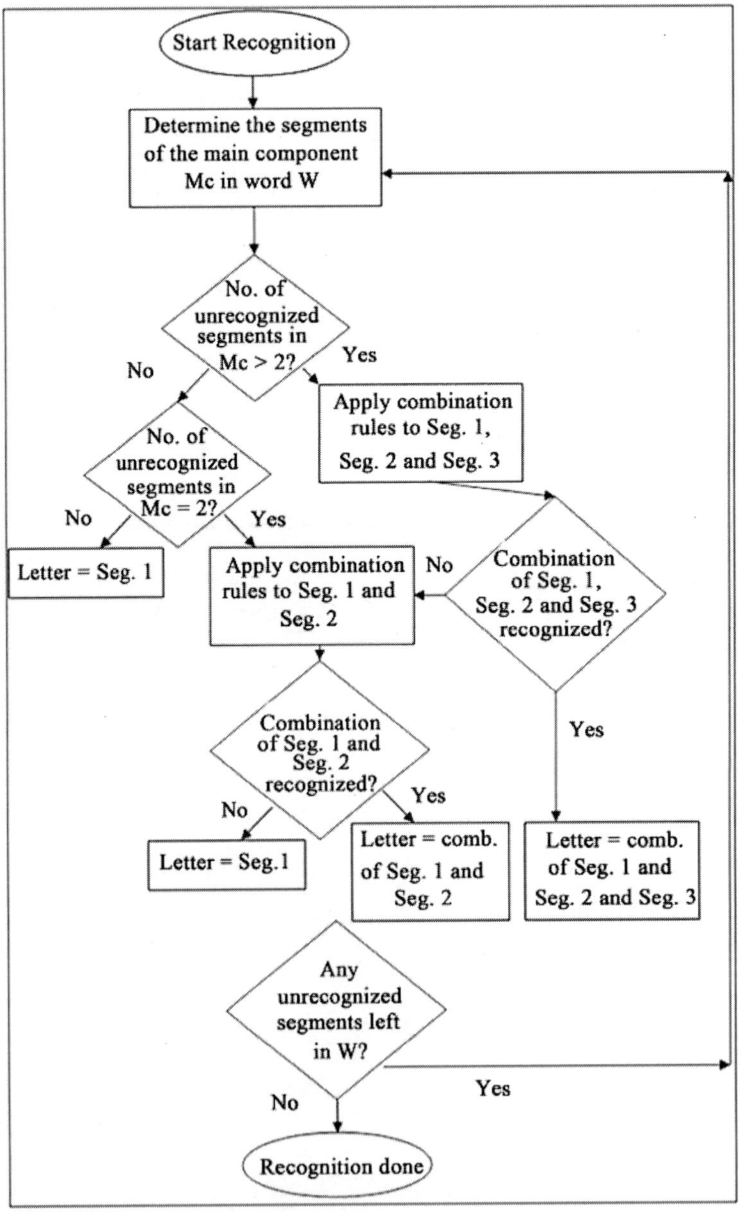

Figure 5. The grouping rules used with the recognition model.

First, the number of resulting segments was determined. Grouping rules were applicable only when the number of segments is equal to or greater than two. Initially, the first two segments or three segments, if any, are passed to the neural network and recognized separately. If the first segment was recognized as a letter which can be a part of any other letter that may over-segmented into three parts, this first segment is combined with the second segment and the third segment and passed again to the neural network. If this grouping was well recognized, then the final character will be the grouping form of the three segments. Otherwise, only the first two segments are combined and passed to the neural network. If the first segment can be a part of any other letter that may over-segmented into two parts, then The final character will be the one with the higher recognition result of the first segment alone and its grouping with the second segment. Finally, this process of grouping and recognition repeated starting from the next unrecognized segment until all resulting segments are recognized as letters or combined into recognized letters. Figure 6 illustrates an over-segmented letter “ث”, where the second segment was classified as class 5 and the grouping form of the two segments was classified as class 6.

Figure 7 also shows a triple-segmented letter “ص”, where the first segment was classified as class 43 and the combined form of the first, second, and the third segments was returned as class 22.

5. EXPERIMENTAL RESULTS

More than 600 of over-segmented words were tested using the proposed recognition system aided by the above grouping rules. The obtained results are very encouraging, as illustrated in Table 2. The percentage of correct segmentation increased from 86% before recognition and grouping rules application to 95% after recognition and grouping. On the other hand, the over-segmentation percentage decreased from 14% to 5% whereas the under-segmentation percentage remained constant.

The majority of the over-segmented characters are combined and recognized correctly. Figure 8depicts segmented words before and after recognition and grouping rules application.

As demonstrated above, both double and triple segmented letters are combined correctly. The letter “ش” which appears in the words “ال شوامخ” and “ب وعطوش” was segmented into three parts and each part is a candidate letter. However, the grouping and recognition processes yield to one strong candidate letter instead of the three parts. A different example of double segmented letters can be observed in letters “ث” and “ي” that belong to words "مارث" and "صحراوي", respectively. Similarly, the combined segments had higher recognition rate, compared to each segment separately. The same case can be observed in the rest of examples.

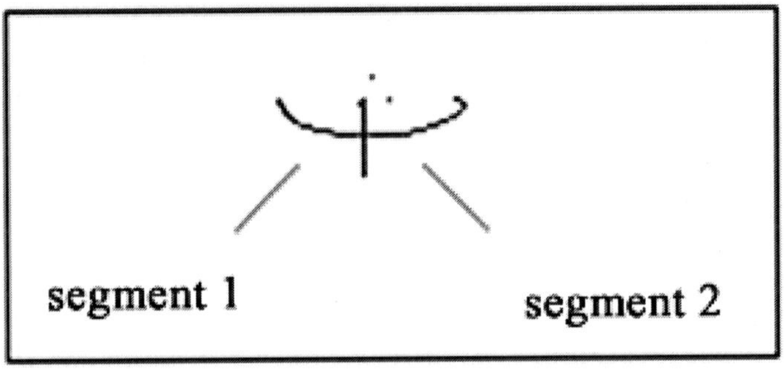

Figure 6. Applied grouping rules to double-segmented letter.

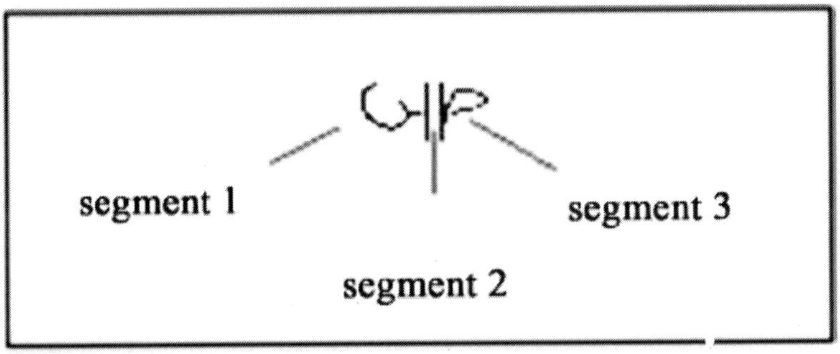

Figure 7. Applied grouping rules to triple-segmented letter.

Table 2. The segmentation results using the selected sample.

	No recognition	After recognition & grouping
% of correct segmentation	86%	95%
% of over segmentation	≈14%	≈5%
% of missing/wrong segmentation	0.3%	0.3%

Figure 8. Over-segmented words before and after applying grouping rules.

Because the grouping rules are strongly based on the recognition result of each segment, those which are misrecognized may not help in handling the over-segmented letters. This case appears in the letters of classes: 3, 6, 29, 32, 43, and 44, where the left segment of the over-segmented letter is wrongly recognized as letter alif "ا", which belongs to class 1. One example is shown in Figure 9, in the letter "ـف" of the word "تـ كريـ ف" and in the letter "ن" in the word "بـ وع ثمان".

The under-segmentation problem may also occur because of letter misrecognition. Adjacent letters that form shapes similar to those of classes 15, 16, 17, 18, 19, 20, 21 and 22 may wrongly be combined although they are correctly classified before grouping. This scenario is very clear in Figure 9, in the word "سـ يدي", where the adjacent letters "يـ" and part of the letter "سـ" were recognized and classified as letter "سـ", and the remaining part of "سـ" was classified as letter "لـ". Similar case was also detected in the words "مدنـ ين" and "حا سـي", with different classification of the combined segments. In the word "جومـ ين", the two letters "يـ" and "مـ" were combined and classified as letter "صـ".

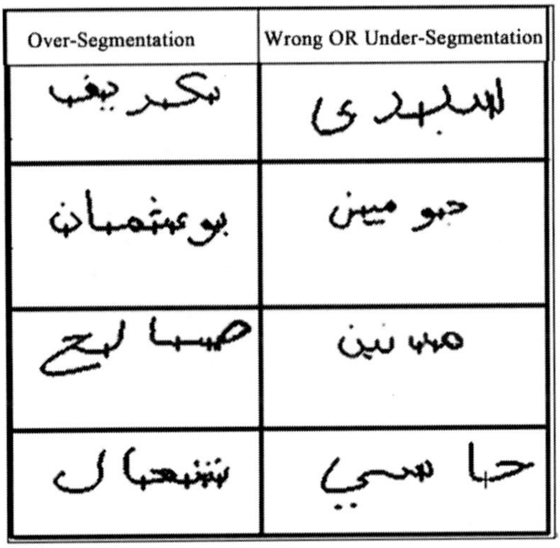

Figure 9. The problems of character misrecognition.

However, these results still fair because the combined segments form a body shape similar to that of an existing alphabetical letter. Moreover, the recognizer is not an interpreter to search for the meaning of the word based on the recognition results of its letters. Therefore, the obtaining outcomes are acceptable since no recent work could solve these situations.

6. CONCLUSION

In this paper, an effective segmentation method for Arabic handwriting was developed. The method used a multi-agent approach to segment words and relied on recognition to verify the validity of the candidate segmentation points. The use of an artificial neural network along with grouping rules lead to a good treatment of the over-segmentation problem in Arabic handwritings. Furthermore, it achieved better results, when compared to similar works, by reducing the effect of under segmentation. This is attributed to the decision agent, which makes the proper decisions to identify the candidate segmentation points. The resulting segments are passed to the recognizer, which will invoke and apply the grouping-rules agent on the unrecognized segments before passing it to the recognizer again. The experimental results (~95%) were very satisfactory and promising. Our future direction will focus on improving this approach and including other styles of Arabic handwritings. On the improvement front, currently we are studying the use of SVM and HMM recent and relevant techniques.

REFERENCES

1. Elnagar, A. and Bentrecia, R. (2012) A Multi-Agent Approach to Arabic Handwritten Text Segmentation. Journal of Intelligent Learning Systems and Applications, 4, 207-215.
2. Cheriet, M., Kharma, N. and Lui, C.-L. and Suen, Y. (2007) Character Recognition Systems: A Guide for Students and Practitioners. John Wiley & Sons, Inc., Hoboken.
3. Elnagar, A. and Alhajj, R. (2003) Segmentation of Connected Handwritten Numeral Strings. Pattern Recognition, 36, 625-634.
4. Vellasques, A.E. Oliveira, L.S., Britto Jr., A.S., Koerich, A.L. and Sabourin, R. (2008) Filtering Segmentation Cuts for Digit String Recognition. Pattern Recognition, 41, 3044-3052.
5. Al-Badr, B. and Mahmoud, S.A. (1995) Survey and Bibliography of Arabic Optical Text Recognition. Signal Processing, 41, 49-77.
6. Amin, A. (1998) Offline Arabic Character Recognition: The State of the Art. Pattern Recognition, 31, 517-530.
7. Eldin, A.S. and Nouh, A.S. (1998) Arabic Character Recognition: A Survey. SPIE Proceedings: Optical Pattern Recognition IX, 3386, 331-340.
8. Khorsheed, M.S. (2002) Off-Line Arabic Character Recognition: A Review. Pattern Analysis and Applications, 5, 31-45.
9. Parhami, B. and Taraghi, M. (1981) Automatic Recognition of Printed Farsi Texts. Pattern Recognition, 14, 395-403.
10. Amin, A. and Masini, G. (1986) Machine Recognition of Multi-Font Printed Arabic Texts. Proc. of the 8th IEEE International Joint Conference on Pattern Recognition, 392-395.
11. Gillies, A., Erlandson, E., Trenkle, J. and Schlosser, S. (1999) Arabic Text Recognition System. Proceedings of the Symposium on Document Image Understanding Technology, Annapolis, 14-16 April 1999, 253-260.

12. Hamami, L. and Berkani, D. (2002) Recognition System for Printed Multi-Font and Multi-Size Arabic Characters. The Arabian Journal for Science and Engineering, 27, 57-72.

13. Dehghan, M., Faez, K., Ahmadi, M. and Shridhar, M. (2001) Handwritten Farsi (Arabic) Word Recognition: A Holistic Approach Using Discrete HMM. Pattern Recognition, 34, 1057-1065.

14. Al-Qahtani, S.A. and Khorsheed, M.S. (2004) An Omni-Font HTK-Based Arabic Recognition System. Proceedings of the 8th IASTED International Conference on Artificial Intelligence and Soft Computing, Marbella, 1-3 September 2004.

15. Al-Qahtani, S.A. and Khorsheed, M.S. (2004) A HTK-Based System to Recognize Arabic Script. Proceedings of the 4th IASTED International Conference on Visualization, Imaging, and Image Processing, Marbella, 6-8 September 2004.

16. Al-Badr, B. and Haralick, R. (1998) A Segmentation-Free Approach to Text Recognition with Application to Arabic Text. International Journal on Document Analysis and Recognition, 1, 147-166.

17. Al-Badr, B. and Haralick, R. (1995) Segmentation-Free Word Recognition with Application to Arabic. Proceedings of the 3rd International Conference on Document Analysis and Recognition, Montreal, 14-16 August 1995, 355-359.

18. Khorsheed, M.S. and Clocksin, W.F. (1999) Structural Features of Cursive Arabic Script. British Machine Vision Conference, Nottingham, 13-16 September 1999, 422-431.

19. Amin, A. (2000) Recognition of Printed Arabic Text Based on Global Features and Decision Tree Learning Techniques. Pattern Recognition, 33, 1309-1323.

20. Pechwitz, M. and Maergner, V. (2003) HMM-Based Approach for Handwritten Arabic Word Recognition Using the IFN/ENIT-Database. Proceedings of the 7th International Conference on Document Analysis and Recognition, ICDAR, Edinburgh, 6 August 2003, 890-894.

21. Gonzalez, R.C. and Wintz, P. (1987) Digital Image Processing. 2nd Edition, Addison-Wesley, Boston.

22. Teuber, J. (1991) Digital Image Processing. Prentice Hall International Series in Acoustics, Speech and Signal Processing, Prentice Hall, Upper Saddle River.

8

CHAPTER

Robust Recognition of Specific Human Behaviors in Crowded Surveillance Video Sequences

Masaki Takahashi, Mahito Fujii, Masahiro Shibata and Shin'ichi Satoh

[1]*Human & Information Science Research Devision, Science and Technology Research Laboratories, Japan Broadcasting Corporation, Tokyo 157-8510, Japan*

[2]*Department of Informatics, The Graduate University for Advanced Studies, Kanagawa 240-0193, Japan*

[3]*Multimedia Information Research Devision, National Institute of Informatics, Tokyo 101-8430, Japan*

ABSTRACT

We describe a method that can detect specific human behaviors even in crowded surveillance video scenes. Our developed system recognizes specific behaviors based on the trajectories created by detecting and tracking people in a video. It detects people using an HOG descriptor and SVM classifier, and it tracks the regions by calculating the two-dimensional color histograms. Our system identifies several specific human behaviors, such as running and meeting, by analyzing the similarities to the reference trajectory of each behavior. Verification techniques such as backward tracking and calculating optical flows contributed to robust recognition. Comparative experiments showed that our system could track people more robustly than a baseline tracking algorithm even in crowded scenes. Our system precisely identified specific behaviors and achieved first place for detecting running people in the TRECVID 2009 Surveillance Event Detection Task.

1. INTRODUCTION

There have been many studies of human motion recognition through video content analysis. This work has gained widespread interest for both academic and industrial purposes [1]. These techniques can be applied to motion-based video searches or to man-machine interfaces that use human gestures, for example.

To achieve these goals, some fundamental technologies have to be established. For recognizing human motions, the capability to detect and track humans in video is essential. A human detector and tracker based on feature points as represented by the Kanade-Lucas-Tomasi Feature Tracker (KLT tracker) has been studied [2, 3]. Moreover, gradient-based features as represented by histograms of oriented gradient (HOG) are currently being used for human detection [4, 5].

In addition, the rapid spread of surveillance cameras has increased demand for cameras that can not only track people but can also automatically identify their specific motions. A number of technologies identify specific motions by detecting a particular image feature value that is unlike the other major features. For example, Shiraki et al. have developed a technology to detect a specific motion from a video sequence using cubic higher-order local auto correlation (CHLAC) image features [6]. However, many of these technologies assume relatively simple videos in which it is relatively easy to detect and track people. A great deal of work has been done analyzing human behavior in simpler datasets (KTH [7], Weizmann [8]) where the motions are performed in controlled situations [9–12]. The features used in these algorithms are corner points, optical flows, and shape. These are not enough available due to the occlusion, different lighting conditions, or varying object sizes. Practical algorithms that can be applied to complicated sequences such as surveillance video from train stations or airports are required [13, 14].

Although some studies have targeted crowded surveillance video sequences, they have been limited to tracking human objects or detecting the overall motion of a great number of people [15–17]. No technology has been established that can robustly detect specific behaviors within crowded sequences in real videos.

We describe a method that can detect specific human behaviors, such as running and meeting, even within crowded sequences. Although tracking all human objects in a crowded scene is a difficult problem, it could be possible to detect specific human behaviors by searching for a certain unique feature value from major normal feature values. The trajectory of a moving person contains rich information about the person's behaviors, such as velocity or travel distance, so we used this trajectory for recognizing human behaviors. No previous technology has recognized human behaviors based on their trajectory in crowded scenes.

For tracking people in complicated sequences, we used a HOG and a support vector machine-(SVM-) based human detection algorithm [18,19] that is known to be relatively robust. In addition, we used a Kalman filter based tracking algorithm that contributes to robust tracking, even with occlusion, by predicting the position of the person.

Our system recognizes specific behaviors by analyzing the similarities to the reference trajectory of each specific behavior in the trajectory feature space. The feature space was generated from ten-dimensional features that were extracted from a trajectory based on principal component analysis (PCA) [20]. Our system can sensitively detect particular behaviors from minimal evidence using the feature space. Though it sometimes incorrectly identifies nontargeted behaviors as the targeted behaviors, most of these so-called false detections are rejected by the verification process. This verification technique is one of the unique features of our system.

We compared our method with a baseline tracking algorithm using two different datasets: the KTH dataset and the TRECVID dataset [21]. The results of these comparative experiments showed that our method more robustly tracked people even in crowded scenes. In addition, the TRECVID 2009 surveillance event detection task showed that our system recognized several specific behaviors precisely and that it was highly effective.

We introduce conventional techniques in Section 2, describe our motion recognition method in Section 3, show results of several experiments in Section 4, and conclude in Section 5.

2. CONVENTIONAL TECHNIQUES

Many researchers have studied human appearance and motion recognition in the field of computer vision [1]. In particular, studies detecting specific motions using surveillance cameras have increased with the number of crimes and instances of terrorism.

Most conventional techniques that recognize particular objects or human motions follow a two-step process: (1) cut out objects or human shapes precisely or calculate low-level image features from a video, (2) apply the cutout objects to detailed shape or motion models prepared beforehand [22–25]. These methods can track people or detect human motions with a low error rate and can precisely recognize even small motions, such as hand waving and jumping, by considering kinematic models or spatio-temporal images. To cut out human shapes, advanced background subtraction methods and contour definition methods have also been developed for precise segmentation of the human shape [26,27].

However, most of this work has assumed simple situations in which large images of people appeared in front of a smooth background as in the KTH dataset [7] and the Weizmann dataset [8], as shown in Figures 1 and 2. Therefore, these techniques are limited to the target video sequences, and it is difficult to apply them to actual video sequences. An autosurveillance system that can detect specific behaviors in practice has not yet been developed.

Figure 1. Samples of KTH dataset.

Figure 2. Samples of Weizmann dataset.

The KTH motion sequences have been frequently used in motion recognition papers. The dataset consists of 2391 low resolution videos (160×120, 25 fps) showing six types of human motions each performed 4 times by 25 persons. The motions are walking, jogging, running, boxing, hand waving, and hand clapping. Only one person appears in each sequence, which is shot by an almost-fixed camera in front of a smooth background, as shown in Figure 1.

The Weizmann dataset is 90 low-resolution video sequences (180×144, 25 fps) showing nine different people, each performing 10 natural motions such as running, walking, skipping, jumping, and hand waving. Though this set contains somewhat more complicated situations such as occlusions, the sequences are controlled, with only one person per sequence, and they were shot by a fixed camera as shown in Figure 2.

In contrast, the TRECVID dataset contains video sequences of real situations. The dataset for the surveillance event detection task was shot in a crowded airport with five different angled surveillance cameras as shown in Figure 3. The video is in PAL format ($720 \times 576, 25$ fps). It consists of 100 hours of video sequences for development and 44 hours of video sequences for evaluation.

Figure 3. Samples of TRECVID dataset.

The TRECVID is a workshop for evaluating information retrieval technologies using a common video corpora. It is organized by the US National Institute of Standards and Technology (NIST) [28]. Once a year, participants, such as research groups from universities and companies, are invited to the evaluation. The participants compete at tasks specified by the TRECVID. The submitted results are evaluated and compared by the TRECVID organizers. The principal tasks are high-level feature extraction, copy detection, and surveillance event detection.

The surveillance event detection is a task to detect sequences of specific human motions. The ten required specific motions are called PersonRuns, CellToEar, ObjectPut, PeopleMeet, PeopleSplitUp, Embrace, Pointing, ElevatorNoEntry, OpposingFlow, and TakePicture. Participants should output detection results for any three events from the required set. NIST annotated the videos with the correct human motion data.

We used complicated videos for detecting specific human behaviors using the TRECVID dataset. We devised a sensitive method for detecting human behaviors by evaluating the trajectory of a person. Though this method also misidentifies many nontargeted behaviors, most of these are then rejected during the verification process. This approach has not been studied in the past.

3. PROPOSED SYSTEM

3.1. Overview

We propose a system that can recognize several human behaviors even in a crowded scene. We mainly focused on human behaviors associated with traveling, such as PersonRuns and PeopleMeet. Figure 4 shows the system configuration. We use the term *human region* to refer to any region in an image that contains one person.

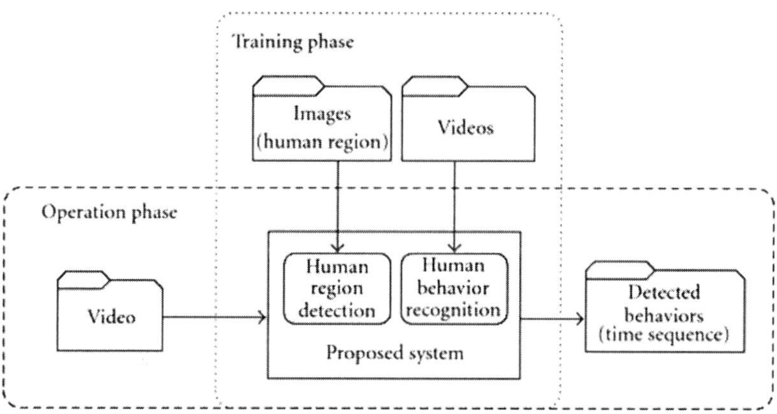

Figure 4. System configuration.

In the training phase, the functions of human region detection and human behavior recognition are created from human region images and video sequences from fixed cameras. We describe human region detection in Section 3.2 and human behavior recognition in Section 3.4. In the operation phase, the system automatically detects specific behaviors from a video sequence shot by the same camera as the training phase. As input, we assume digitized video files that can be played repeatedly. The system outputs a file that has a time sequence of detected specific behaviors. The beginning time and ending time of the specific behaviors are written in the file. Though our system needed to be trained in advance, it could be applied to any surveillance video sequences without any camera calibration.

The method for recognizing specific human behaviors consists of four steps, as shown in Figure 5. Step 1 is human region detection. The system detects the regions that contain a human from the input image using HOG descriptors and an SVM classifier. Step 2 is human region tracking. The system tracks a region by evaluating a two-dimensional color histogram in the region. It robustly tracks human regions using a Kalman Filter. Step 3 is human behavior recognition. The system judges behaviors on the basis of the trajectory of the human region. It recognizes behaviors by analyzing the similarities to a reference trajectory of each specific behavior. Step 4 is human behavior verification. The system verifies the detected human behaviors by analyzing the followed trajectory or optical flows. In the following subsections, we describe the processing of each step in detail.

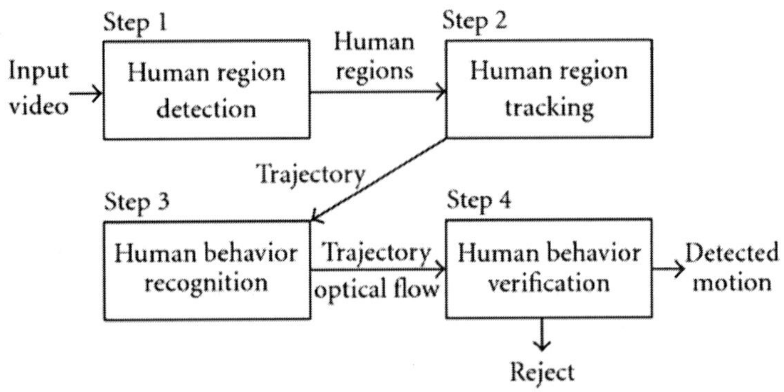

Figure 5. Flow for recognizing specific human behaviors.

3.2. Human Region Detection

3.2.1. Processing Flow

The system follows the flow in Figure 6 to detect human regions. The preprocessing and postprocessing are performed before and after this human detection processing. The preprocessing (changed area detection) contributes to reducing the total processing cost and noise objects by limiting the area searched. The postprocessing (clustering) contributes to stabilizing the human region tracking.

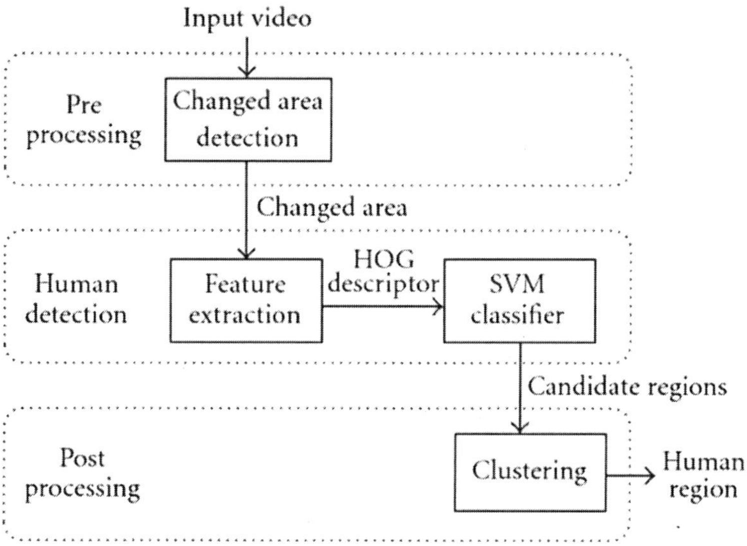

Figure 6. Flow for human region detection.

3.2.2. Changed Area Detection

If the system searched for human regions in all ranges of the input image, the processing cost would be extremely high. In addition, the noise objects interrupt robust detection of human regions. Therefore, it searches for human regions only where there are frame differences or luminance differences from the background. Figure 7 shows a sample of background subtraction. The system can detect even a standing person by referring to the image. Frame differences are used for detecting the changed areas when a background subtraction image cannot be used because of the illumination change.

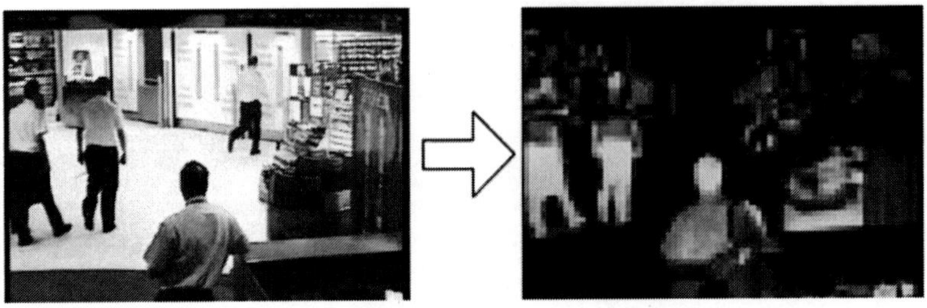

Figure 7. Detection of changed area.

3.2.3. Human Detection Processing

Our human detector searches for human regions by calculating image features around the changed region. We used a human detector that combines the histograms of oriented gradient (HOG) feature descriptors and a support vector machine (SVM).

HOG descriptors are used for object detection. Many studies have reported that the HOG is suitable for detecting human regions because it is robust to a wide range of variations of poses [4, 5]. The technique counts occurrences of gradient orientation in localized portions of an image. It computes on a dense grid of uniformly spaced cells and uses overlapping local contrast normalization for improved performance.

We normalized all target regions at 25×50 pixels. The HOG descriptor is calculated by shifting a block by one cell. We defined a cell as 5×5 pixels and a block as 3×3 cells, so 81 (9 directions × 9 cells) dimensional histograms of gradient directions are obtained in a block. The cells and blocks concept is shown in Figure 8. The normalization is performed for 24 blocks (3 horizontal × 8 vertical blocks) so that a 1,944-dimensional descriptor (24 blocks × 81 dimensions) is obtained for each target region.

The human detector (SVM classifier) uses the HOG descriptor to determine whether a target region contains a person. We trained the classifier with about 1,000 HOG descriptors in human regions (positive data) and about 2,000 HOG descriptors in other regions (negative data) for every camera of the TRECVID dataset. All sample data were extracted manually from the development datasets. The detected regions were treated as candidate human regions. A scheme for detecting candidate human regions is shown in Figure 9.

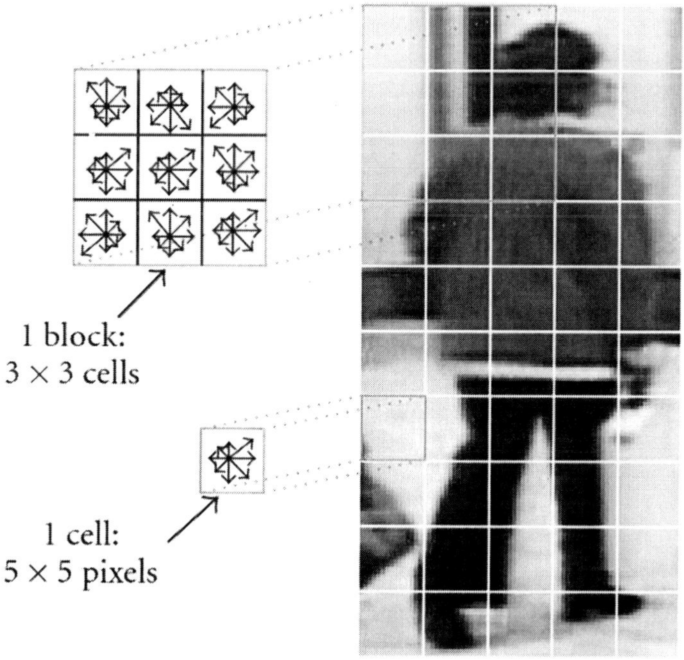

Figure 8. Cells and blocks.

3.2.4. Clustering Human Regions

More than one candidate human region is usually detected around one person. The system should detect one human region for each person in order to track robustly and recognize human behaviors accurately. Therefore, the system clusters the candidate human regions and determines a representative human region for one person from each of the candidate human regions in each cluster. This function stabilizes the tracking of human regions.

The similarity of candidate human regions is evaluated by calculating two distances: (1) the simple Euclidean distance between the centers of gravity of two human regions and (2) the Bhattacharyya distance between two color histograms of candidate human regions [29]. First, the system calculates a simple distance d by (1). (x_1, y_1) and (x_2, y_2) represent the centers of gravity of two human regions in (1). After that, the distance of the color histogram is calculated only for nearby candidate human regions

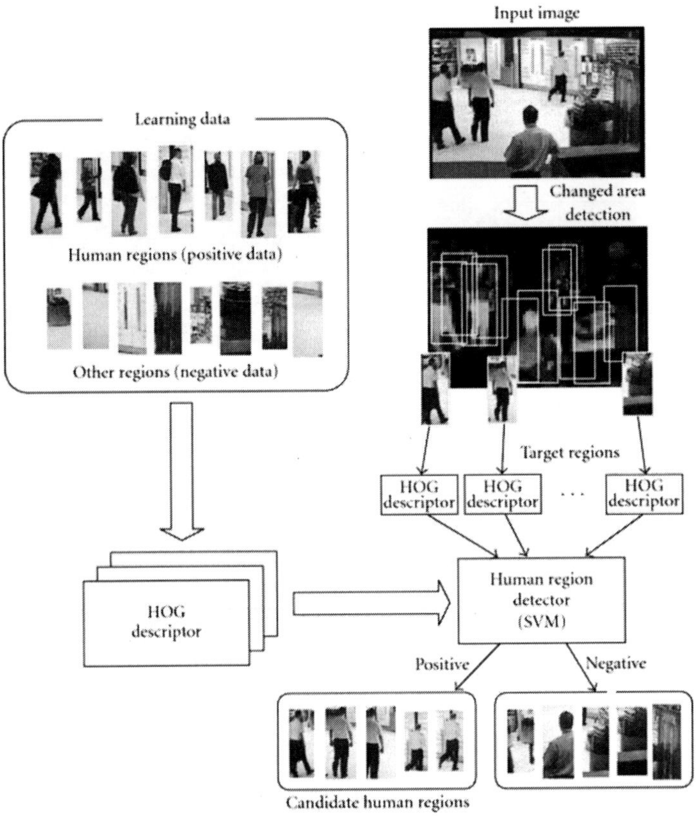

Figure 9. Detecting candidate human regions.

$$d = \sqrt{(x_1 - x_2)^2 + (y_1 - y_2)^2}. \tag{1}$$

We used HSV color space for creating color histograms. HSV stands for hue, saturation, and value. The hue and saturation are intimately related to the way human eye perceives color, so they are suitable as components of the histogram. The value is the brightness of the color. A histogram that is influenced by luminance should not be used because it changes depending on the positions of people. We used two-dimensional (2D) color histograms of HSV color space (H, S). The sum of a histogram is normalized to deal with the difference of the size of target regions.

Figure 10 shows samples of visualized 2D color histograms corresponding to the left target region. The horizontal axis shows hue, and the vertical axis shows saturation. The figure indicates that 2D color histograms differ according to colors in a target region.

Figure 10 Target regions and 2D color histograms.

The similarity of the 2D color histograms is calculated by Bhattacharyya distance, which is normally used to measure the separability of classes in classification. The distance is calculated from a Bhattacharyya coefficient that shows the similarity of two normalized histograms (3). The coefficient is calculated by (2) from normalized color histograms p and q. The ρ, m, and D_B denote the Bhattacharyya coefficient, the number of color components, and the Bhattacharyya distance

$$\rho = \sum_{x=0}^{m} \sqrt{p(x)q(x)}, \tag{2}$$

$$D_B = \sqrt{1 - \rho}. \tag{3}$$

A candidate human region located in the center of its cluster is selected as the representative human region of the cluster.

3.3. Human Region Tracking

3.3.1. Processing Flow

A human region is tracked following the flow of Figure 11. The system tracks human regions by searching for a similar human region in previous image frames. The similarity is evaluated by a simple Euclidean distance and a Bhattacharyya distance of 2D color histograms in the same way as the clustering process in human region detection.

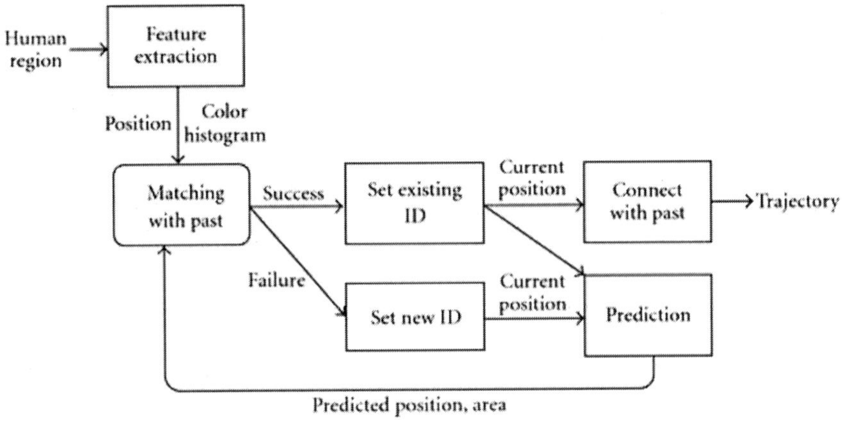

Figure 11. Flow for human region tracking.

If a similar human region is detected, the same ID as the past frame is set to the current human region. Otherwise, a new ID number is set. By connecting the center positions of the same ID region from past frames to the current frame, we can obtain the trajectory of the human region. Figure 12 shows sample trajectories of human regions.

It is difficult for a motion vector-based tracker to track all human regions in a crowded area because large numbers of the same motion vectors are detected. In our system, each human region can be tracked relatively robustly, even in a crowded scene, because of the 2D color histograms.

3.3.2. Prediction Processing

That approach, however, does not necessarily give the position of the human region in every frame. Detections can fail when an occlusion occurs in a crowded scene. Therefore, we supplemented the system with a prediction-based retrack function. The prediction continues even after a

Figure 12. Samples of human region trajectories.

detection failure, so it is possible to pick up the human region again after it passes through an area where extraction is difficult.

A Kalman filter [30, 31], which assumes uniform straight-line motion, is used for prediction. It estimates the state of a linear dynamic system from a sequence of measurements that contain noise. It predicts the vectors $\mathbf{X}$, $\mathbf{Y}$, and $\mathbf{P}$ for each frame using

$$\mathbf{X}_t = \mathbf{F}\mathbf{X}_{t-1} + \mathbf{v}_t,$$
$$\mathbf{Y}_t = \mathbf{H}\mathbf{X}_t + \mathbf{w}_t,$$
$$\mathbf{P}_t = \mathbf{F}\mathbf{P}_{t-1}\mathbf{F}^T + \mathbf{Q}_t. \quad (4)$$

Here t is a frame number, and matrix $\mathbf{F}^T$ expresses the transposition of matrix $\mathbf{F}$. $\mathbf{X} = [x, y, x', y']^T$ is the state estimation vector that consists of the position coordinates and speed, and $\mathbf{P}$ is the covariance matrix of the prediction error. $\mathbf{F}$ is the state propagator matrix whose elements express uniform straight-line motion for the linear prediction. $\mathbf{v}$ is a covariance matrix of the process noise $(p(\mathbf{v}) \sim N(0, \mathbf{Q}))$, and $\mathbf{w}$ is a covariance matrix of the observation noise $(p(\mathbf{w}) \sim N(0, \mathbf{R}))$.

Furthermore, if the system extracts a region, the process updates $\mathbf{X}$, $\mathbf{P}$, and the Kalman gain $\mathbf{K}$ using

$$\mathbf{X}' = \mathbf{X} + \mathbf{K}(\mathbf{Y} - \mathbf{H}\mathbf{X}),$$
$$\mathbf{P}' = (\mathbf{I} - \mathbf{K}\mathbf{H})\mathbf{P},$$
$$\mathbf{K} = \mathbf{P}\mathbf{H}^T(\mathbf{H}\mathbf{P}\mathbf{H}^T + \mathbf{R})^{-1}. \tag{5}$$

where $\mathbf{Y} = [p_x, p_y]^T$ is the measurement state (detected position coordinates), and $\mathbf{X}'$ and $\mathbf{P}'$ are updated values of $\mathbf{X}$ and $\mathbf{P}$. $\mathbf{H}$ is a matrix that converts a state vector into a measurement vector. $\mathbf{R}$ is the covariance matrix of the measurement error. When the tracking goes wrong, the diagonal elements of $\mathbf{P}$ become large values, and when it succeeds, the elements become small. Therefore, the process controls the size of the image area searched for people on the basis of the values of $\mathbf{P}$.

There usually exist many missing trajectories due to occlusion in crowded scenes. When a trajectory disappears, the system estimates the speed and moving direction of the missing person and predicts the future position of the person by calculating $\mathbf{X}$ frame by frame. The system matches the 2D color histogram information of the missing human region with any new human regions around the predicted position. If a match succeeds, the system connects the new detected position with the missed trajectory. This prediction processing contributes to robust tracking of human regions. Figure 13 shows a sample of retracking. Though two people crossed and an occlusion occurred at the center of the image, both people were extracted again and retracked after they separated.

3.4. Human Behavior Recognition

3.4.1. Normalization of the Length of Motion Vector

A trajectory of detected human regions contains rich information about human behavior, such as moving speed and travel distance. Our system recognizes specific human behaviors from their trajectories. However, the length of the motion vector differs depending on the detected position in the image coordinates. For example, the motion vectors of people who are detected at positions near the camera are large, and the motion vectors of people who are detected at a distance are small. To address this, we devised an average velocity map to normalize the motion vectors.

Figure 13. Retracking after occlusion.

The average velocity map is created by calculating the average velocities of the small blocks in the image coordinates using (6). Motion vectors (v_x, v_y) at the center of gravity of a person about 170 cm tall were gathered automatically and the average velocity V_{ij} in each block was calculated. The variable n is the number of motion vectors gathered in block i,j. The concept of generating an average velocity map is shown in Figure 14. The lengths of motion vectors are accumulated in blocks, filled in dark in the figure. The average velocity for each block is calculated by averaging the length of all accumulated motion vectors during a certain period of time

$$V_{ij} = \frac{1}{n} \sum_{p=1}^{n} \sqrt{v_{x_p}^2 + v_{y_p}^2} \,. \tag{6}$$

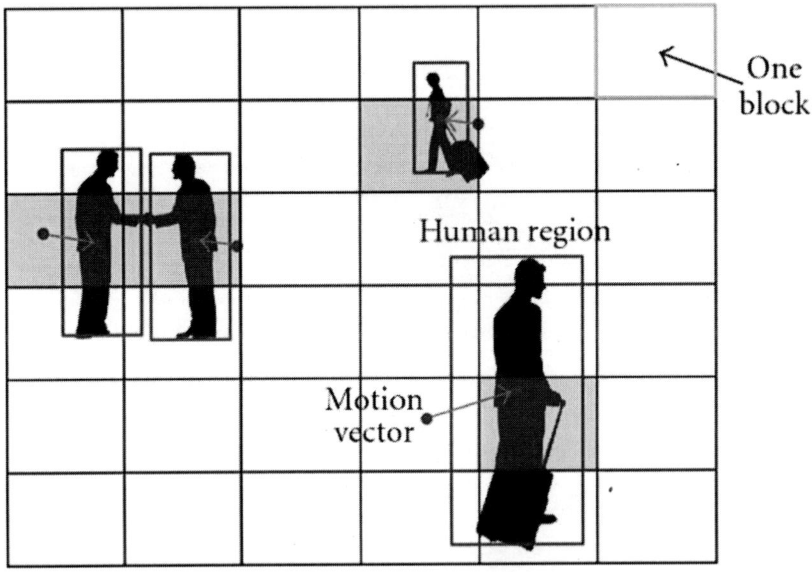

Figure 14. Concept of calculating an average velocity map.

We created average velocity maps from four hours of video sequences for each camera of the TRECVID dataset. A sample of an average velocity map is shown in Figure 15. In the figure, each number indicates the average velocity in the block. The values of the average velocities at the bottom are large because the motion vectors in the blocks were large. The values become smaller toward the top. The system found no human regions in any of the top row blocks, so the average velocities in these blocks are zero.

By referring to this average velocity map, the system can normalize an input motion vector, so it can treat all trajectories equally regardless of their detected position in the image. This technique does not need any calibration or positional information of the camera, so it can be applied to every video sequence shot by a fixed camera.

The system can normalize the motion vectors more accurately when the blocks are set to be small. However, the suitable block size depends on the resolution of the video, the distance from the camera to people, and the number of motion vectors used for training. If the resolution was low, the camera was near people, and the training sample vectors were poor, block size should be large, because the average velocity might be influenced by unusual motion vectors.

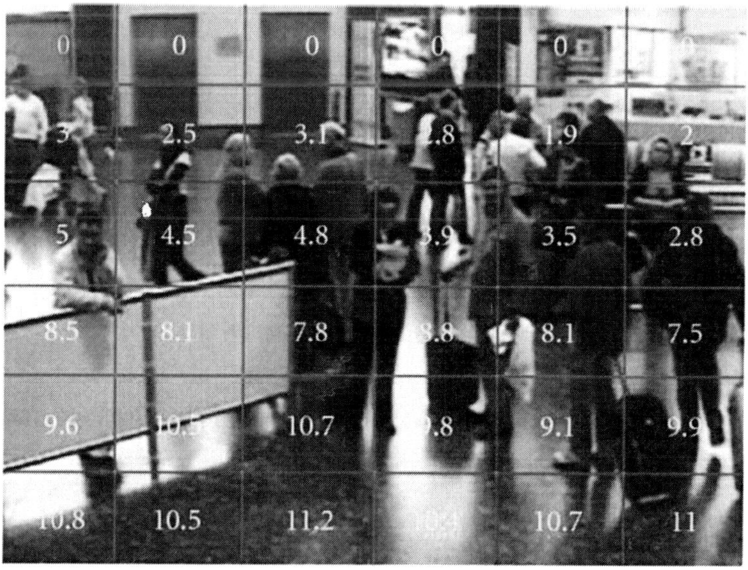

Figure 15. Sample of average velocity map.

3.4.2. Feature Extraction from a Trajectory

We extracted the following ten-dimensional features from a trajectory.

1. *(i)* first detected position (x, y),

2. *(ii)* last detected position (x, y),

3. *(iii)* total vector (x, y),

4. *(iv)* travel distance,

5. *(v)* average velocity,

6. *(vi)*acceleration,

7. *(vii)*linearity.

The total vector is calculated by accumulation of the motion vectors of each frame in a trajectory. The feature indicates the direction of the trajectory. The system calculates the vector horizontally (x) and vertically (y). The travel distance means the distance from the first detected position to the last detected position. The distance is normalized in the same way as the motion vectors. The average velocity is the average length of motion vectors in a trajectory. The acceleration is a shift in velocity. We can calculate this feature by differentiating velocities. The system can detect a person who stopped or started suddenly with this feature. The linearity is the average distance from each detected position to a regression line. If a person has moved straight ahead, the linearity is close to zero.

If the system extracts these features from the full length of a trajectory, the features fade away by averaging them. Therefore, we divided the trajectories of an ID by every one second. Figure 16 shows the relations between a detected human trajectory and its features.

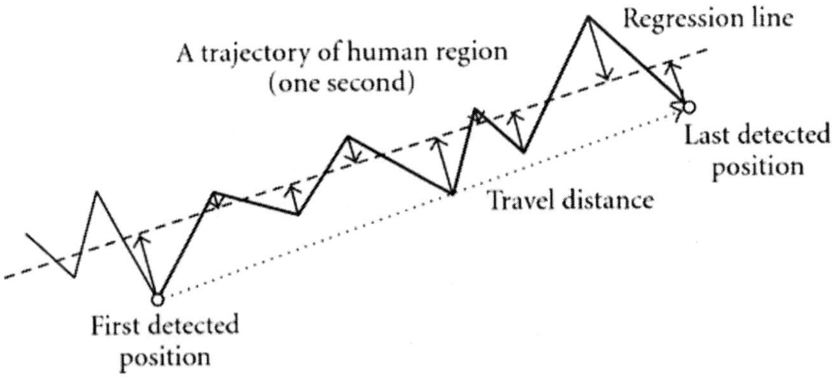

Figure 16. Features of a trajectory.

Generally, it is difficult to precisely estimate the moving speed and direction. However, the system can calculate these features as suitable for recognizing the specific behaviors from a human region trajectory that has been normalized with the average velocity map.

3.4.3. Detecting Behaviors from the Trajectory Feature Space

To cluster trajectories, we projected each trajectory onto a trajectory feature space that was generated using principal component analysis (PCA) [20]. We calculated eigenvalues and eigen vectors from the ten-dimensional features of each trajectory. We narrowed down the dimensions from ten to five. The first principal component was strongly influenced by the average velocity and the travel distance, the second one was influenced by the vertical position and the total vector, and the third one was influenced by the horizontal position, the total vector, and the acceleration.

Figure 17 shows a scatter diagram of trajectories in the trajectory feature space of the axis of primary components one to three. Each point denotes one trajectory in the video sequences for training. Almost all of the normal trajectories gathered at the original point in the feature space and specific trajectories tended to be plotted far from the original point.

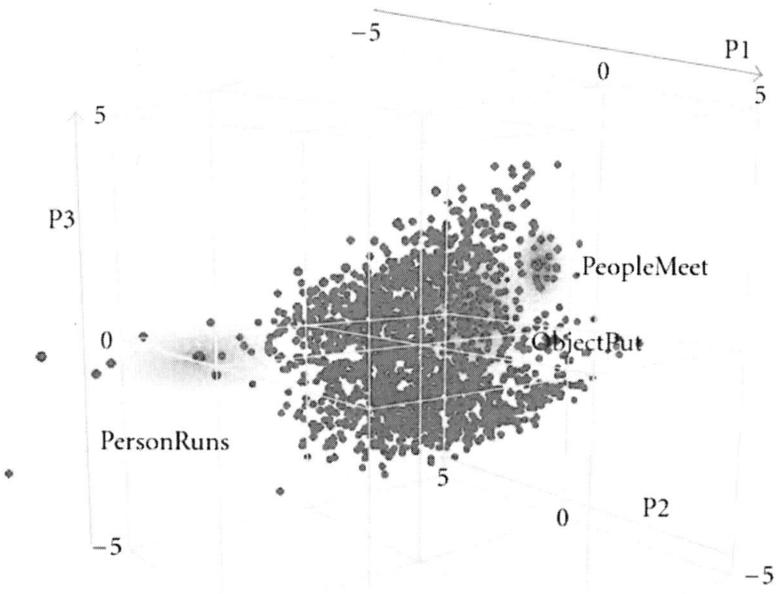

Figure 17. Scatter diagram of the trajectory feature space.

In addition, trajectories of the same behaviors tended to be plotted near each other. So, we created classes called PersonRuns, PeopleMeet, and ObjectPut by calculating their average positions $\boldsymbol{\mu}$ and standard deviations $\boldsymbol{\sigma}$ in the feature space. Ellipses denote classes of specific behaviors, and their radii denote standard deviations. A large bias is seen at the trajectories of the specific behavior PersonRuns. This showed that the PersonRuns behavior could be reliably detected from this feature space. On the contrary, the ObjectPut class was positioned near the original point and its variance was large. This showed that it is difficult to detect the ObjectPut behavior from only features of a trajectory.

The system detects specific behaviors by calculating the Mahalanobis distance from the position of an input trajectory $\mathbf{x}$ to each behavior class [32]. The Mahalanobis distance $D_M(\mathbf{x})$ is calculated with the following:

$$D_M(\mathbf{x}) = \sqrt{(\mathbf{x} - \boldsymbol{\mu})^T \Sigma^{-1} (\mathbf{x} - \boldsymbol{\mu})}, \qquad (7)$$

where $\boldsymbol{\mu}$ is an average position of a behavior class in the trajectory feature space. Σ is a covariance matrix of each class.

The system sets decision scores according to the closeness for each behavior class. If a decision score exceeds the particular threshold for the motion, the system recognizes that the specific behavior might occur in the ID that contains the trajectory. The threshold is experimentally decided for each camera during the learning process. However, the system does not identify the behavior immediately. It verifies whether the behavior truly occurred by a verification process that we describe in the next section.

3.5. Human Behavior Verification

3.5.1. Verification of Fast Motion by Backward Tracking

People move in various ways in the surveillance video sequences. The movements can be roughly classified into three types: (1) fast motions that have large motion vectors such as PersonRuns, (2) big motions associated with traveling such as PeopleMeet and PeopleSplitUp, and (3) small motions not associated with traveling such as ObjectPut, TakePicture, and CellToEar. Our proposed system uses several methods to verify behavior depending on the motion type.

The system sometimes makes a mistracking, especially when the motion is fast, because of the large motion vectors. In addition, false detections for

PersonRuns frequently occurred when the system misextracted a distant region because the motion vectors also tended to be large at greater distances. Thus, the system verifies the trajectory by searching backward after the PersonRuns behavior is identified in forward tracking. Tracking results between forward tracking and backward tracking are different in a crowded scene because the predicted positions of persons in each frame are different for forward and backward tracking, so the system tends to extract different regions.

Figure 18 shows a timeline of backward tracking. Once a PersonRuns event is detected in forward tracking (t_{f1}), the system starts backward tracking from the frame when the forward tracking finished (t_{f2}). The system tracks the person in the same way as in forward tracking. If the PersonRuns behavior is detected in backward tracking as well, the system identifies a PersonRuns event (t_{b1}). If the behavior could not be detected over the time when forward tracking was started (t_{f0}), it rejects the event by decreasing the decision score (t_{b2}). After that, the system restarts the processing from the time the tracking finished in forward tracking (t_{f2}).

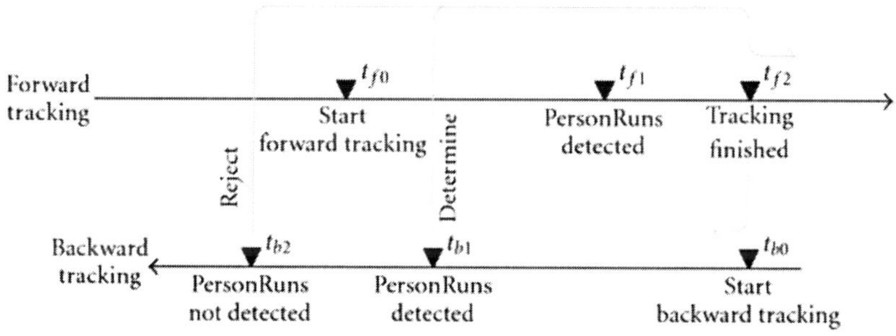

Figure 18. Timeline of backward tracking.

Figure 19 shows sample images of the backward tracking. A PersonRuns event was detected by both forward and backward tracking. This technique reduces the number of false detections.

Figure 19. Sample backward tracking trajectory (right).

3.5.2. Verification of Big Motion by Following Trajectories

Continuing to follow a trajectory after a behavior is detected can be used to verify big motions, such as PeopleMeet and PeopleSplitUp. Our system does not stop tracking a person even after detecting a big motion with the human behavior recognition process. If a followed trajectory does not match one or more of the criteria decided experimentally in the training phase, our system rejects the occurrence of the behavior by decreasing the decision score. For example, if a trajectory with a travel distance greater than T_d was extracted just after detecting a PeopleMeet event as (8), our system rejects the behavior because most people do not walk far away immediately after meeting someone. T_d is the threshold decided in the training phase, (x_p, y_p) is the position of the detected PeopleMeet event, and (x_c, y_c) is the current position of the person in (8). This technique contributes to reducing false detections in the same way as backward tracking

$$\sqrt{\left(x_c - x_p\right)^2 + \left(y_c - y_p\right)^2} > T_d. \tag{8}$$

3.5.3. Verification of Small Motion by Optical Flows

It is difficult to detect small motions from only a trajectory, because a trajectory contains little information about small motions. Thus, it is hard to distinguish the trajectory from other normal trajectories in the trajectory feature space. Therefore, the system also uses optical flows [33] in the human region as a local feature for detecting small motions.

We tried to detect the ObjectPut behavior using optical flow. After a person stops moving (the motion can be detected from a trajectory), the system calculates optical flows within the detected human region. If the average of the vertical flows v_y was large and more downward than a threshold T_p that we set experimentally as (9), the system detected the ObjectPut behavior. The variable *n* in (9) denotes the number of optical flows in the human region. Figure 20 shows a sample of the optical flows in an ObjectPut scene. Though we can also apply this method to other small motions, particular criteria have to be set for each behavior

$$\frac{1}{n}\sum_{i=1}^{n} v_{y_i} < T_p. \tag{9}$$

Figure 20. Optical flow in ObjectPut sequence.

4. EXPERIMENTS

4.1. Comparison of Tracking Accuracy

We compared the tracking accuracy of our system with a baseline method that was created based on the KLT tracker. The KLT tracker is an algorithm that selects and keeps track of feature points that are optimal for tracking. It is widely used in visual feature tracking and the method can be used with the OpenCV video library [34]. The KLT tracker detects motion vectors around moving objects; motion vectors that have the same length and direction tend to be detected around one person. Thus, the baseline method uses motion vectors to cluster human regions.

We used two different datasets for the experiment; the KTH dataset and the TRECVID event detection dataset. The KTH motion sequences have been used in many motion recognition studies. The dataset contains sequences of a person walking in front of a smooth background, and only one person appears in each sequence. We used 100 sequences of walking people for the experiment. The TRECVID event detection dataset is a series of video sequences from five surveillance cameras set at different angles in an airport. A large number of people appear in each sequence and many occlusions occur. We used 14 sequences of the TRECVID dataset in which 120 people appeared.

Table 1 lists the tracking accuracy results of the two methods using the two different datasets. The success rate S was calculated by

$$S = \frac{N_{\text{success}}}{N_{\text{detect}}}. \tag{10}$$

Table 1. Success rate of two methods with different datasets.

	KTH	TRECVID
Baseline method	84.03%	33.9%
Proposed method	86.21%	47.62%

N_{success} is the number of trajectories that were successfully tracked, and N_{detect} is the total number of trajectories that the system detected. People in both datasets appeared for 3–5 seconds on average. Thus, we considered it a success when the system tracked a person correctly for more than 75 frames (3 seconds).

The baseline method was slightly worse than the proposed method for the KTH dataset. This is because the KTH dataset was not shot by completely fixed cameras, so motion vectors appeared even in the background as well as around people. However, both success rates of the two methods in the KTH dataset were quite high, indicating that both methods are accurate enough to track human regions in simple video sequences. Figure 21 shows samples of tracking results with the baseline method using the KTH dataset.

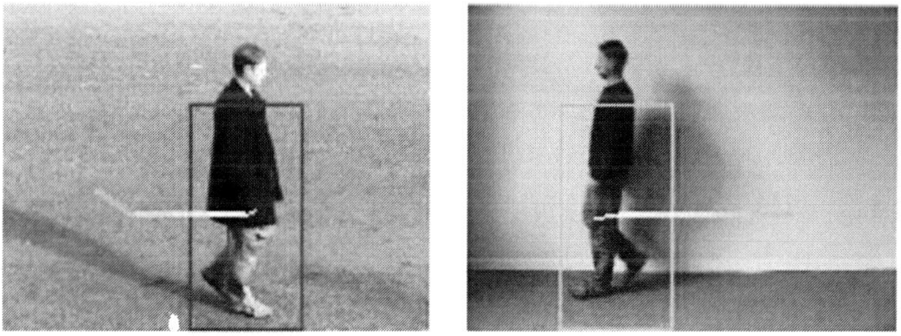

Figure 21. Tracking samples of baseline method using KTH dataset.

We can see the differences in the two methods in the results of the TRECVID dataset. Our method was 13.72% better than the baseline method. This indicates that our method can track human regions relatively robustly even in crowded scenes.

Both methods were sensitive to detect human regions so there were few false negative errors. Thus, the overwhelming majority of errors were false positive. To clarify the factors of the false positive error, we conducted another experiment using the TRECVID dataset. We defined two types of errors.

1. *Mistracking*: tracking a human region for less than 75 frames (includes tracks jumping from one person to another).
2. *False alarm*: tracking a noise region that does not contain a human for more than 75 frames.

Table 2 shows that mistracking occurred more frequently than false alarm. The baseline method tracks human regions based on motion vectors. It identifies objects based on the lengths and the directions of the motion vectors. Because many people walk in the same direction at approximately the same speed in a crowded scene, the tracking method tended to mistrack people because of the difficulty of distinguishing between adjacent or overlapping human regions. To overcome this, our method clusters human regions considering color histograms so that it can track human regions relatively robustly even in crowded scenes. In addition, our prediction process helped prevent a tracking region from shifting from one person to another. Consequently, our system had 10.21% fewer tracking errors than the baseline method.

Table 2. Comparison of two methods.

	Error		Processing speed
	Mistracking	False alarm	
Baseline method	48.31%	17.80%	219 msec/frame
Proposed method	38.10%	14.29%	429 msec/frame

The baseline method also had many false alarms. The method was very sensitive not only to human regions but also to other objects, such as shadows or baggage, because it does not distinguish people from other objects. On the other hand, our classifier can identify whether a region contains people or not because it was trained using supervised machine learning on examples of regions containing people (positive) and examples of regions not containing people (negative). This is one reason that our error rate of false alarm was 3.51% better than the baseline method.

At the same time, the processing time of our methoa could be a disadvantage. Table 2 shows that the proposed method takes about twice as long as the baseline method. The data is calculated by averaging the processing time for about 2 hours in the TRECVID dataset. Although the proposed method is slower due to the complexity of the processing, the performance improvement outweighs the disadvantage.

In addition, the baseline method is easier to apply to a new video sequence than our method because it does not need to learn human regions. The proposed method needs much prior knowledge such as background information and an average velocity map. However, most of the data is calculated automatically in the training phase, so the proposed system does not require much preparation.

4.2. Effectiveness of Verification Process

Our system has fewer false detections of specific behaviors than other systems because the verification process reduces this type of error. To confirm this fact, we conducted an experiment. Table 3 lists the number of false detections with and without the verification process for three behaviors. The false detections were extracted from about 16 hours of video sequences in the TRECVID dataset. The table also lists the reduction rate with the verification process.

Table 3. Occurrence of false detections.

	The number of false detections without verification process	The number of false detections with verification process	Reduction rate (%)
PersonRuns	1572	440	72.01
PeopleMeet	2198	1124	48.86
ObjectPut	37275	754	97.98

The verification process for the PersonRuns behavior reduced false detections to less than one third, from 1572 to 440. This indicates that backward tracking avoided two of three false detections. The process was effective for the PeopleMeet behavior as well. The false detections were reduced from 2198 to 1124.

These results show the effectiveness of the verification process. Even though the process restricts our system to not being able to be applied in real time, the accuracy rather than the processing speed should be emphasized.

Though false detections were reduced to only about 2% of the first decision for the ObjectPut behavior, the detecting accuracy of the behavior was low. We should also search for effective features for identifying small motions.

4.3. Recognition Accuracy of Specific Behaviors

We evaluated the recognition accuracy of our system for specific human behaviors in the TRECVID 2009 surveillance event detection task. We trained our detecting, tracking, and recognition algorithm using 100 hours of a development dataset. NIST evaluated our algorithm from submission data that was made using 44 hours of evaluation dataset.

We tried to detect three specific behaviors: PersonRuns, PeopleMeet, and ObjectPut using fast motion, big motion, and small motion. Table 4shows the results. Detection cost rate (DCR) was used to evaluate the system performance. It was calculated using missed detection probability P_{Miss} and false alarm rate R_{FA} as shown in (11). The $Cost_{Miss}$, the $Cost_{FA}$, and the R_{Target} are constants with values set by NIST

$$\mathrm{DCR}(\theta) = P_{\mathrm{Miss}}(\theta) + \beta * R_{\mathrm{FA}}(\theta),$$

$$P_{\mathrm{Miss}}(\theta) = \frac{N_{\mathrm{Miss}}(\theta)}{N_{\mathrm{Targ}}}, \qquad R_{\mathrm{FA}}(\theta) = \frac{N_{\mathrm{FA}}(\theta)}{T_{\mathrm{Source}}},$$

$$\beta = \frac{\mathrm{Cost}_{\mathrm{FA}}}{\mathrm{Cost}_{\mathrm{Miss}} * R_{\mathrm{Target}}},$$

$$\mathrm{Cost}_{\mathrm{Miss}} = 10, \qquad \mathrm{Cost}_{\mathrm{FA}} = 1, \qquad R_{\mathrm{Target}} = 20, \tag{11}$$

where $N_{\mathrm{Miss}}(\theta)$ is the number of missed detections at decision score θ, N_{Targ} is the number of event observations, $N_{\mathrm{FA}}(\theta)$ is the number of false alarms at decision score θ, and T_{Source} is the total duration of the video segments in hours.

Table 4. Results in TRECVID 2009 event detection task.

Event	Reference	Our system	Correct	FalseAlarm	Miss	R_{FA}	P_{Miss}	DCR
PersonRuns	107	354	15	339	92	22.234	0.860	0.971
PeopleMeet	449	960	55	905	394	59.355	0.877	1.174
ObjectPut	621	488	19	469	602	30.760	0.969	1.123

The results indicate that many false detections and missed detections occurred. However, our system performed better than other systems developed by participants for the TRECVID 2009 surveillance event detection task.

Figure 22 shows the detection error tradeoff (DET) curve for each behavior. The DET curve plots a series of event-averaged missed detection probabilities and false alarm rates that are a function of a detection threshold, θ. This θ is applied to the system's detection scores, meaning the system observations with scores. The θ is declared to be the set of detected observations. If the P_{Miss} and the R_{FA} are low, the line is drawn around lower left in the figure. Filled points on the lines show the DCR.

Table 5 compares our results to systems developed by other participants. Our system was first place out of thirteen systems for the PersonRuns behavior. Our DCR (0.971) was much better than the average DCR of all systems (2.651). This shows that our system is reliable and effective.

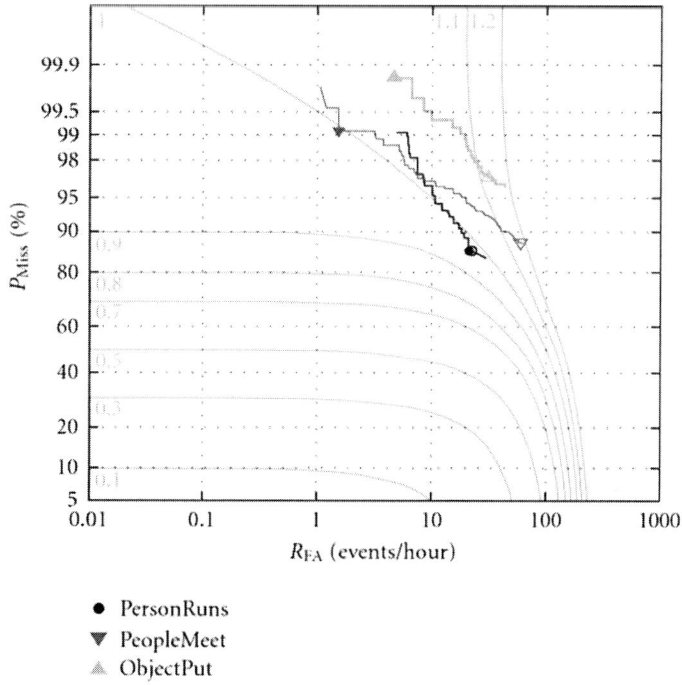

Figure 22. Results of our system in DET curve.

Table 5. Comparison with other systems.

	Average of all DCR	Standard deviation of all DCR	Our DCR	Our rank
PersonRuns	2.651	2.700	0.971	1/13
PeopleMeet	2.349	1.705	1.174	4/8
ObjectPut	1.186	0.292	1.123	6/8

An important technique for detecting the PersonRuns behavior is robust tracking of fast moving objects. The Kalman filter based prediction process accomplished this. The process set the search area for a tracked person depending on the speed of the person and the tracking situation so that our system could track running people robustly even if an extraction failure occurred in a few frames. The recognition process also contributed to good results. We could confirm a large bias on the axis of the first principal component in the trajectory feature space. The first principal component weighed heavily on the features of the average velocity and the travel distance. These features could be sufficiently extracted from a trajectory. Thus, our system was able to detect the PersonRuns behavior. In addition to the above two processes, our verification process was also effective in helping reduce false detections.

Our system could not detect the PersonRuns behavior when a person ran temporally (for less than one second) because the averaged velocity tended to be low in that case. It was particularly difficult to detect temporal dashing by children. However, the time length of trajectories can be configured freely so that we can set an appropriate length depending on the target person.

For the PeopleMeet behavior, our result was fourth place out of eight systems. The average DCR of all systems was 2.349. Our DCR was 1.174, so our system detected the PeopleMeet behavior relatively accurately compared to the other systems.

The places where one person can meet another are limited, because people do not stop where traffic density is high. Before meeting someone, a person tends to slow down his walking speed before stopping. A slight bias in the third principal component was confirmed in the trajectory feature space. The third principal component weighed heavily on the features of position and acceleration. So, we could divide the trajectory of a suspected PeopleMeet behavior from people who are moving without stopping. However, the distance from the center of major normal trajectories to this behavior class was relatively small in the trajectory feature space, causing many false detections. Even though the verification process reduced the number, the recognition accuracy was worse than for the PersonRuns behavior.

For the ObjectPut behavior, our result was sixth place out of eight systems. Our DCR was worse than the average DCR of all the systems. Our system is not reliable for detecting the ObjectPut behavior because that behavior is small compared to the other two behaviors, and it was difficult to recognize it from only a trajectory. In addition, there are many potential actions that fall under the category of ObjectPut. The behavior includes putting heavy baggage on the floor, picking up money at a register, and leaning on a luggage cart. Though the system accounts for optical flows in the human region, it considered only downward motion. There is still room for improvement in the detection of small motions. In future work, we should set assumptions more strictly or extract more effective features for detecting small motions.

5. CONCLUSIONS

We proposed a method that can detect specific human behaviors even in crowded surveillance video sequences, and we developed a system that detects the NIST-defined behaviors PersonRuns, PeopleMeet, and ObjectPut. The system recognizes these behaviors by identifying a human region trajectory, which is created by detecting and tracking areas that contain people, which we call human regions, in video sequences. The system detects these human regions using HOG descriptors and an SVM classifier and uses a Kalman filter to track them robustly. The similarity of two human regions is evaluated by the simple Euclidean distance between them and the Bhattacharyya distance of 2D color histograms.

The system determines an occurrence of a specific behavior based on the distance from a trajectory to each class of specific behaviors in the trajectory feature space created using PCA. The system also has functions to verify detected behaviors. For example, it uses backward tracking to verify fast motions, and it calculates optical flows to verify small motions. These functions contribute to robust recognition of specific types of behavior.

We evaluated the tracking accuracy of our system by comparing it with a baseline tracking method. Our system was able to track human regions more robustly than the baseline method even for crowded scenes. We also showed that the verification process could reduce false detections effectively. In addition, the results of the TRECVID 2009 surveillance event detection task showed that our system could recognize human behaviors robustly; our recognition capability won first place for detecting the PersonRuns behavior.

The system is suitable for detecting fast motion and big motions because it recognizes behaviors based on motion trajectories, which contain rich information about these motions. We plan to analyze local features, such as optical flows, in detail to expand the range of human behaviors that can be recognized.

REFERENCES

1. Bradski G, Davis J: Modeling people: vision-based understanding of a person's shape, appearance, movement, and behavior. *Computer Vision and Image Understanding* 2006, 104: 87-89.

2. Tomasi C, Kanade T: *Detection and tracking of point features.* Carnegie Mellon University; 1991:91-132.

3. Moore D: *A real-world system for human motion detection and tracking, Undergraduate Thesis.* California Institute of Technology; May 2003.

4. Dalal N, Triggs B: Histograms of oriented gradients for human detection. *Proceedings of IEEE Computer Society Conference on Computer Vision and Pattern Recognition (CVPR '05), June 2005, San Diego, Calif, USA* 886-893.

5. Han F, Shan Y, Cekander R: A two-stage approach to people and vehicle detection with HOG-based SVM. *PerMIS* 2006, 133-140.

6. Shiraki T, Saito H, Kamoshida Y, *et al.*: Real-time motion recognition using CHLAC features and cluster. *Proceedings of IFIP International Conference on Network and Parallel Computing (NPC '06), 2006* 50-56.

7. Schüldt C, Laptev I, Caputo B: Recognizing human actions: a local SVM approach. *Proceedings of the 17th International Conference on Pattern Recognition (ICPR '04), August 2004, Cambridge, UK* 3: 32-36.

8. Blank M, Gorelick L, Shechtman E, Irani M, Basri R: Actions as space-time shapes. *Proceedings of the IEEE International Conference on Computer Vision, October 2005* 2: 1395-1402.

9. Fathi A, Mori G: Action recognition by learning mid-level motion features. *Proceedings of the 26th IEEE Conference on Computer Vision and Pattern Recognition (CVPR '08), June 2008, Anchorage, Alaska, USA* 1-8.

10. Sun X, Chen M, Hauptmann A: Action recognition via local descriptors and holistic features. *Proceedings of IEEE Conference on Computer Vision and Pattern Recognition (CVPR '09), June 2009, Miami, Fla, USA* 58-65.

11. Li Z, Fu Y, Huang TS, Yan S: Real-time human motion recognition by luminance field trajectory analysis. *Proceedings of ACM*

International Conference on Multimedia, October 2008, Vancouver, Canada 671-676

12. Mikolajczyk K, Uemura H: Action recognition with motion-appearance vocabulary forest. *Proceedings of the 26th IEEE Conference on Computer Vision and Pattern Recognition (CVPR '08), June 2008, Anchorage, Alaska, USA*
13. Efros AA, Berg AC, Mori G, Malik J: Recognizing action at a distance. *Proceedings of the 9th IEEE International Conference on Computer Vision, October 2003, Nice, France* 2: 726-733.
14. Niebles JC, Fei-Fei L: A hierarchical model of shape and appearance for human motion classification. *Proceedings of IEEE Conference on Computer Vision and Pattern Recognition (CVPR '07), June 2007* 1-8.
15. Lien K-C, Huang C-L: Multiview-based cooperative tracking of multiple human objects. *Eurasip Journal on Image and Video Processing*2008., 2008:
16. Tsai Y-T, Shih H-C, Huang C-L: Multiple human objects tracking in crowded scenes. *Proceedings of the 18th International Conference on Pattern Recognition (ICPR '06), August 2006, Hong Kong* 3: 51-54.
17. Hu M, Ali S, Shah M: Learning motion patterns in crowded scenes using motion flow field. *Proceedings of the 19th International Conference on Pattern Recognition (ICPR '08), December 2008, Tampa, Fla, USA* 1-5.
18. Schölkopf B, Platt JC, Shawe-Taylor J, Smola AJ, Williamson RC: Estimating the support of a high-dimensional distribution. *Neural Computation* 2001, 13(7):1443-1471.
19. Chen P-H, Lin C-J, Schölkopf B: A tutorial on v-support vector machines. *Applied Stochastic Models in Business and Industry* 2005, 21(2):111-136.
20. Besse P, Ramsay JO: Principal components analysis of sampled functions. *Psychometrika* 1986, 51(2):285-311.
21. TREC Video Retrieval Evaluation http://www-nlpir.nist.gov/projects/trecvid/
22. Bradski GR, Davis JW: Motion segmentation and pose recognition with motion history gradients. *Machine Vision and Applications* 2002, 13(3):174-184.

23. Dedeoğlu Y, Uğur Töreyin B, Güdükbay U, Enis Çetin A: Silhouette-based method for object classification and human motion recognition in video. *Proceedings of the Computer Vision in Human-Computer Interaction, May 2006, Graz, Austria* 3979: 64-77.

24. Ke Y, Sukthankar R, Hebert M: Event detection in crowded videos. *Proceedings of the 11th IEEE International Conference on Computer Vision (ICCV '07), October 2007, Rio de Janeiro, Brazil*

25. Pavlovic V, Rehg JM, Cham T-J, Murphy KP: A dynamic Bayesian network approach to figure tracking using learned dynamic models.*Proceedings of the 7th IEEE International Conference on Computer Vision (ICCV '99), September 1999, Kerkyra, Greece* 1: 94-101

26. Stauffer C, Grimson WEL: Adaptive background mixture models for real-time tracking. *Proceedings of the IEEE Computer Society Conference on Computer Vision and Pattern Recognition (CVPR '99), June 1999, Collins, Colo, USA* 2: 246-252.

27. Garrett Z, Saito H: Live video object tracking and segmentation using graph cuts. *Proceedings of International Conference on Image Processing (ICIP '08), October 2008, San Diego, Calif, USA* 1576-1579.

28. National Institute of Standards and Technology http://www.nist.gov/index.html

29. Xuan G, Chai P, Wu M: Bhattacharyya distance feature selection. *Proceedings of the International Conference on Pattern Recognition (ICPR '96), 1996* 2: 195-199.

30. Grimble MJ: *Robust Industrial Control: Optimal Design Approach for Polynomial Systems*. Prentice-Hall, Upper Saddle River, NJ, USA; 1994.

31. Yu X, Xu C, Tian Q, Leong HW: A ball tracking framework for broadcast soccer video. *Proceedings of IEEE International Conference on Multimedia & Expo, 2003* 2: 273-276.

32. Mahalanobis P: On the generalized distance in statistics. *Proceedings of the National Academy of Sciences of the United States of America*1936, 2: 49-55.

33. Horn BKP, Schunck BG: Determining optical flow. *Artificial Intelligence* 1981, 17(1–3):185-203.

34. Shi J, Tomasi C: Good features to track. *Proceedings of the IEEE Computer Society Conference on Computer Vision and Pattern Recognition (CVPR '94), June 1994, Seattle, Wash, USA* 593-600.

9

CHAPTER

A Perceptual Masking Approach for Noise Robust Speech Recognition

Hari Krishna MagantiEmail author and Marco Matassoni

ABSTRACT

This article describes a modified technique for enhancing noisy speech to improve automatic speech recognition (ASR) performance. The proposed approach improves the widely used spectral subtraction which inherently suffers from the associated musical noise effects. Through a psychoacoustic masking and critical band variance normalization technique, the artifacts produced by spectral subtraction are minimized for improving the ASR accuracy. The popular advanced ETSI-2 front end is tested for comparison purposes. The performed speech recognition evaluations on the noisy standard AURORA-2 tasks show enhanced performance for all noise conditions.

INTRODUCTION

Enhancement of noise corrupted speech signals is a challenging task for speech processing systems to be deployed in real-world applications. In practice, speech signals are usually degraded by additive background noises, reverberation effects and speech signals from other speakers[1]. The primary goal of robust speech processing techniques is to improve intelligibility and quality of noise corrupted speech in perspective human listeners and modify the same and extract robust features that lead to improved performance for speech recognition systems.

Apart from extracting robust features which represent parameters less sensitive to noise by modifying the extracted features[1], other research directions aimed at increasing the performance of speech recognizers in noise are: speech signal enhancement, model adaptation and hybrid methods[2–5]. The model adaptation techniques fail to perform in constantly changing environments where little or no adaptation data is available and hybrid methods attempt to preprocess speech signals and depend on reliability of estimations of those segments. On the other hand the signal enhancement techniques require no training, and provide "real-time" enhancement of the recognition accuracy. The spectral subtraction method of speech enhancement is the most widely used conventional method for reducing additive noise. Many improvements are proposed to deal with the problems typically associated to spectral subtraction such as residual broadband noise and narrow band tonal noise referred as musical noise[4]. Other variants of spectral subtraction for this purpose include spectral subtraction with over subtraction, non-linear spectral subtraction, multi-band spectral subtraction, MMSE spectral subtraction, and extended spectral subtraction[3, 6].

Spectral subtraction based on perceptual properties has been investigated to improve intelligibility and quality of the speech signals[7–9]. The masking properties of human auditory system are incorporated into the enhancement process in order to attenuate the noise components that are already inaudible due to masking. In[7], the selected masking threshold level is high, so that the residual noise will be masked and will be inaudible. In[8], a psycho-acoustical spectral weighting rule is proposed which utilizes only estimates of the masking threshold and noise power spectral density for complete masking of distortions of the residual noise. The application of using human auditory masking in Kalman filtering to speech enhancement is considered in[9]. Furthermore, another novel approach based on sub-band variance normalization technique was proposed where speech frames are characterized by high variance and noise frames by low variance, which are suppressed to improve the ASR performance in presence of both additive noise and reverberation[10].

In the present study, an alternate approach based on psycho-acoustical model for reducing the artifacts associated with spectral subtraction for improving speech recognition performance in the presence of additive noise is proposed. Based on the human auditory system, the noise below the audible threshold is suppressed which reduces the amount of modification to the spectral magnitude, and hence the amount of distortion introduced into the cleaned speech signal. Further, critical band variance normalization is performed to minimize the musical noise which is caused by increased variance at random frequencies. The features derived from the combination of techniques are effective in providing robustness. The studied features are shown to be reliable and robust to the effects of the additive noise. The effectiveness of the proposed features is demonstrated with experiments on noisy AURORA-2 database. For comparison purposes the recognition results obtained by using the standard spectral subtraction and ETSI advanced front-end are tested[11].

The article is organized into the following sections. Section 2 briefly summarizes the principle spectral subtraction using over subtraction. Section 3 describes psycho-acoustic motivated features including tone and noise masking and critical band variance normalization. Section 4 discusses the spectral subtraction with perceptual post-filter and Section 5 describes the database, experiments and results. Finally, Section 6 concludes the article.

Spectral subtraction for speech enhancement

Spectral subtraction algorithms are based on subtraction of the noise estimate from original speech. The power spectral density (PSD) of a clean speech signal is estimated by subtracting the PSD of the noise from the PSD of the noisy speech signal[12]. Each estimate of the PSD is performed within a short-time segment based on the assumption that noise is stationary or slowly varying, and that the noise spectrum does not change significantly between the updating periods. The noisy speech signal can be expressed as

$$y(t) = s(t) + d(t) \tag{1}$$

where $y(t)$ is the degraded speech signal, $s(t)$ represents the clean signal, $d(t)$ is the additive noise, which is uncorrelated with the speech signal and unknown.

The power spectrum of the noisy speech signal is represented as:

$$|Y(\omega)|^2 = |S(\omega)|^2 + |D(\omega)|^2 + S(\omega) \cdot D(\omega)^* + S(\omega)^* \cdot D(\omega) \tag{2}$$

where $D(\omega)^*$ and $S(\omega)^*$ represent the complex conjugates of $D(\omega)$ and $S(\omega)$, respectively. If noise and speech are uncorrelated then the terms $S(\omega) \cdot D(\omega)^*$, $S(\omega)^* \cdot D(\omega)$ can be neglected. The power spectral subtraction estimate of the enhanced speech $S(\omega)$ is given by

$$|\hat{S}(\omega)|^2 \approx |Y(\omega)|^2 - |\bar{D}(\omega)|^2 \quad (3)$$

where||D̄ (ω)||2$|\bar{D}(\omega)|^2$ is the average value of noise square-magnitude taken during non-speech activity. The performance of this technique depends on the accuracy of noise estimation and is limited by the processing distortions caused by random variations of the noise spectrum. The non-linear mapping of spectral estimates that fall below a threshold, where noise has been overestimated results in some randomly located negative values for the estimated clean speech magnitude. This leads to undesired residual noise called musical noise (narrow band spectrum with randomly distributed tones over time and frequency).

An important variation of spectral subtraction proposed in[4] in order to alleviate the problem of musical noise is

$$|\hat{S}(\omega)|^2 = \begin{cases} |Y(\omega)|^2 - \alpha|\bar{D}(\omega)|^2, & \text{if } |\hat{S}(\omega)|^2 > \beta|\bar{D}(\omega)|^2 \\ \beta|\bar{D}(\omega)|^2, & \text{otherwise} \end{cases} \quad (4)$$

where α, β are the subtraction factor and spectral floor parameter. To reduce the speech distortion caused by large values of α, its value is adapted from frame to frame depending on the segmental noisy signal to noise ratio (NSNR) of the frame. In general, less subtraction is applied for frames with high NSNR and vice versa. For the estimate of the noise power spectrum, minimum statistics technique is used[13]. The NSNR is computed using a decision directed approach as proposed in[14].

As described in[4], the oversubtraction factor α can be calculated as

$$\alpha_m = \begin{cases} 1, & \mathrm{NSNR}_m \geq 20\,\mathrm{dB} \\ \alpha^0 - \frac{3}{20}\mathrm{NSNR}_m, & -6\,\mathrm{dB} \leq \mathrm{NSNR}_m < 20\,\mathrm{dB} \\ 4.9, & \mathrm{NSNR}_m < -6\,\mathrm{dB}, \end{cases} \quad (5)$$

where m is the frame index and α^0 is the value of α at 0 dB NSNR. With the higher over-subtraction, the stronger components with a low SNR are attenuated which prevent musical noise. But, too strong over-subtraction may suppress too many components causing distortion to the signal.

Psychoacoustical masking model

The oversubtracted spectral subtraction reduces the noise to some extent but the musical noise is not completely eliminated, effecting the quality of the speech signal. There is a trade-off between the amount of noise reduction and speech distortion. The perceptual based techniques help in reducing the noise by taking advantage of the masking properties of the auditory system. In order to further enhance the quality, the noise and tones are masked and critical band variance normalization is performed by incorporating the masking properties of human auditory system. The human auditory system does not perceive all the frequencies in the similar way, and is limited to mask certain sounds in the presence of competitive sounds. The two main properties of the human auditory system that make up the psychoacoustic model are: absolute threshold of hearing and auditory masking.

Absolute threshold of hearing

The absolute threshold of hearing defines the minimum sound level that can be heard by an active listener in absence of other sounds. The quiet threshold can be expressed by the following equation:

$$\mathrm{ATH}(f) = 3.64\left(\frac{f}{1000}\right)^{-0.8} - 6.5e^{-0.6\left(\frac{f}{1000}-3.3\right)^{2}} + 10^{-3} \times \left(\frac{f}{1000}\right)^{4} \quad (6)$$

The frequency components of the signal with power levels that fall below the absolute threshold of hearing (ATH) can be discarded, as they do not contribute in improving perceptibility of the signal.

Auditory masking

The inability of the human auditory perception system to identify the minute differences in frequency when played at the same time is known as masking. A strong 1 kHz signal masks the nearby frequencies, making them inaudible to the listener. For a masked signal to be heard, its power has to be increased to a level greater than that of a threshold that is determined by the frequency of the masker tone and its strength.

The masking analysis method described in MPEG1 audio coder is used to detect the tonal and nontonal components[15]. The tonal and noise masking threshold that give the maximum level of noise that is inaudible in the presence of speech is computed. The calculation steps as described in[15] are:

The frequency analysis along the critical band scale is performed by mapping the power spectrum onto an auditory frequency axis, by combining FFT bins into equally-spaced intervals on the Bark scale defined by:

$$\text{Bark}(f) = 13\arctan(0.00076f) + 3.5\arctan\left(\left(\frac{f}{7500}\right)^2\right) \tag{7}$$

where f is the frequency in linear domain. The relationship between frequency in Hertz and Bark scales is shown in Figure1.

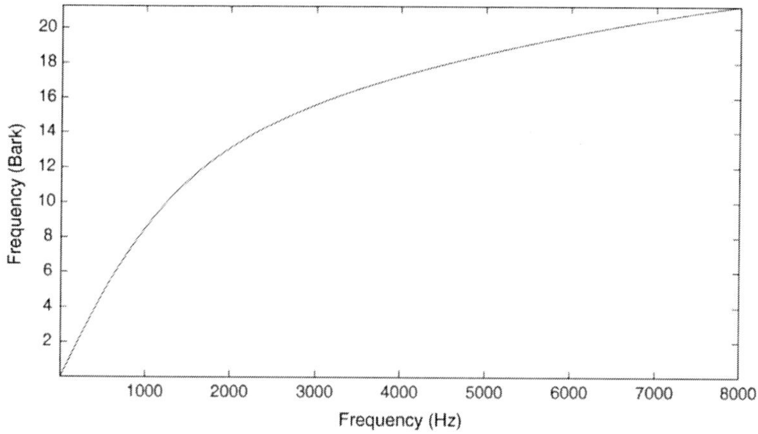

Figure 1. Relationship between frequency in Hertz and Bark scales.

The masking threshold is computed from the short-term power spectral density estimate of the input signal. The power density spectrum is obtained from the FFT of the input signal, following multiplication by a Hann window. The magnitude of each spectral component is converted to a decibel scale, to obtain the estimate $P[k]$. The power spectrum is normalized to a level of 96 dB SPL, such that the maximum spectral component corresponds to this value.

The following step involves the discrimination between tonal and noise maskers. This accounts for the dependence of masking thresholds on the nature of the maskers. First, tonal components are identified through the detection of local maxima within the power spectrum. A component is labeled as a local maximum if $P[k] > P[k-1]$ and $P[k] \geq P[k+1]$. Components are declared as tonal if $P[k] - P[k+j] \geq 7$ dB, where j lies within a neighborhood that is dependent on the center frequency, k. The sound pressure level of the tonal masker, $P_{TM}(z)$, where z is the Bark value of the frequency bin k, is computed as follows:

$$P_{TM}(z) = 10\log_{10}\left(10^{P[k-1]/10} + 10^{P[k]/10} + 10^{P[k+1]/10}\right) \tag{8}$$

Tonal maskers are removed from the power spectrum $P[k]$, by setting all frequency lines within the examined range to $-\infty$. The sound pressure levels of noise maskers are obtained by summing the energies of spectral lines within each critical band to compute $P_{TM}(z)$.

Subsequently, the number of maskers considered for threshold computation is reduced. At first, only maskers having a level above the absolute threshold of hearing are retained. A decimation process then occurs between multiple tonal maskers that lie within half of a critical band. The tonal masker having the highest level is maintained while the other elements are removed from the directory of maskers. The tone and noise maskers for part of the utterance "three six seven" corrupted with subway noise of 5 dB SNR is shown in Figure 2.

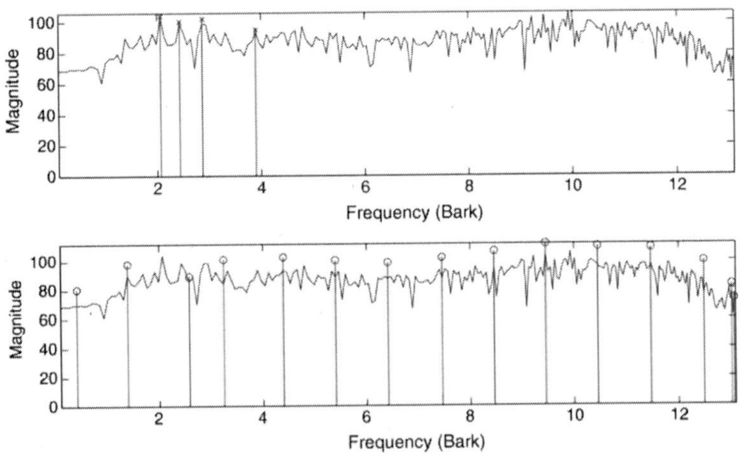

Figure 2. Tone and noise maskers for part of the utterance "three six seven" corrupted with subway noise of 5 dB SNR.

The contribution of each masker to the overall masking threshold is evaluated. The spread of masking effects is modeled using the spreading function described below:

$$s(z_j, \Delta z, P_M(z_j)) = \begin{cases} 17\Delta_z - 0.4P_M(z_j) + 11, & -3 \leq \Delta_z < -1 \\ (0.4P_M(z_j) + 6)\Delta_z & -1 \leq \Delta_z < 0 \\ -17\Delta_z & 0 \leq \Delta_z < 1 \\ (0.15P_M(z_j) - 17)\Delta_z - 0.15P_M(z_j) & 1 \leq \Delta_z < 8 \\ -\infty & \text{otherwise,} \end{cases} \tag{9}$$

where $z_j, \Delta z$, and $P_M(z_j)$ represent, respectively, the masker Bark frequency, the Bark frequency separation between the masker and target and the sound pressure level of the masker. The spread of masking is only considered within the range of $-3 \leq \Delta z < 8$, for reasons of implementation complexity.

The masking indices (in dB) for tonal maskers $a_{TM}(z)$, and noise maskers $a_{NM}(z)$, expressed below in Equations (11) and (12) are both frequency dependent. They represent the offset to be subtracted from the excitation pattern of the masker to obtain the masking pattern. The checked tone and noise maskers for part of the utterance "three six seven" corrupted with subway noise of 5 dB SNR is shown in Figure 3.

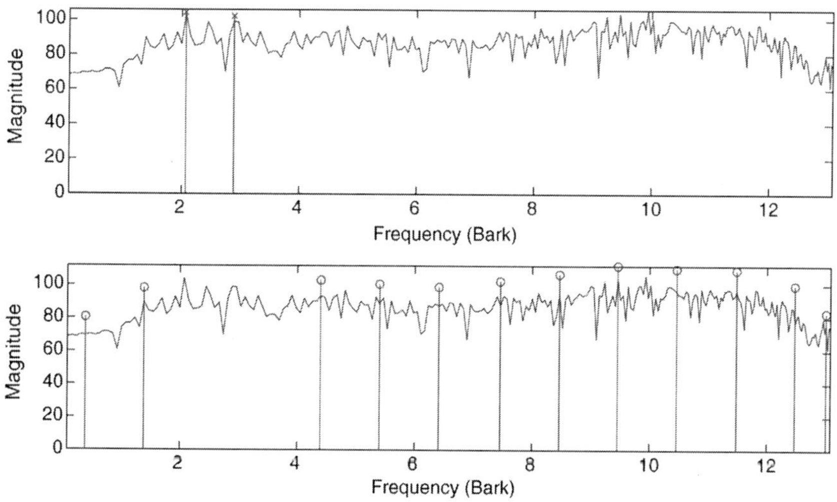

Figure 3. Checked tone and noise maskers for part of the utterance "three six seven" corrupted with subway noise of 5 dB SNR.

$$a_{TM}(z) = -1.525 - 0.257z - 4.5 \tag{10}$$

$$a_{NM}(z) = -1.525 - 0.175z - 0.5 \tag{11}$$

The individual masking thresholds from each masker calculated according to:

$$M_{TM}(z_j, \Delta z) = P_{TM}(z_j) + a_{TM}(z_j) + s(z_j, \Delta z, P_{TM}(z_j)) \tag{12}$$

$$M_{NM}(z_j, \Delta z) = P_{NM}(z_j) + a_{NM}(z_j) + s(z_j, \Delta z, P_{NM}(z_j)) \tag{13}$$

The individual making thresholds are computed for each sub-band, using all the maskers. The global masking threshold per sub-band is computed by summing the individual masking contributions from each masker along with the absolute threshold of hearing, $T_Q(z)$

$$M_g(z_i) = 10\log_{10}\left(10^{T_Q(z_i)/10} + \sum_{j=1}^{m} 10^{M_{TM}(z_j z_i)/10} + \sum_{j=1}^{n} 10^{M_{NM}(z_j z_i)/10}\right) \tag{14}$$

The ATH, original PSD, noise and tone maskers, and global masking threshold for part of the utterance "three six seven" corrupted with subway noise of 5 dB SNR is shown in Figure4.

Variance normalization

Further, to reduce the effect of any present tones which are caused by increased variance at random frequencies, variance normalization across the critical bands is performed[10]. The variance is computed as

$$v(m) = \frac{1}{K-1}\sum_{i=1}^{K}\left(v_i(m) - \hat{v}(m)\right)^2 \tag{15}$$

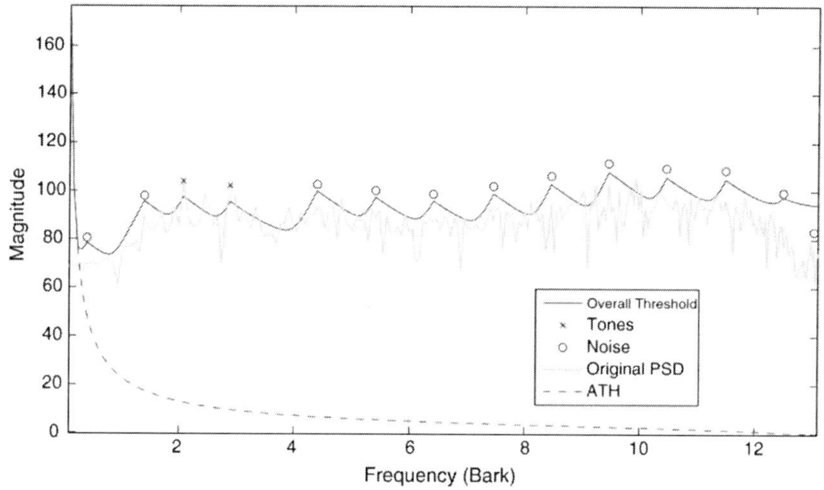

Figure 4. The ATH, original PSD, noise and tones, and global masking threshold for part of the utterance "three six seven" corrupted with subway noise of 5 dB SNR.

where K is the number of bands, m is the frame index,v^$\hat{\nu}$ is the mean, and v_i is the element number i. To suppress the peaks of noise, these values are normalized with respect to the maximum value across the bands

$$w(m) = \frac{v(m)}{\max\{v(m)\}} \quad (16)$$

Spectral subtraction with perceptual post-filter

The description provided in previous Section 3 provided a theoretical foundation for combining the masking properties of human auditory system in a spectral subtraction framework used for speech recognition. The proposed feature extraction methodology is shown in Figure5. First, the 8 kHz speech signal undergoes pre-emphasis and short segments of speech are extracted with a 25 ms rectangular window, shifted by 10 ms. After the spectral subtraction (spectral floor parameter $\beta = 0.02$, α as defined in Equation (5) with $\alpha^0 = 4$) with oversubtraction, the signal is then filtered by a bank of 24 critical-band bark filters. The global masking threshold is applied, then variance normalization is performed to further suppress the tones at random frequencies. Later, these normalized values are used as weights which are then multiplied with the filter bank energies as shown

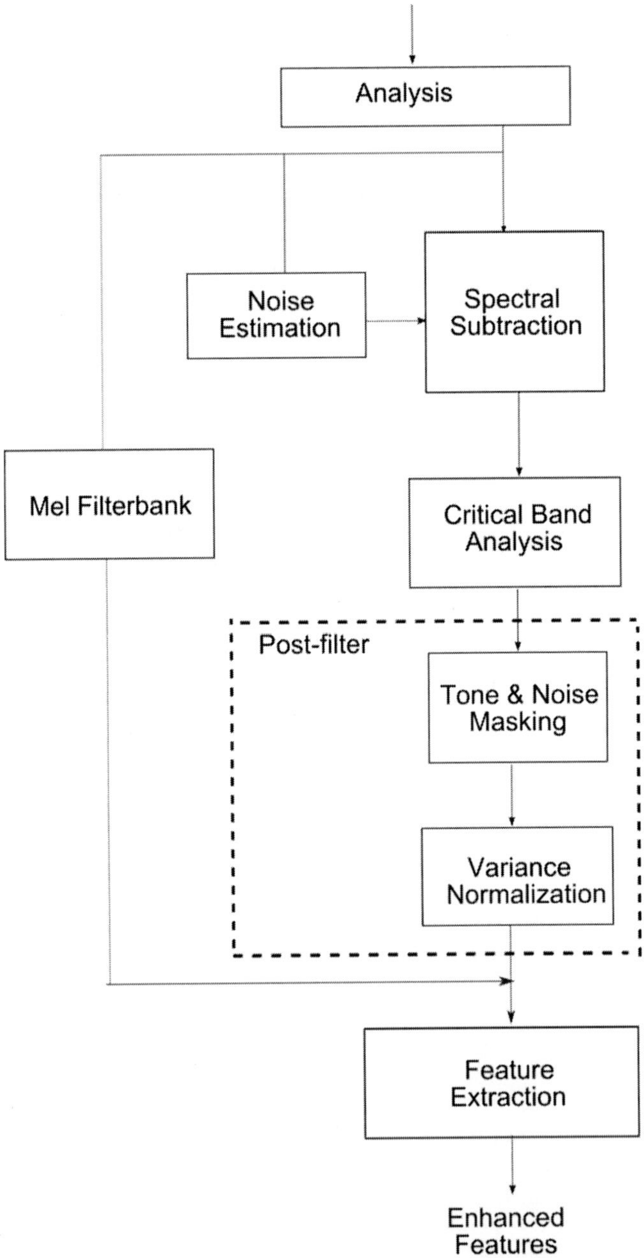

Figure 5. Processing stages of the proposed features.

$$\tilde{Y}_k(m) = Y_k(m) \cdot w(m) \tag{17}$$

MFCC features are extracted from the log Mel spectrum by applying a discrete cosine transformation. First thirteen cepstral coefficients along with their first- and second-order derivatives are used.

Experiments and results

The ASR experiments are performed with the proposed approach using a full HTK based recognition system[16] on connected digit recognition task using the Aurora 2 database[17]. The database was designed to evaluate the front-end of ASR systems in noisy conditions, and the training and testing follow the specifications described in[17]. The task is speaker independent connected digit recognition.

Testing data include eight types of realistic background noise subway, babble, car, exhibition hall, restaurant, street, airport and train station noise at various SNRs (clean, 20, 15, 10, 5, 0, and −5 dB). There are three test sets. Set A contains 4004 utterances in the first four types of noise, set B contains 4004 utterances in the other four, and set C contains 2002 utterances, where only subway and street noise are present.

The Aurora 2 task defines two different training modes: training on clean condition only, and training on multi-condition which include both clean and noisy conditions. Experiments with training on both conditions are considered to demonstrate the efficiency of the proposed approach. A word-based ASR system for digit string recognition where each HMM word model has 16 emitting states is adopted. A three-state silence model and a one state short pause model are used. The details about the training set, test set and HTK recognizer can be found in[17]. Results on Aurora 2 test sets A, B, and C with training on clean data and multi-condition data are reported in Figures6 and7, respectively.

From Figures6 and7, it can be seen that spectral subtraction has the highest word error rates (WER) for both clean and multi-condition training. Also, it can be observed that for a minimal average loss in case of clean speech for both clean and multi-condition training, an improvement is obtained with the proposed features for all the noise conditions. The improvement is particularly large for −5, 0, 5, 10 and 15 dB SNRs. It can also be observed that the improvements are better for training on clean data than multi-condition data which is consistent with[17]. For both the cases, the approach is precisely able to remove noise as much as possible improving the recognition accuracy

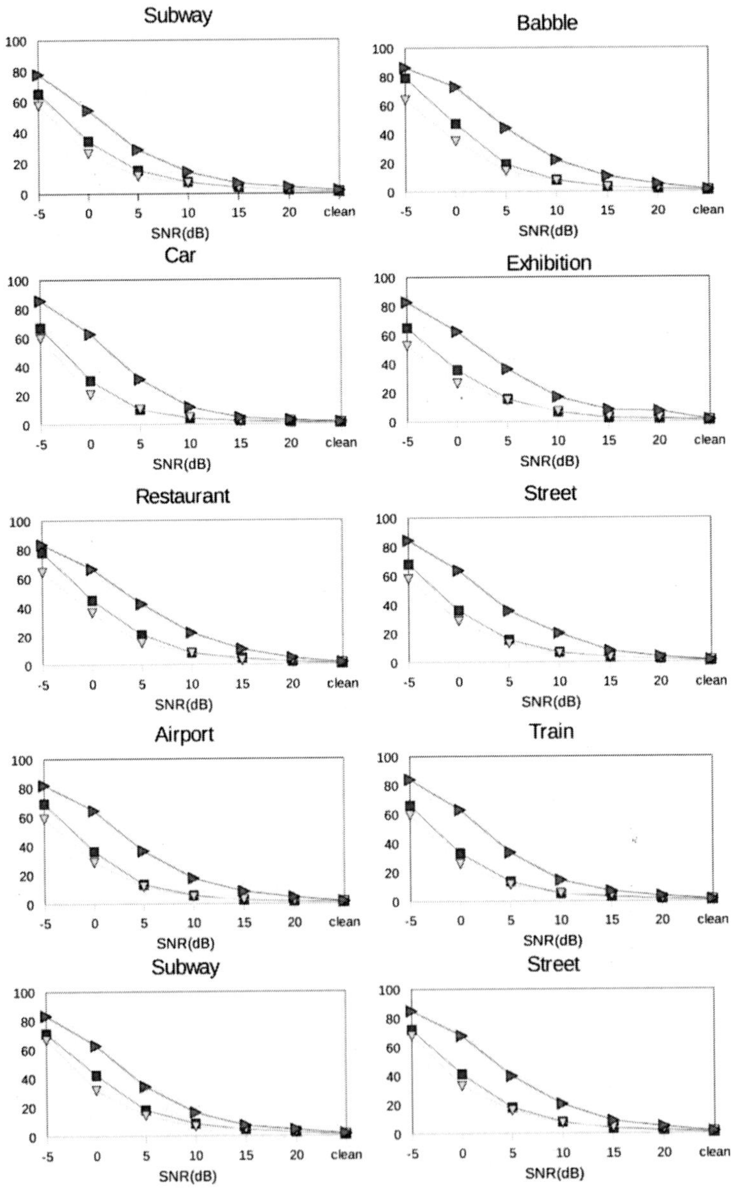

Figure 6. Comparison of WER (%) performance for ETSI-2 (□), proposed features (▽) and spectral subtraction (▻) for all noises of test sets A, B, and C trained on clean data.

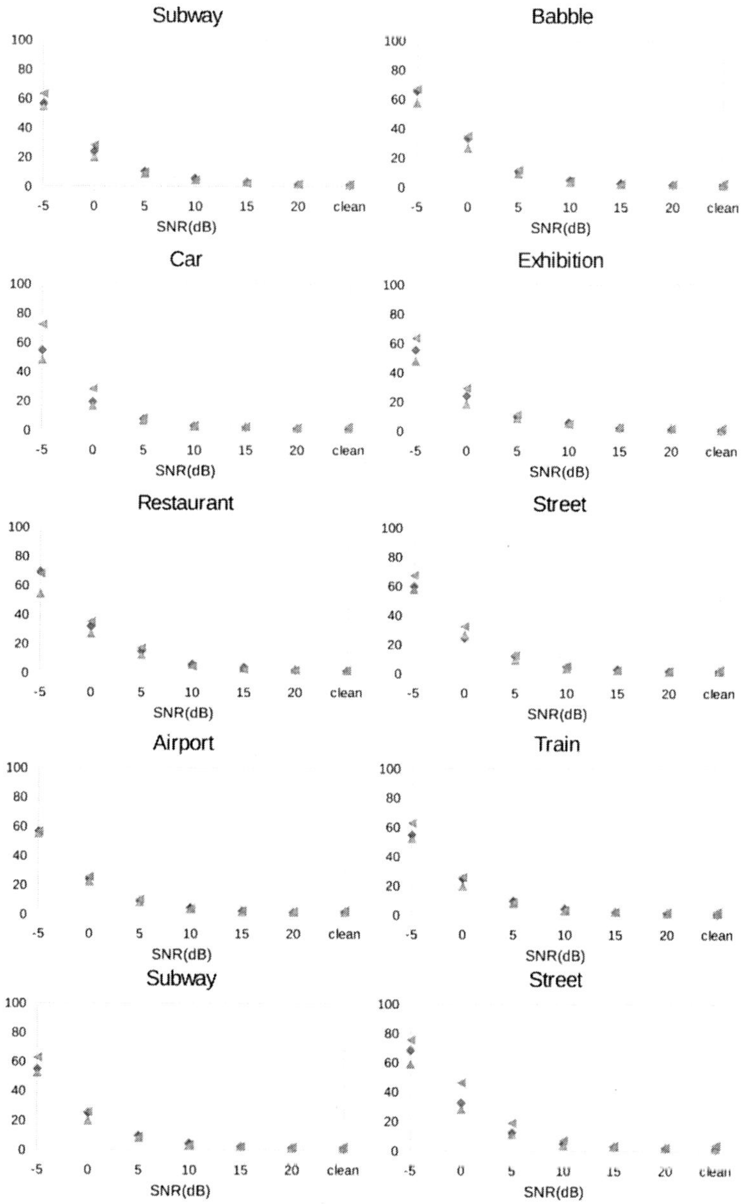

Figure 7. Comparison of WER (%) performance for ETSI-2) (◇) , proposed features (△) and spectral subtraction (⊲) for all noises of test sets A, B, and C trained on multi-condition data.

Figure8 shows comparison of the performance for average calculated over 0 to 20 dB SNR's for all the test sets A, B, and C, respectively. The first and second bars indicates the average result obtained with spectral subtraction and ETSI-2 frontend trained on clean data. The third bar denotes the performance of proposed approach for clean condition training. The fourth, fifth, and sixth bars show the results obtained with spectral subtraction, ETSI-2 frontend and proposed approach for multi-condition training. It can be observed that for all the test sets the performance of the proposed approach is better than spectral subtraction and ETSI-2 frontend for both training on clean data and multi-condition data.

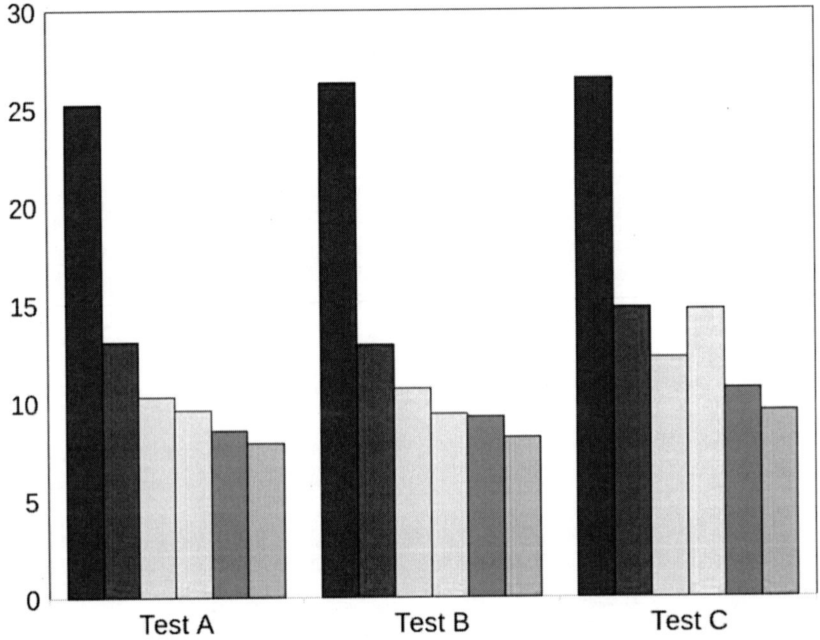

Figure 8. Comparison of average WER (%) performance calculated from 0 to 20 dB for spectral subtraction, ETSI-2 frontend and proposed approach for test sets A, B, and C. The first and fourth and second and fifth bars indicate performance of spectral subtraction and ETSI-2 frontend for training on clean data and multi-condition data. The third and sixth indicate performance of proposed approach for training on clean data and multi-condition data.

It can be clearly observed from the Figures6,7, and8 that the performance of proposed features is consistently the best for all noise conditions irrespective of the training. To overcome the basic limitation and application of spectral subtraction technique for recognition tasks, the combination of psychoacoustical masking and critical band variance normalization is effective in minimizing the artifacts without causing distortion to the original speech signal, thereby improving the ASR accuracy.

CONCLUSIONS

This article presented a psychoacoustical masking and critical band variance normalization based spectral subtraction approach to improve the speech recognition performance in noisy environments.

The spectral subtraction method was used to reduce the broadband noise due to peaks, and the combination of masking and variance normalization technique was effective in reducing the artifacts by reducing the dynamic range of its magnitude spectrum, which resulted in the improved speech recognition performance. The proposed approach has been evaluated on a standard Aurora-2 database. Results were compared with standard ETSI-2 advanced front-end which show that the proposed features perform consistently better both in terms of robustness and reliability for all types of noises.

In future investigations, improvement of auditory based features to deal with both additive noise and reverberation simultaneously will be investigated. Also, evaluation of these features on large vocabulary tasks to deal with real world noisy speech will be studied..

REFERENCES

1. Droppo J, Acero A: Environmental robustness, chapter 33. In *Springer Handbook of Speech Processing* Edited by: Benesty J, Sondhi MM, Huang (eds) Y. (2008), 653-680.

2. Furui S, Sondhi M: Marcel Dekker, Inc. In *Advances in speech signal processing*. New York; 1991.

3. Ephraim Y, Cohen I: *Recent advancements in speech enhancement*. The Electrical Engineering Handbook, CRC Press; 2006.

4. Berouti M, Schwartz R, Makhaul J: Enhancement of speech corrupted by acoustic noise. In *Proc. IEEE International Conf. on*

Acoustics, Speech, and Signal Processing (ICASSP). Washington, USA; 1979:208-211.

5. Gales MJF: Robust Speech Recognition of Uncertain or Missing Data, chapter 1. In *Springer series of Signal, Image and Speech Processing* Edited by: Kolossa D, Umbach (eds) RH. 2011, 101-125.

6. Krishnamoorthy P, Prasanna SRM: Reverberant speech enhancement by temporal and spectral processing. *IEEE Transactions on Speech Audio Processing* 2009, 17(2):253-266.

7. Virag N: Single channel speech enhancement based on masking properties of the human auditory system. *IEEE Transactions on Speech Audio Processing* 1999, 7(2):126-137.

8. Gustafsson S, Jax P, Vary P: A novel psychoacoustically motivated audio enhancement algorithm preserving background noise characteristics. In *Proc. IEEE International Conf. on Acoustics, Speech, and Signal Processing (ICASSP)*. Washington, USA; 1998:397-400.

9. Ma N, Bouchard M, Goubran RA: Speech enhancement using a masking threshold constrained kalman filter and its heuristic implementations. *IEEE Transactions on Speech Audio Processing* 2006, 14(1):19-32.

10. Maganti HK, Zanon S, Matassoni M: Sub-band spectral variance feature for noise robust ASR. In *Proc. 19th European Signal Processing Conference (EUSIPCO)*. Barcelona, Spain; 2011:2114-2118.

11. ETSI ES 202050 STQ: *Distributed Speech Recognition, Advanced Front-End Feature Extraction Algorithm, Compression Algorithm, ETSI ES 202 050 v1.1.3*. 2003-11.

12. Boll S: Suppression of acoustic noise in speech using spectral subtraction, IEEE Transactions on Acosutics. *Speech Signal Processing*1979, 27(2):113-120. 10.1109/TASSP.1979.1163209

13. Martin R: Noise power spectral density estimation based on optimal smoothing and minimum statistics. *IEEE Transactions on Speech Audio Processing* 2001, 9: 504-512.

14. Ephraim Y, Malah D: Speech enhancement using a minimum-mean square error short-time spectral amplitude estimator. *IEEE Transactions on Acosutics, Speech Signal Processing* 1984, ASSP-32(6):1109-1121.

15. Painter T, Spanias A: Perceptual coding of digital audio. *Proc. of the IEEE* 2000, 88: 451-513.

16. Young SJ, Evermann G, Gales MJF, Kershaw D, Moore G, Odell JJ, Ollason DG, Povey D, Valtchev V, Woodland PC: *The HTK book (version 3.4)*. Cambridge University Engineering Department, Cambridge, UK; 2006.

17. Hirsch HG, Pearce D: *Applying the Advanced ETSI Frontend to the Aurora-2 task, in version 1.1*. 2006.

Index